Constructing Cultural Tourism

PEFC
PEFC/16-33-111
CATG-PEFC-052
www.pefc.org

LIVERPOOL JMU LIBRARY

3 1111 01367 6976

TOURISM AND CULTURAL CHANGE
Series Editors: Professor Mike Robinson, *Centre for Tourism and Cultural Change, Leeds Metropolitan University, Leeds, UK* and Dr Alison Phipps, *University of Glasgow, Scotland, UK*

Understanding tourism's relationships with culture(s) and vice versa, is of ever-increasing significance in a globalising world. This series will critically examine the dynamic inter-relationships between tourism and culture(s). Theoretical explorations, research-informed analyses, and detailed historical reviews from a variety of disciplinary perspectives are invited to consider such relationships.

Full details of all the books in this series and of all our other publications can be found on http://www.channelviewpublications.com, or by writing to Channel View Publications, St Nicholas House, 31–34 High Street, Bristol BS1 2AW, UK.

TOURISM AND CULTURAL CHANGE
Series Editors: Professor Mike Robinson
and Dr Alison Phipps

Constructing Cultural Tourism
John Ruskin and the Tourist Gaze

Keith Hanley and John K. Walton

CHANNEL VIEW PUBLICATIONS
Bristol • Buffalo • Toronto

Library of Congress Cataloging in Publication Data
A catalog record for this book is available from the Library of Congress.
Hanley, Keith.
Constructing Cultural Tourism: John Ruskin and the Tourist Gaze/Keith Hanley and
John K. Walton.
Tourism and Cultural Change: v.25
Includes bibliographical references and index.
1. Heritage tourism--Great Britain--History. 2. Heritage tourism--Europe,
Western--History. 3. Ruskin, John, 1819-1900--Travel--Great Britain, 4. Ruskin, John,
1819-1900--Trave--Europe, Western. 5. Ruskin, John, 1819-1900--Criticism and inter-
pretation. 6. Travel in literature. I. Walton, John K. II. Title. III. Series.
G156.5.H47H36 2010
338.4'79141–dc22 2010026359

British Library Cataloguing in Publication Data
A catalogue entry for this book is available from the British Library.

ISBN-13: 978-1-84541-155-8 (hbk)
ISBN-13: 978-1-84541-154-1 (pbk)

Channel View Publications
UK: St Nicholas House, 31–34 High Street, Bristol, BS1 2AW, UK.
USA: UTP, 2250 Military Road, Tonawanda, NY 14150, USA.
Canada: UTP, 5201 Dufferin Street, North York, Ontario M3H 5T8, Canada.

Copyright © 2010 Keith Hanley and John K. Walton.

All rights reserved. No part of this work may be reproduced in any form or by any
means without permission in writing from the publisher.

The policy of Multilingual Matters/Channel View Publications is to use papers
that are natural, renewable and recyclable products, made from wood grown in
sustainable forests. In the manufacturing process of our books, and to further support
our policy, preference is given to printers that have FSC and PEFC Chain of Custody
certification. The FSC and/or PEFC logos will appear on those books where full
certification has been granted to the printer concerned.

Typeset by Techset Composition Ltd., Salisbury, UK.
Printed and bound in Great Britain by the MPG Books Group.

Contents

Illustrations vii
Acknowledgements xi
1   Introduction: The Joy of Travel 1
2   The Ruskin Moment 24
3   Sightseeing with Ruskin 55
4   The Interpretation of Places 91
5   Ruskin and Tourist Destinations 133
6   Ruskin and Popular Tourism 154
7   Ruskin and Brantwood 179
8   Conclusion 201
Index 204

Illustrations

1.1   John Ruskin. From *The Growth of Leaves*.

2.1   *Map of Thomas Cook's First Tour of Switzerland*, from *Miss Jemima's Swiss Journal*.

2.2   *The Mer de Glace, Chamonix*, from *Miss Jemima's Swiss Journal*.

2.3   Samuel Prout. *Abbeville*.

2.4   John Ruskin. *Casa Contarini Fasan*.

2.5   J.M.W. Turner. *Lake of Como*.

2.6   John Ruskin. *The Jungfrau from Interlaken*.

2.7   David Roberts. *The Alhambra in Granada*.

2.8   F. Crawley. *Aiguilles, Chamonix*.

2.9   Ruskin's double brougham.

2.10 *Mornings in Florence*.

2.11 Finely bound Ruskin Guidebooks.

3.1   John Ruskin. *Loch Achray and Ben Venue*.

3.2   John Ruskin. *Troutbeck*.

3.3   John Ruskin. *Trees and Rocks*.

3.4   John Ruskin. *Cottage near Altdorf*.

3.5   John Ruskin. *Villa, Sommariva, Cadenabbia*.

3.6   *St Mark's and Clock Tower*.

3.7   *Detail of S. Denis and Angels, Rheims Cathedral*.

3.8   Unknown photographer and John Ruskin. *Maria della Spina, Lucca*.

3.9   J.M.W. Turner. *Near Blair Athol, Scotland*.

3.10 John Ruskin. *Spanish Chestnut at Carrara*.

3.11 John Ruskin. *Study of Portal and Carved Pinnacles, Cathedral of St Lô, Normandy*.

3.12 John Ruskin. *Ornaments from Rouen, St Lô, and Venice*.

3.13 John Ruskin. *Temperance and Intemperance in Curvature*.

3.14 Thomas Rowlandson. *Dr Syntax Tumbling into the Water*.

3.15 John Ruskin. *The Pass of Faido*.

3.16   John Ruskin. *Simple Topography* and *Turnerian Topography.*

3.17   John Ruskin. *Crests of the Slaty Crystallines.*

3.18   John Ruskin, *Ca' d'Oro, Venice.*

3.19   J.M.W. Turner. *Edinburgh, from St Anthony's Chapel.*

3.20   *Potifices. Clerus. Populus. Dux Mente Serenus,* St Mark's.

3.21   A.H. Mackmurdo. *Sepulchral Slab of Galileus de Galileis, Santa Croce, Florence.*

3.22   J.M.W. Turner. *Kirby-Lonsdale Church Yard.*

4.1   John Ruskin. *State of Snow on Mont Blanc.*

4.2   John Ruskin. *Le Glacier des Bois, Chamonix.*

4.3   Unknown artist. *The Geissbach Falls 1816.*

4.4   John Ruskin. *Detail from Tintoretto's 'Adoration of the Magi'.*

4.5   Louise Virenda Blandy. *Copy of Fra Angelico.*

4.6   John Ruskin. *Copy of the central part of Tintoretto's 'Crucifixion'.*

4.7   John Ruskin. *The Vine, Free and in Service* and *Leafage in the Vine Angle.*

4.8   John Ruskin. *Lily Capital, St Mark's.*

4.9   Unknown photographer. *Adam and Eve and the Fig Tree, the Ducal Palace.*

4.10   John Ruskin. *The Vine Angle, the Ducal Palace.*

4.11   Unknown Photographer. *The Judgement of Solomon, the Ducal Palace.*

4.12   Unknown Photographer. *The columns of San Marco and San Teodoro, the piazzetta.*

4.13   H.S. Uhlrich. *Bas-relief of the Apostles and the Lamb, St Mark's.*

4.14   H.S. Uhlrich. *St George, St Mark's.*

4.15   *St George and the Dragon, Venice.*

4.16   Paulo Veronese. *The Queen of Sheba and Solomon.*

4.17   Giotto. *The Marriage of St Francis and Poverty.*

4.18   Vittore Carpaccio. *The Dream of St Ursula.*

4.19   Vittore Carpaccio. *Presentation in the Temple.*

4.20   John Ruskin. *Amiens from the river.*

4.21   John Ruskin. *St Wulfran, Abbeville.*

4.22   *The Last Judgement Tympanum, St Maclou, Rouen.*

4.23   John Ruskin. *Sculptures for Bas-reliefs of the North Door of the Cathedral of Rouen.*

4.24   Unknown photographer. *S. Denis and angels (detail of sculpture), Rheims Cathedral.*

4.25 John Ruskin. *Northern Porch, West Front, Amiens Cathedral, Before Restoration.*

4.26 David Roberts. *The West Front, Amiens Cathedral, France.*

4.27 Charles Hugot. *Vue Générale d'Amiens, Prise de la Citadelle.*

4.28 Kaltenbacher. *General View of Amiens Cathedral.*

4.29 [Kaltenbacher]. *The Three Western Porches, Amiens Cathedral.*

4.30 *The Golden Virgin, Amiens Cathedral.*

4.31 *The Choir Stalls, Amiens Cathedral.*

4.32 John Ruskin. *Plan for the Western Porches, Amiens Cathedral.*

Maps

1 The Old Roads

2 The Swiss Tours

3 The Italian Tours

4 The French Tour of 1848

Acknowledgements

This book is a dissemination of the three-year research project, *John Ruskin, Cultural Travel and Popular Access*, based at The Ruskin Centre, Lancaster University, and funded by the Arts and Humanities Research Council. The activities and outcomes were led by Keith Hanley, Director of the Ruskin Centre, in collaboration with co-investigators Brian Maidment, Salford University, and John Walton, then of Leeds Metropolitan University, and were assisted by the AHRC postdoctoral Research Associate, Rachel Dickinson. Lauren Proctor, Administrator of The Ruskin Centre, and Emma Sdegno of the University of Ca' Foscari, Venice, were indispensable in organising the related events and conferences, in particular that on *Ruskin, Venice and 19th Century Cultural Travel*, 25–29 September 2008, in co-operation with The Department of European and Postcolonial Studies of the University of Ca' Foscari, Venice, the Scuola Grande Arciconfraternita di San Rocco and Venice International University.

For their support in all aspects of our research we wish to thank Stephen Wildman, Director, and Diane Tyler, Assistant Curator, at the Ruskin Library, Lancaster University; Jacqueline Ayrault, Directrice, Bibliothèque Louis Aragon, Bibliothèque d'Amiens Métropole, Amiens; Heather Birchall and Dionysia Christoforou, The Whitworth Gallery, Manchester; Helen Clish, Rare Books Collection, Lancaster University Library; Prisca Hazebrowck, Bibliothèque Municipale, Abbeville; Claude Marin, Director of Cultural Affairs, Chamonix Mont-Blanc, France; Matthieu Pinette, Directeur, Musée de Picardie, Amiens; Catherine Poletti, Musée Alpin, Chamonix Mont-Blanc; Grand Master, Arch. Franco Posocco, Scuola Grande Arciconfraternita di San Rocco; Louise Pullen, The Guild of St George, Sheffield; Paul Smith, The Thomas Cook Archives, Peterborough; Walter Tschopp, Musée d'Art et d'Histoire, Neuchâtel; Verena Villinger, Directrice adjointe, Musée d'Art et d'Histoire, Fribourg. Thanks also to Howard Hull, Director at Brantwood, and to Bridie Diamond for conversation and insights.

We are grateful to R. Martin Seddon who designed the maps and provided the photographs for a catalogued exhibition, *Journeys of a Lifetime: Ruskin's Continental Tours*, curated by Keith Hanley and Rachel Dickinson at The Ruskin Library, Lancaster University, 19 April–28 September 2008, many of which are included in this book. We are indebted also to the trustees of the institutions which have permitted us to print illustrations from their holdings: The Ruskin Foundation, The Ruskin Library, Lancaster University; The Brantwood Trust; The Guild of St George, Sheffield Galleries and Museums Trust; The Thomas Cook Archives, Peterborough; The Whitworth Art Gallery, The University of Manchester; and private owners.

Arts & Humanities
Research Council

Chapter 1
Introduction: The Joy of Travel

Ruskin and Tourism Studies

This book examines the role of John Ruskin in the development of tourism in Britain and Western Europe during and after the second half of the 19th century. Ruskin was a major figure in setting the agenda and directing the gaze, not only for the upper- and middle-class British tourists who played such an important part in the consolidation of international tourism in the age of the railway, but also for the emergent working-class explorers of hills and countryside within Britain in the late 19th and early 20th century. His own journeys did not cover new ground: indeed, he followed the orthodox routes of the Grand Tour in Europe and the conventional pathways of the picturesque traveller in upland Britain. But what he provided were new ways of seeing and imagining, new contexts and meanings and a new moral vision which transformed the rhetoric of experience, and, at least for some people, its actual nature. Ruskin was one influence among many, and the task of teasing out the nature and significance of his contribution is complex and nuanced; but it has never been undertaken, and its importance is indubitable. It is all the more problematic, because Ruskin's own attitude to tourism was ambivalent and demanding, eager to encourage the enquiring mind, but suspicious of anything superficial or with any connotations of 'Cook's tours' or what came to be known as 'mass tourism'. For this reason, among others, the relationships between Ruskin's writings, practices and influences, and the existing agenda of writing about tourism, need to be explored at the outset. We begin by arguing that incorporating a Ruskin perspective into tourism studies has the potential to change the face and agenda of the discipline.

Tourism studies have been mainly preoccupied with the rise and contemporary practices of the tourist industry, which is seen to have started in the early 19th century and to have been developed along with 'increases in free time, more disposable income and advances in technology' (Sharpely, 1999: 22). The different disciplinary approaches within the field seem to have been mostly dominated by that closed focus, and 'the value' of tourism is most often described in firmly economic terms. Any contrary agendas and value systems, such as religious or educational motives, are usually treated as market specialisms. Otherwise they have been left to be covered by their own disciplines as, for example, part of cultural, educational and religious history. Academically, tourism studies have been comprehensively appropriated by neo-classical economics and functionalist sociology, with an admixture of anthropology, concerned with defining the general social forces and norms which determine the individual's behaviour. A great deal of published work has been practical and instrumental in orientation. History, as a critical discipline grounded in evidence, has only recently begun to enter the frame (Walton, 2009a, 2009b). In this way, tourism studies have been primarily concerned with describing and accounting for the workings of an industry, which, especially in the context of theories of globalisation, has been fundamentally unproblematised and may even be argued to have produced in some cases the industrialisation of tourism studies themselves. It is surprising, for example, that George Ritzer's critical concepts of McDonaldisation and glocalisation have not been pursued more energetically in tourism studies, while the long survival of the tourism area life cycle as a key organising principle suggests an inertia which is only now being overcome (Ritzer & Butler, 2006). From some humanities perspectives, the dominant approaches in tourism studies relegate the consideration of individual agency and development through tourism to consumer choice (Wright, 2002).

The following work offers a fresh humanities-based intervention founded on the case history of an influential voice during the time of the rise of the tourist industry, John Ruskin. Ruskin's cultural constructions were set against the practices of capitalist production which Rudy Koshar has argued were replicated in leisure activities:

> Tourism ... [i]s not self-directed but externally directed. You go not where you want to go but where the industry has decreed you shall go. ... Tourism requires that you see conventional things, and that you see them in a conventional way. (Koshar, 2002: 39; see also Fussell, 1980)

His approach to cultural tourism and its afterlives in leisure and travel practices offers important versions of the well-established distinction between the 'tourist' and the 'traveller' and of what James Buzard terms 'anti-tourism', an 'exemplary way of regarding one's own cultural experiences as authentic and unique, setting them against a backdrop of always assumed tourist vulgarity, repetition, and ignorance' (Buzard, 1993: 5). Most approaches to cultural tourism acknowledge, either directly or indirectly, the predominance of the market as the defining motor of tourism per se, and view the conflicted aspirations behind the more actively self-determined and self-determining 'travel' as the content of a superior product rather than being freed from market forces. Related research has most commonly been shaped by the phenomenal expansion of 20th-century tourism which made it 'arguably the largest of multinational activities', leading to 'the increased blurring of the distinctions which once marked out tourism and culture as separate spheres of activity' (Robinson & Boniface, 1999: 1, 2), as cultural experience has become overwhelmingly commodified. It is in the context of what Mike Robinson writes of as the globalisation of the 'new world order … dominated by progressive, Western neo-modern ideologies in which economic relationships are central' (Robinson, 1999: 23) that Priscilla Boniface reduces the achievement of a possible 'consensus' between 'Tourism and Cultures' to an outcome in which 'cultures play a crucial role because in their differences they offer variety and the possibility of product differentiation' (Boniface, 1999: 287). The only role of 'culture' is thus seen to lie in the management of demand through branding and marketing. As part of this process, tourism studies as a discipline has focused overwhelmingly on the so-called 'mass tourism' and on the international package holiday industry as organised and marketed by tour operators in various guises. Such perspectives rarely make contact with the historical rise of tourism when that trajectory was less inevitable, when culture and tourism were not entirely conflated, and when adversarial cultural projects that were non-complicit with the market, and in Ruskin's case opposed to it, were still imagined to be both available and desirable. We distinguish Ruskin's approach to 'travel' from that of the service industry of tourism, regarding it as individually validated experience, characterised by activism in perception, entering into different or alternative cultural formation, and with sufficient complexity and depth to lead to an enriching educational or learning outcome.

Writing in the tradition of Romantic anti-capitalism, Ruskin stands for the opposition to much that the industry embodied, expressed and was bringing about, and he took his stance in the name of drawing out individual potential, advocating a quality of cultural experience and moral education which the industry was not simply neglecting but in his view actively undermining, and doing so precisely in the area of aesthetic perception which was most crucial to their beneficial impact. While acknowledging the obvious historical, social and institutional investments in Ruskin's constructions of cultural experience, we are keen to avoid the classist tag of elitism as ascribed by many sociologists including Boorstin (1961: 85–88), and in particular we would argue that the religious and educational motives which were attached in Ruskin's day to the residues and transformations of pre-modern travel, represented by pilgrimage and the Grand Tour, represent complex and contradictory class investments in the self-fulfilment of people in all social positions. In particular, we begin to explore in this book both practical and theoretic continuities from Ruskin's interventions. Europe, for example, to which his travelling was confined, is still the region which attracts most international tourism, and the debates opened up by Romantic anti-capitalists such as Wordsworth and Ruskin concerning the uses and abuses of rail travel and the first rise of something that might be labelled 'mass tourism' are still current in the age of the airborne package tour, when 'The consumers (mass tourists) are, arguably, deceived by the lure of a holiday that promises escape from the capitalist system yet which is, in effect, an extension of it' (Sharpley: 12; see Hanley, 1993: 228–229; Hanley, 2007: 65–68).

The seriousness of Ruskin's critique and his alternative agenda may be seen in terms of Dean MacCannell's and others' treatment of tourism as a quest for authenticity in modern alienated societies. Eric Cohen, for example, writes that the frustrated lack of authenticity 'may well be a structural consequence of the pluralization of modern life-worlds' (Cohen, 1988: 376). Historically, Ruskin was battling just that dawning situation and the significance of his travelling chimes with the behaviour MacCannell describes as a model for 'modern-man-in-general' (1989: 1): 'sightseeing is a kind of collective striving for a transcendence of the modern totality, a way of attempting to overcome the discontinuity of modernity, of incorporating its fragments into unified experience' (13). But Ruskin's destinations promise more than just flights from materialism, mass production and consumption. As transformations of pilgrimage, less secularised than MacCannell argues, his travels to the pre-modern countryside and the architecture of the Middle Ages offer the restoration of insights into integrated communities of belief.

Ruskin was a famous polymath whose cultural interventions covered a wide range of interests and disciplines. Though a gifted draughtsman, scientific commentator and celebrated writer of Romantic prose, it was as a critic of art, architecture and society that he achieved his chief cultural function and influence. His defining project was to found a comprehensive critique of contemporaneous culture and society on aesthetics, and to offer a deeply satisfying aesthetic integration of his period's leading discourses, of science and religion, which had become painfully and confusingly fragmented for his fellow Victorians. But in order to locate the superior social model by which his present was to be judged, and arrive at the positions advocated in his teachings, he went in search of places which still represented values and potential experiences opposed to those of the developing industrial capitalism of 19th-century Britain. He identified its touchstones and then conducted the gaze of his contemporaries to representations of an alternative, more fulfilling society which he recuperated from the historical geography of a European past of western Christianity. As a radical anti-capitalist critic, he had to travel against his age. It will be clear that we do not subscribe to the 'Wiener thesis' that, even at its industrial apogee, Britain never fully embraced the cultural logic of industrialism, and that hierarchical assumptions of rural superiority remained enshrined in dominant values. Ruskin's work and influence might indeed be enlisted in support of such an argument, and Wiener does indeed do so; but he was always working against the grain of an increasingly industrial and commercial *zeitgeist*, rather than taking comfort from a supportive traditionalist dominant ideology (Wiener, 1981: 37–40).

It is true that Ruskin directed his readers to a very circumscribed, western eurocentric area of travel. He worked to have them participate in a shared heritage which was specifically pre-Renaissance and Christian, and to that end endeavoured to reduce the sense of differentiation in time and place to a condition that was unified by a shared moral tradition. But that cultural enlargement was conceived as a reform of 19th-century British values, to be achieved by the restitution of what was an *other* Europe, represented for example by Swiss pastoralism, northern French Gothic and early Renaissance Italian painting. This could, he urged, turn out to be the radical origin of his own re-imagined national tradition, though one which had become an alien culture for his contemporary British traveller. Whereas the leading guidebooks of his day, issued by Murray and Baedeker and the leading tour operator, Thomas Cook, were concerned in facilitating the educational and recreational appropriation of 'abroad' by their British consumers, making the alien cultural experience of historic Europe a commodity, Ruskin insisted on a respectful submission to, and only then the assimilation of, its values. He describes and attempts to promote a profound and challenging cultural negotiation which demands a distinct set of practices, including sufficient periods of time and adequately studious attitudes to allow for the informed selection and active interpretation of representative sites and monuments. Such were the programme and methods of what may be called his 'critical tourism'.

Opting out of the tourist market can too easily be unhelpfully confused with what John Urry describes as the privatised and anti-social assumptions and practices of the 'romantic gaze' (Urry, 2002b: 44). Of course, the tendency to self-centred absorption is not absent from Ruskin's cultural responses. Of an Italian tour of 1846, Ruskin remorsefully recounts an anecdote which speaks for the rift which opened up between himself and his father, a hard-headed businessman, who was to be irritated and embarrassed by his son's denunciation of the capitalist system in later economic works. On a 'sunny afternoon at Pisa',

> just as we were driving past my pet La Spina chapel, my father, waking out of a reverie, asked me suddenly, 'John, what shall I give the coachman?' Whereupon, I, instead of telling him what he asked me … took upon me with impatience to reprove, and lament over, my father's hardness of heart, in thinking that moment of sublunary affairs. (35.419)[1]

Ruskin was aware of the self-indulgences of his privileged situation which he never completely overcame, yet the kind of aesthetic epiphany he was experiencing took him into a cultural imagination far beyond navel

LIVERPOOL JOHN MOORES UNIVERSITY
LEARNING SERVICES

gazing. He was most interested in objectifying and communicating his own experience to others, as Buzard argues of the 'romantic gaze':

> There is a dialectical relationship between the elaboration of 'crowd' and 'tourist', on the one hand, and the anti-tourist's privileging of 'solitude', which is less a valuing of private experience than it is a rhetorical act of role-distancing in need of its audience, real or imaginary.... Even celebrated moments of solitude (e.g. in travel books) must be seen as in some measure *existing to be celebrated*. (Buzard, 1993: 153)

These were representative experiences of individual interiority which he felt everyone was entitled to and should be helped to enjoy.

The varieties of Urry's 'tourist gaze', which he has explored in several works and which he writes 'marks the beginning of the modern era in terms of landscape' in 1840 when it becomes 'endlessly devouring', are all reinforced by product differentiation for 'The "consuming" of Place' (Urry, 2005: 21). But such an account lacks the recalcitrances of cultural history, and the chemistry of historical experience. The gazes, of course, are not always separate and distinct in reality, and the polarisation he posits between the self-centred 'romantic gaze' and the social solidarity of his 'collective gaze' (Urry, 2002b: 43–44) is importantly unreal, for example, in the case of what may be termed Wordsworth's *communal* gaze, representing both shared and varied experiences. While Urry's antithesis edges on pitting solipsism against mass culture, represented by the random 'presence of large numbers of other people' (Urry, 2002b: 43), Wordsworth (and Ruskin after him) rejected the kind of anonymous social experience of the crowd he described in his vision of the modern metropolis, London, as epitomised in Bartholomew Fair: '... melted and reduced/To one identity, by differences/That have no law, no meaning, and no end /.../By nature an unmanageable sight' (Wordsworth, 1984: 486, ll.703–705, 709) for the interconnected local community of Grasmere Fair, bound together by affection over generations for the 'Fellow-beings' (Wordsworth, 488, l.70) who gathered there. Ruskin, in his turn, was more concerned with the cultural exclusion of the labouring classes and their economic exploitation than with the stimulations of collective consumerism that he encountered at Furness Abbey in 1871 (see Hanley, 2007: 67–68). He knew that the railway there, as elsewhere in the Lake Counties, was intended primarily for mineral exploitation, and then for exploitation of the workforce:

> ... all that your railroad company can do for them is only to open taverns and skittle grounds round Grasmere, which will soon, then, be nothing but a pool of drainage, with a beach of broken ginger beer bottles; and their minds will be no more improved by contemplating the scenery of such a lake than of Blackpool. (34.141)

He made a distinction between '*giving* to the poor' and 'making a dividend out of the poor', between opening up access to fresh experiences and flattening them all out: let engineers and contractors live, he echoed

Wordsworth, 'in a more useful and honourable way than by keeping Old Bartholomew Fair under Helvellyn' (141). Wordsworth's aesthetic of imaginative experience is not that of the detached picturesque tourist but still participates in that already available to the native residents, like the old shepherd, Michael. His land is filled with 'thoughts' (226, 1.64), and it represents much more than unconscious immersion in his farm land:

> Fields, where with cheerful spirits he had breathed
> The common air; the hills, which he so oft
> Had climbed with vigorous steps; which had impressed
> So many incidents upon his mind
> Of hardship, skill or courage, joy, or fear. (Wordsworth, 1984: ll.65–69)

The intellectual tradition that this alternative Romantic gaze appeals to is that of philosophical realism, in its intricate recuperations as the undercurrent of the British imagination. The early Romantics appealed to the psychological machinery of associationism, whereby sense impressions combined to generate complex ideas, in 'the manner in which we associate ideas in a state of excitement' (1984: 597). For such an outlook, Urry's severance of land and landscape, the 'physical, tangible resource' (Urry, 2005: 19) and the spectacle, is not absolute. Michael's land is inscribed with social memory, and over time images become invested with the accumulation of more evolved meanings, as Wordsworth writes in 'Tintern Abbey' of new scenes viewed on his travels: 'Though absent long,/These forms of beauty have not been to me,/As is a landscape to a blind man's eye', so that those originating 'sensations sweet' have gradually '[passed] into [his] purer mind' (Wordsworth, 1984: 132, ll.23–25, 28, 30). Wordsworth's paradigmatic traveller is the Wanderer in the aptly entitled *The Excursion*, 1814, who, having first read the potential of expanding significance in the horizon of his locality, '. . . the least of things/Seemed infinite; and there his spirit shaped/Her prospects, nor did he believe, – he saw' (Wordsworth, 2007: 55, ll.251–253), continues on his journeying to sustain an axis between centre and periphery, home and abroad, self and other. He is, as Urry recognises, a *returning* traveller (Urry: 202). He comes from, as well as goes to, the ownership of a cultural identity without which there would be no agency of interaction in all his encounters, enabling him to go on adding to and modifying a set of shared meanings and values. The community of this gaze, which spreads among Wordsworth's readership, has a cultural substance not represented by Urry's approach to the 'mediatised gaze' (Urry, 2005: 22), but one preserved by the works of its major mediators who provide an imaginative map back to its real origins. There is all the difference in the world between the writings of Wordsworth and Ruskin and a picture postcard.

Ruskin was never rooted in the same way as Wordsworth, and he travelled farther in every sense. Indeed, he eventually became impatient with the restricted cultural vision of Wordsworth, 'a Westmoreland peasant'

(34.318) (see Hanley, 1993: 224). The process of deracination which Buzard describes in Wordsworth's poem, 'The Brothers', 1800, along with several poems of the time concerning the breakdown of the agrarian economy and the rise of industrialism, as 'the beginning of modernity ... a time when one stops belonging to a culture and can only *tour* it' (Buzard: 26), had become embedded by the end of the 1830s when Ruskin began his own cultural tourism. But his own touring began on the cusp of a world which had far from passed away, and Ruskin's dependence on horse-drawn transport and pre-mechanical mediations, especially drawing, were to remain in tension with the innovations which Urry treats as definitive of the ways 'places of land became places of visual desire' (Urry, 2005: 20) by 1840. Ruskin looks for more than 'the desire of the eyes' (10.141): his gaze has a deep historical content which includes the perception of a layering of cultural alienations from Renaissance capitalism onwards, as well as the economic traumas of the early 19th century (see Chapter 3). Ruskin lived and wrote through a transitional period which was marked by a series of stages and developments, all of which were received with the conflicted responses and internal divisions which marked Victorian culture, leading to its characteristic antithetical mode: Carlyle's *Past and Present*, Disraeli's 'Two Nations', Gaskell's *North and South*, Newman's *Loss and Gain*. As Matthew Arnold wrote, the age had its feet planted in two different worlds; and as Ruskin wrote, the market – certainly not alone – could not reconcile them. Urry's 'tourist gaze' was not suddenly undivided in actuality, as Ruskin bears witness, but occupies an underlying dilemma which is still representative of our social and cultural reality. Perhaps it is symptomatic of Urry's reduction that in his various writings he always refers to Wordsworth's representative poem 'The Brothers' as 'The Brother'. There are, of course, *two* Ewbank brothers who belong to both sides of the land/landscape divide: one dies on the land he never leaves, and the other travels endlessly on, unable to return home. They occupy diverging impulses – to restrictive allegiances on the one hand, and to enterprising desires on the other, which can however prove insatiable and hollow. Indeed, Urry concludes his most recent commentary on 'The "consuming" of place' with what seems like an uncomfortable kind of fatalism: 'The consuming of place as landscape is thus our destiny and our dilemma. It cannot be avoided' (Urry, 2005: 26). Really? The word 'dilemma' does actually acknowledge alternatives, however repressed, and this book is addressed to entertaining and amplifying that awareness.

Superficially, Ruskin's central concern with the aesthetic, focused on museums, galleries and historic buildings, may appear to offer itself for categorisation in terms of Pierre Bourdieu's reductive binary of 'popular' and 'pure' taste in his highly influential *Distinction: A Social Critique of the Judgement of Taste* (1979), which informs much sociological analysis, including Buzard's, arguing for the constructedness of elitist cultural taste in basically social and economic terms. Whereas Bourdieu's 'high culture' is simply a class construct of capitalism, however, Ruskin's most certainly is not, and indeed presciently identifies precisely that operation which it radically opposes. Buzard, for example, 'endorses' what Bourdieu calls '"*habitus*", the internalized system of "dispositions" which, among other things, prepare one for the satisfactory appropriation of cultural goods' (Buzard, 1993: 7), and sees tourism accordingly as

> an exemplary cultural practice of modern liberal democracies, for it has evolved an appearance of being both popularly accessible and exclusive at once. In spite of its 'meritocratic' ideology, however – and also because of it – modern tourism has tended to reinforce existing privileges, reproducing assumptions about the special suitedness of well-to-do northern European men for fully realized acculturation. (Buzard, 1993: 6–7)

This analysis is in effect an unfolding of Ruskin's own critique of his contemporary tourist industry, and he worked right against the grain of this mindset, notoriously denouncing the industrialists of Bradford and Manchester on their own territory for trying to consume and appropriate 'high culture' in this way, as a sign of economic success.

In particular, Bourdieu's treatment of the aesthetic connects it to a specifically Kantian idealism, whereas the British Romantic tradition which underpins Ruskin's thought has a dissimilar genealogy, based on philosophical and social realism. In his unsystematic way, Ruskin adhered to Locke's definition of the 'idea', quoting his *Essay Concerning Human Understanding* to the effect that it '[extends] even to the sensual impressions themselves as far as they are "things which the mind occupies itself about in thinking;" that is, not as they are felt by the eye only, but as they are received by the mind through the eye' (3.91–92), and that the act of 'perception' requires the mental internalisation of sense 'impressions' (141). It is the worldview embedded in the English Romantic imagination and which finds its most explicit expression in Wordsworth's poetry: 'How exquisitely the individual Mind/ ... to the external world/Is fitted; and how exquisitely, too–/ ... /The external world is fitted to the mind' (Wordsworth, 1984: 198, ll.1006, 1008–9, 1011). The framework Bourdieu constructs, for example, in his 'Postscript: towards a "vulgar" critique of "pure critiques"', is out of touch when applied to English Romantic texts. He writes that:

> 'Pure' taste and the aesthetics which provides its theory are founded on a refusal of 'impure' taste and of aesthesis (sensation), the simple, primitive form of pleasure reduced to a pleasure of the senses, as in what Kant calls 'the taste of the tongue, the palate and the throat'. (Bourdieu, 1979: 486)

Ruskin's associationism, which the Romantics derived from the empiricist psychology of Hume and David Hartley, simply does not make this absolute division between the 'taste of reflection' and the 'taste of sense' (Bourdieu, 1979: 490). Associationist taste, defined by a school of British aesthetics represented by Archibald Alison's *Essays on the Nature and Principles of Taste* (1790), and Richard Payne Knight's *Analytical Inquiry into the Principles of Taste* (1805), views the perceiving mind as actively seeking correspondence with the intrinsic order in natural forms (see 'Visual Representation', Chapter 3).

In order to clarify Ruskin's worldview it is necessary to separate his writings from some of their misleading assimilations, however prestigious. Proust was an ardent disciple of Ruskin and spent six years studying his works as he developed his own great writing project and aesthetic theories. In the concluding section of 'The pleasure of the text', Bourdieu (1979) refers his argument to Proust's 'lucid description' of his guilty competence in allusive fields which depend on elitist access to privileged knowledge. Proust had made his confession in relation to a charge of 'idolatry' he had come to make against what he felt was Ruskin's subtly self-deceiving prioritisation of the aesthetic over the moral, even resulting in a pretence of finding a moral and pious discourse inscribed within the real objects of his admiring perception. He quotes a well-known virtuoso passage on St Mark's basilica from Ruskin's 'Causes of Venetian Decadence' in the *Stones of Venice*, starting

> Not in wantonness of wealth, not in vain ministry to the desire of the eyes or the pride of life, were those marbles hewn into transparent strength, and those arches arrayed in the colour of the iris. There is a message written in the dyes of them, that once was written in blood; and a sound in the echoes of their vaults, that one day shall fill the vault of heaven .... (10.141)

Ruskin proceeds to castigate the moral decline of the state as a betrayal of the virtues embodied in the architecture of its past: '... for amidst them all, through century after century of gathering vanity and festering guilt, that white dome of St Mark's had uttered in the dead ear of Venice, "Know thou, that for all these things God will bring thee to judgment"' (10.142). Proust finds the alleged continuities between the real objects and the moral scheme to be 'artificialities' (Proust, 1987: 58), and accordingly he considers Ruskin's ostensible aesthetic values to be insincere. Always absorbed in Ruskin's allegorical reading of things, Proust had come to question the latter's prioritisation of the spirit over the letter and the asserted capacity of real experience to produce anything other than tissues of re-interpretation rather than the truths Ruskin claimed (see Macksey, 1982: 185–190). Nevertheless, he does attribute a 'kind of truth' to 'the very vivid aesthetic pleasure we experience when reading such a page', and Proust detects within this pleasure a self-satisfaction in being able to construe 'the text that had appeared in Byzantine letters around [the] haloed brows', and 'A sort of egotistical self-evaluation [which] is unavoidable in those joys in which erudition and art mingle and in which aesthetic pleasure may become more acute, but not remain as pure' (Proust, 1987: 53). Bourdieu is not interested in Proust's theory of a disinterested sense of beauty so much as in his recognition of what for him is an extended definition of 'idolatry': the give-away of the exclusivist workings of

> Cultivated pleasure [which] feeds on these intertwined references, which reinforce and legitimate each other, producing, inseparably, belief in the value of works of art, the 'idolatry' which is the very basis of cultivated pleasure, and the inimitable charm they objectively exert on all who are qualified to enter the game.... (Bourdieu, 1979: 499)

Proust's refusal to accept Ruskin's moral aesthetic, derived from real sense experience, and leading the latter definitively to refute the imposition of mental constructions not so based, has become attached by Bourdieu to a different philosophical universe in which mediation is simply and inevitably a sign of social empowerment. Proust himself partially unmoored the workings of what was to become his famous 'involuntary memory', his central theoretical formulation, from its dependence on the realist base claimed by both Wordsworth and De Quincey, who both helped to evolve the basis and context for Ruskin to invent the expression in describing the secret of 'all great inventors', such as Dante, Scott, Tintoretto and Turner (see 'The Ruskin Gaze', Chapter 3): '... their imagination consisting, not in a voluntary perception of new images, but an involuntary remembrance, exactly at the right moment, of something they had actually seen' (6.42). For Proust the object of sensation which originated the operations of memory was arbitrary and did not possess inherent meaning, yet Proust did concede that Ruskin's own vicarious perception had an exemplary and founding relation to the real thing, as opposed to his own premonition of Baudrillard's argument about the consumption of mere signs or representations:

> For Ruskin's thought is not like that of Emerson, for example, which is entirely contained in a book, that is to say an abstract thing, a pure sign of itself. The object to which thought such as Ruskin's is applied, and from which it is inseparable, is not immaterial, it is scattered here and there over the surface of the earth. One must seek it where it is, in Pisa, Florence, Venice, the National Gallery, Rouen, Amiens, the mountains of Switzerland. Such thought has an object other than itself, which has materialised in space, which is no longer infinite and free, but is limited and subdued, which is incarnated in bodies of sculptured marble, in snowy mountains, in painted countenances, is perhaps less sublime than pure thought. But it makes the universe more beautiful for us .... (Proust, 1987: 58–59)

It is Ruskin's insistence on the teleology of sensation – after all the upshot of all his travels – which divides his agenda from what Bourdieu describes as the socio-economic elite's 'disgust at the facile' in merely sensationalist taste:

> The refusal of what is easy in the sense of simple, and therefore shallow, and 'cheap', because it is easily decoded and culturally 'undemanding', naturally leads to the refusal of what is facile in the ethical or aesthetic sense, of everything which offers pleasures that are too immediately accessible and so discredited as 'childish' or 'primitive' (as opposed to the deferred pleasures of legitimate art). (Bourdieu, 1979: 486)

The Weberian critique that protestant Christianity is inherently bourgeois hovers around Bourdieu's analysis, but Ruskin's (evangelical) stress on hard work was innovatively directed to self-expressive creativity in all walks of society. This is in sharp contrast with the expectation of effortless superiority, of cultural capital as acquired almost by osmosis, which recurs in the conventional portrayal of the gentleman as tourist, a legacy of the Grand Tour which helps to exclude those born outside the charmed circle. Ruskin's central endeavour was to recover the pre-Reformation European Christianity which preceded Renaissance capitalism and which he strove to model socially in his utopian Guild of St George. All his own works are dedicated to the message which was most clearly articulated in *Unto This Last* that work should be about making men not profit, enabling the energy of self-expression rather than subdued to the terms of employment. His deeply ruminated counter to utilitarian pleasure was imbued, like Turner's landscapes, with a recognition of inescapable suffering which strove to find comprehensive meaning in the redemptive Christian scheme. His very English Romantic word, after Blake, Keats and Wordsworth, for the internalised architecture of commonly available experience, was 'joy'.

The Argument

We are attempting to examine the historical influence of Ruskin on the rise of the middle-class practice of what he helped to define as cultural tourism and its different continuities. Ruskin's is the peculiar case of a leading English cultural critic who is a major Romantic writer, a significant draughtsman and a scientific commentator whose travels were the basis of his aesthetic and social teaching and moral guidance. His creativity and interdisciplinary researches were fed by a historical geography which he explored on journeys in time as well as space, as he re-entered through them a civilisation which he considered under process of destruction and sought to recover a past, largely medieval, which he held up against the fall of modernity, for him the product of free market capitalism. The cultural tourism he practised and advocated on an imaginary basis in all his writings as well as in formal guides to his most epitomising destinations led away from the ugly and immoral progeny of industriali- sation and mechanisation, and was by definition particularly, if not always successfully, directed at avoiding its own commodification.

Looking back to, and overlapping with, the educational and aesthetic agenda of the aristocratic Grand Tour, Ruskin's approach was founded on the traditions of the Picturesque Tour and Romantic literary tourism, which passed into increasingly critical relation with the popular access enabled by new modes of transport and publication together with the aspirations for self-improvement encouraged by an age of social, political and educa- tional reform. While Ruskin responded positively to the widening of par- ticipation in traditional culture and the arts, in the course of his life and travels he witnessed the rise of industrial modernism and secularism which accompanied it, and strenuously condemned the industrialisation of the arts as of tourism itself as effectively destroying complex and valuable kinds of experience rather than opening them up. His practices as a travel- ler, his chosen centres and all his ways of visiting were directed to a pro- phetic rebuttal of those forces in his contemporary Europe which were to generate two world wars and the ecological disasters of the 20th century. Symptomatic is his rejection of contemporary tourism, its entanglement in the capitalist machine, and his appeal to those he guides to awaken an imagination of the potential for a greater self and society represented in the great art works, buildings and landscapes of other times and places.

The combination of Ruskin's radicalism and his Victorian 'high serious- ness' made the artefacts, cultural monuments and natural scenes he visited matter intensely, and gave them moral and political urgency. Taken together they constituted his invention of what may be called 'critical tourism', set against the predominant utilitarian mentality of his times, and informing it positively. He had inherited and struggled to sustain two worldviews which he attempted to reconcile: the British Romanticism of Byron, Wordsworth and Turner which he had imbibed during his highly preco- cious teenage years, and the Evangelicalism he learned at his mother's knee. Specifically, for Ruskin, they represented the holistic tradition of a mind deeply imbued with a conservative reading of the historical past and nourished by a natural world with which it felt at one. The reading of his- tory was to open out over time into an interpretation of the Middle Ages as a cultural model for a non-industrial society, free from the fall into the alienated production and competitive capitalism of the Renaissance. It led him to an increasingly less sectarian vision of pan-European Christianity and a moral and social critique of British imperialism. (If, in common with a string of other eminent Victorians of various political stamps, he sided with Carlyle in the notorious controversy over Governor Eyre's brutal sup- pression of the Jamaican insurrection, he did so in a perverse and ignorant misapplication of his own principles which in almost every other case led

him consistently to a sound diagnosis of the workings of the military industrial machine.) A profound respect for the natural environment and a scrupulous attention to the laws of nature developed from his original belief in
natural theology, the deist, pre-evolutionary apprehension that God's hand
could be seen in the created world and his purposes inferred from natural
design. Any of these huge issues can and do surface in Ruskin's critical
tourism, but whether his rejection of the workings and products of capitalism is stressed, or his nostalgia for fuller and more wholesome forms of
living and creating, Ruskin's travels opened the door to encounters with
cultural otherness which carried drastic and life-enhancing lessons for his
home nation and which have motivated followers from many different cultures (Dickinson & Hanley, 2006: xxii–xxvi).

Because of his critical agenda, it is impossible to separate Ruskin's cultural guides and guidebooks from the body of his aesthetic, social and
economic criticism. Artworks, architectural monuments and landscapes
were to be the focus of the formal guides which he produced later in his
career: *Mornings in Florence,* in six parts, each describing a morning's walk
in the city, issued separately from 1875 to 1877, *Guide to the Principal Pictures
in the Academy of Fine Arts at Venice. Arranged for English Travellers* (1877), *St
Mark's Rest. The History of Venice, Written for the Help of the Few Travellers
who still care for her Monuments* (1877–84), the two-volume edition of the
Stones of Venice . . . for the Use of Travellers while staying in Venice and Verona,
issued in 1879–1881, and *The Bible of Amiens. Chapter IV. Interpretations.
(Separate Travellers' Edition, to serve as a Guide to the Cathedral)* (1881). But all
his writings share an ethical base, and his principal works such as *Modern
Painters, The Seven Lamps of Architecture* and *The Stones of Venice* were all
offered as cultural guides to recent British landscape painting, Northern
French and Italian Gothic architecture and early Renaissance Venetian
religious painting which distinctively demonstrated the moral content of
artworks and monuments.

Ruskin particularly wished to mark out his own approach from assimilation into the contemporaneous cultural market. Directing the attention of
the middle class and later the working man to the touchstones of European
art, he became increasingly aware that his promotion of cultural reference
was becoming appropriated by the new industry of cultural tourism. Just
as his advocacy of Gothic order architecture became overtaken by commercial fashion when what for him were deeply significant ecclesiastical features appeared on public houses and banks, so the tastes his writings had
fostered became part of the consumerist package served up by the burgeoning tourist industry as symbolised by Thomas Cook, with the accom-
paniment of the indispensable *vade mecums* published by Murray and
Baedeker. He was literally absorbed into that market when he provided
notes on art for the 1847 edition of Murray's *Handbook for Northern Italy,*
some of which are attributed to him, only to conduct thereafter a mocking

campaign in his writings against the kind of consumption those guides encouraged. It was too easy to confuse his own agenda with theirs.

His style can be off-putting. His adherence to the culture of evangelical Christianity was firmly grounded in the Bible, and his language is extraordinarily infused with scriptural allusions and rhetorical echoes, expressing the prophetic role which he and particularly Carlyle exercised as denouncers of the spiritual and imaginative death of their times. Because his cultural publications are after all examples of imaginative literature, there is a mythic and metaphorical dimension to the historical representation in their construction of pre-Renaissance mentality. They promise a sense of cultural wholeness that, as Peter D. Osborne writes, had been lost in the earlier period, which was traumatically reiterated in the moment of 19th-century alienation, crucially connected with 'the fading away of Christianity's "shared symbolic order"...':

> While competitive self-interest and the force of social change continually ignited the vigour and cruelty of the Renaissance and its aftermath, what also drove its people to explore in every direction was the need to fill a great emptiness that had opened up in the cosmology and the sense of self of many Europeans – the lack at the heart of modernity, the origin of its anxiety but also a source of its dynamism and creativity. This emptiness induced the urge to travel, to fill the spatial void with human presence, or to find whatever was imagined to have been lost. It impelled the creation of images to fill the vacant spaces with human features and meanings or to draw the dreamer or traveller towards a world that might be repossessed. (Osborne, 2000: 4)

Ruskin's writings, with all their rich stratifications and elaborately conceived illustrations, are an attempt at the kind of cultural substitution for a lost past sought by travel, though his critical predicament is inevitably invested with the inescapable knowledge of an altogether transformed society.

The kind of culturally unalienated experience which Ruskin enjoyed and attempted to communicate for his reader-travellers was directed to the enlargement of their *life*, Ruskin's key term for aesthetic and cultural worth. All Ruskin's travels define a journey of self-discovery which he narrates in his ultimate work, the autobiography *Praeterita*, 'Outlines of Scenes and Thoughts Perhaps Worthy of Memory in My Past Life' (1885–1889) (see Hanley, 2009). There he shows how all his scattered experiences were *bound and blended together* by a pattern of recurrent destinations – symbols of a personal geography simplifying to the series of place-names which head most chapters: Schaffhausen and Milan, The Col de la Faucille, Roslyn Chapel, L'Hotel du Mont Blanc ... such places stand for formative moments, when an actual scene becomes a metaphor for a state of realised selfhood, organising future development and deepening over time.

These turning points stayed with him wherever he subsequently travelled. For example, walking on the road to Norwood in 1842 he perceived for the first time the inherent design in 'a bit of ivy round a thorn stem' which, he writes, 'ended the chrysalid days. Thenceforward my advance was steady, however slow' (35.311). Later the same summer, his 'insight into a new silvan world' (315) was fixed when, studying a 'small aspen tree against the blue sky' at Fontainebleau, he conclusively registered how natural objects '"composed" themselves, by finer laws than any known of men' (314). So, in 1845, at Lucca, it was the same 'discipline from the Fontainebleau time ... [t]he accurate study of tree branches, growing leaves, and foreground herbage' (349) which enabled him to 'fasten on the tomb of Ilaria di Caretto ... with certainty of its being a supreme guide to me ever after' (347), as the figure of 'the sleeping Ilaria' faithfully represented the same 'harmonies of line ... under the same laws as the river wave, and the aspen branch, and the stars' rising and setting' (349).

Ruskin shapes and is shaped by a structure of change and continuity attached to sites and scenes – travelling to the same places yet seeing more and different meanings in them over time, or indeed to different places and finding the same meanings – so that, as Elizabeth Helsinger writes, his 'constant travelling is never progress: it is the means by which he revisits the territory of a visually extended self' (Helsinger, 1979: 88). Access to a vaster and richer cultural being was literally an eye-opening process. Again and again he notes his first self-enhancing sights: '... in the eastern light I well remember watching the line of the Black Forest hills enlarge and rise, as we crossed the plain of the Rhine. "Gates of the Hills" [Ruskin's title for Turner's *Pass of Faido*]; opening for me to a new life' (35.113), and the sensation of self-expansion over a widening visual field impels his non-stop mobility for more than 60 years. Like many of Ruskin's major individual works, like his entire *oeuvre*, *Praeterita* remains unfinished. His entire writing project and the travelling on which it is based are characterised by the relentless 'desire of [the] eyes' (10.141), what he calls in the *Stones of Venice* 'that strange *disquietude* of the Gothic spirit', which found its most sympathetic expression in his favourite architecture:

> ...that restlessness of the dreaming mind, that wanders hither and thither among the niches, and flickers feverishly around the pinnacles, and frets and fades in labyrinthine knots and shadows along wall and roof, and yet is not satisfied, nor shall be satisfied. (10.214)

Ultimately his revisited destinations become for him symbols of unending self-augmentation, as through them he enters and reinvigorates a vast tradition of continuous experience and persistent belief.

As his preoccupations widened, from art, to architecture, and social criticism, they were never dropped, but became layered in a cumulative process of interpretation. Nurturing these processes of growth was the tremendous attraction of the greater Europe; or at least, those parts of Western Europe to which he kept returning and which nourished his perceptions and understanding. As soon as he crossed the channel, Ruskin felt its power: 'I cannot find words to express the intense pleasure I have always in first finding myself, after some prolonged stay in England, at the foot of the old tower of Calais church' (6.11). Such monuments admitted him to a living history which he felt the British passion for novelty tended to obscure:

> Abroad, a building of the eighth or tenth century stands ruinous in the open street; the children play round it, the peasants heap their corn in it . . . we feel the ancient world to be a real thing, and one with the new: antiquity is no dream; it is rather the children playing about the old stones that are the dream. But all is continuous; and the words, 'from generation to generation,' understandable there. (6.13)

The configuration of past and present is informed by an inner drive to self-realisation and fruition – the same pattern of growth which he explored in his writings on biological and vegetational forms as they found expression in medieval ornamentation, where 'a leaf might always be considered as a sudden expansion of the stem that bore it; an uncontrollable expression of delight, on the part of the twig' (5.264), and 'the central type of all leaves' will become modified on the same rule according to rank:

> If it be meant for one of the crowned and lovely trees of the earth, it will separate into stars, and each ray of the leaf will form a ray of light in the crown, (Horsechestnut); and if it be a commonplace tree, rather prudent and practical than imaginative, it will not expand all at once, but throw out the ribs every now and then along the central rib, like a merchant taking his occasional and restricted holiday (Elm)' (265).

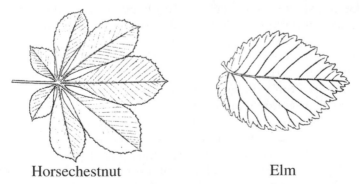

Horsechestnut   Elm

1.1 John Ruskin. From *The Growth of Leaves*. Engraved by R.P. Cuff. (5.facing 264). Photo by R. Martin Seddon.

Ruskin worked to motivate his readers' and students' fullest potential for their equivalent self-realisation, freed from the restraints of mercantilism. In his notes to his translation of Ruskin's *Sesame and Lilies*, Proust describes the 'secret plan' within the ramifications of Ruskin's imagination, unfolded in his extraordinarily sustained sentence structures: 'He goes from one idea to another without apparent order. But in reality the fancy that leads him follows his profound affinities which in spite of himself impose on him a superior logic' (Proust, 1987: 146). Yet it was a secret Ruskin was eager to share. If his travels took on the excitement of a treasure hunt, he published the map of where the booty lay buried in all his writings, encouraging his followers to retrace his actual footsteps, and arranging to import his discoveries for all to see: the best copies, the most accurate architectural casts and the most telling mineralogical specimens for his Oxford students and working men in his regional museums. He jealously promoted national 'treasuries' of art galleries and museums which, he argued, could and should spread the 'Open Sesame' of access for popular cultural education. Above all, he wanted to get a life for his fellow citizens. Believing that mechanisation and economic competition was hollowing out the being of 19th-century men and women, he offered to them the fruits of his own life, fervently believing that 'THERE IS NO WEALTH BUT LIFE' (17.105).

Addressing the appetite for self-improvement of the aspirant and affluent middle classes, his particular approaches both fed and sought to correct that market. His Romanticism and Evangelicalism placed him in a conflicted middle-class position, though from his perspective they generated a kind of reforming version of imaginary feudalism, and a morally enriched nationalism, dominated by an aristocracy and the common folk. The cocktail was eventually to produce Ruskin's invention of his conscientiously conceived neo-feudal/utopian Guild of St George in the early 1870s, combining galleries, museums and art treasures with an agrarian society in which all ranks were to share the wealth and health of unalienated labour. That social and economic vision led him to address his guidance and redirections not only to a middle-class readership but to all serious-minded members of society. His educational agenda was wide-ranging, whether he was lecturing Oxford undergraduates as Slade Professor of Fine Art, or teaching at Winnington private school for girls in Cheshire or Eton College, or mentoring an assortment of would-be female artists or young women in Oxford and elsewhere who were then ineligible to become students; and it was consistently aimed at enlarging popular access to artistic and cultural experience. But, as he argued in his popular lectures intended to redress the crass display of art as wealth which he viewed the Manchester Exhibition to be, published as *Sesame and Lilies*, he recognised a radical cleavage between a programme which genuinely opened the door to a shared experience of cultural work and the specious concessions made to industrial democracy. Together with his work for the London Working Men's College and his series of pamphlet-letters to the working men of Sunderland, *Time and Tide*, and then of Great Britain, *Fors Clavigera*, as also the museum he set up at Walkley near Sheffield, that project represented a reaching out to a far wider social audience than his earlier art and architectural works had most obviously invited.

Like Thomas Cook, Ruskin was dedicated to widening social access to traditional cultural experience. A Non-conformist promoter of the Temperance movement, Cook's 'broad vision of social reform' was for a Whiggish '"levelling upwards" of the social classes into a condition of national (ultimately universal) cultural brotherhood' (Buzard, 1993: 49). In *Cook's Excursionist*, July 1854, he wrote: 'Taste and Genius may look out of third-class windows...' (Buzard: 50). But Cook's tours were themselves to move upmarket to enable middle- and upper-class travel in the next generation, and Ruskin was extremely chary about what genuine access actually entailed. Cultural access was becoming most effectively achieved through travel, and it stood precisely on the divide between, on the one hand, the popular tourism which was industrialising travel, offering a superior market leisure product and indeed serving to constitute and define the new dominant class as its privileged consumers, and, on the other, admitting much larger numbers to the quality and knowledge of an order of experiences which had previously been the exclusive domain of an aristocratic elite. For Ruskin, such class mobilities were subsidiary to, and manipulations of, the inherent benefits of genuine cultural experience in itself.

In the first issue of *Cook's Excursionist*, for example, Cook printed an essay by a weaver from Bolton, 'To the Working Men of England', which advocated the programme of Cook's trips to the Great Exhibition as participating in what Cook proclaimed was 'a great School of Science, of Art, of Industry, of Peace and Universal Brotherhood', by entering into international industrial competition:

> The particular advantage to be derived from visiting the Exhibition by all those employed in preparing and manufacturing cotton goods will be, that Bolton, Manchester, Glasgow, Carlisle and Dundalk, will each and all be in friendly competition in workmanship, raw material and variety of patterns, and will also be found in rivalship with the foreign producers of such goods. (Buzard: 54)

This kind of 'philanthropy and five per cent' was precisely what Ruskin attributed to the manufacturers who sent their workforces on day trips to the Lake District which were spent in junketing and did not result in any actual exposure to landscape beauty. His own letters addressed to the Working Men of Great Britain, *Fors Clavigera*, preached a gospel of moral and imaginative fulfilment beyond the confines of the industrial routine.

Ruskin could have warmed to Cook's rebuttal of Charles Lever's satires on his tourists' habits – and they were representative of much ill-directed snobbery throughout the 19th century – and to his declaration of open democratic access:

> Mr Lever would reserve statue and mountain, painting and lake, historical association and natural beauty, for the so-called upper classes and for such Irish Doctors and German degrees as choose to be their toadies and hangers-on. I see no sin in introducing natural and artistic wonders to all. (Parsons, 2007: 242)

But again and again Ruskin argued that simply shipping tourists out did not in itself enable them to experience anything significant, though for him the realist base of experience did indeed open out potential for popular imaginative perception. So he imported real artefacts and specimens for the eyes of his workers at the Walkley museum as they were unable to make the journey to their original sites. With the important and notable exception of that of the band of copyists he trained and commissioned often from the different institutions he had to deal with (artists like John Wharlton Bunney, Charles Fairfax Murray and Thomas M. Rooke), the cultural 'travelling' took the form of imported exhibits, a few originals, casts and copies. In that way the encounter with a larger continental culture was effected by bringing it home to England in a modification of the importations of the privatised trophies of the Grand Tour.

Ruskin's ideological position is confused and confusing, which is perhaps why his thought has been so widely influential across the political spectrum and has resurfaced in contradictory forms, from high Toryism to communism. The various ranks and split motivations within a social reality which was undergoing rapid and radical change could only be imaginarily reconciled in utopian gestures and communitarian experiments which were to have important and divergent influences beyond his own geographical focus on Western Europe, in India, Russia, Japan and the United States. His most celebrated followers were only the tip of a readership which was wide and extraordinarily varied: Ruskin's imaginative resistance was most effective on anti-capitalist thinking in Gandhi, Tolstoy, the social teaching of Pope Leo XIII's *Rerum Novarum*, the Distributism of Chesterton and Belloc, and Fritz Schumacher, while the implications of his aesthetics were adopted by Proust and his art and architectural criticism fed into impressionism and the designs of Frank Lloyd Wright. His holistic approaches to art and craft were major directives in Japan and, through Morris, Edward Carpenter and religious communes like Eric Gill's Ditchling, in Britain. More diffusely, his teachings applied to education and the cultural tourism which defined it have extended to developments in well-being and leisure represented by bodies such as the Co-operative Holidays Association in Britain and America which shaped the wholesome leisure-time activities of the working classes. The diffusions are yet to be fully researched. His home on Coniston Water, Brantwood, has become an actual tourist destination testing his own kind of cultural travel – as the repository of his art and miscellaneous collections and as the experimental terrain for agricultural experimentation and environmental schemes since his own day. He prepared it in his will deliberately as an epitomising museum and writer's home which has influenced Lake District tourism as well as the practices of other museums and art galleries down to the present.

The authors of this volume have attempted, from the different disciplines of cultural history and literary and aesthetic criticism, to approach these common themes as they have affected the social and cultural spectrum of Ruskin's reader-travellers and unwitting beneficiaries as they have emerged over time. Starting with Hanley's three chapters devoted to Ruskin's experiences, practices and thought as a traveller and travel writer, where the emphasis is on exposition of a highly specific version of the established cruces of cultural tourism – anti-tourism and the tourist/traveller antithesis – the sometimes surprising inheritance of the critique which he constructed is pursued through the book's second half by Walton which addresses popular tourism, the 'outdoor movement' and his continuing presence in the Lake District. We are fully conscious of Ruskin's often off-putting appearance of preaching, and the intemperate and eccentric character of many of his individual opinions, which are also sometimes self-contradictory and inconsistent; and the passage from sensation to idea is frequently open to challenge. But we believe that feeling too great a need to be apologetic about aspects we are happy to leave to Ruskin scholars can act as a distraction from communicating his undervalued significance. Overall, we aim to put Ruskin back on the tourist map in the context of contemporary anti-market politics and theory.

Note

1. Unless otherwise stated, all citations from Ruskin are referred to parenthetically within the text by volume and page number, as here, from *The Works of John Ruskin* (Library Edition), 39 volumes, edited by E.T. Cook and A. Wedderburn (London: George Allen, 1903–12).

References

Alison, A. (1790) *Essays on the Nature and Principles of Taste*. London: J.J. and G. Robinson, Edinburgh: Bell and Bradfute.

Boniface, P. (1999) Cultural conflicts in tourism: Inevitability and inequality. In M. Robinson and P. Boniface (eds) *Tourism and Cultural Conflicts*. Oxford and New York: CABI Publications.

Boorstin, D.J. (1961) *The Image: A Guide to Pseudo-Events in America.* New York: Harper & Row.

Bourdieu, P. (1979) *Distinction: A Social Critique of the Judgement of Taste* (R. Nice, trans.). London: Routledge and Kegan Paul.

Butler, R. (2005) *The Tourist Area Life Cycle.* (Vol. 2). Clevedon: Channel View Publications.

Buzard, J. (1993) *The Beaten Track: European Tourism, Literature and the Ways to Culture, 1899–1918.* Oxford: Oxford University Press.

Cohen, E. (1988) Authenticity and commoditisation in tourism. *Annals of Tourism Research* 15 (3), 371–386.

Dickinson, R. and Hanley, K. (eds) (2006) *Ruskin's Struggle for Coherence: Self-Representation through Art, Place and Society.* Newcastle: Cambridge Scholars Press.

Fussell, P. (1980) *Abroad: British Literary Traveling between the Wars.* New York: Oxford University Press.

Hanley, K. (1993) In Wordsworth's shadow: Ruskin and neo-romantic ecologies. In G.K. Blank and M.K. Louis (eds) *Influence and Resistance in Nineteenth-Century English Poetry.* Basingstoke: Macmillan.

Hanley, K. (2007) *John Ruskin's Romantic Tours 1837–1838: Travelling North.* Lampeter: Edwin Mellen.

Hanley, K. (2010) Becoming Ruskin: Travel writing and self-representation in *Praeterita.* In A. Chantler, M. Davies and P. Shaw (eds) *Literature and Authenticity 1780–1900: William Cowper to Joseph Conrad.* Basingstoke and London: Macmillan.

Helsinger, E. (1979) The structure of Ruskin's *Praeterita.* In G.P. Landow (ed.) *Approaches to Victorian Autobiography.* Athens, OH: Ohio University Press.

Knight, R.P. (1805) *An Analytical Inquiry into the Principles of Taste.* London: T. Payne and J. White.

Koshar, R. (2002) Seeing, traveling, and consuming: An introduction. In R. Koshar (ed.) *Histories of Leisure.* Oxford: Berg.

Locke, J. (1690) *An Essay Concerning Human Understanding.* London: T. Basset.

MacCannell, D. (1973) Staged authenticity: Arrangements of social space in tourist settings. *American Journal of Sociology* 79, 589–603.

MacCannell, D. (1989) *The Tourist: A New Theory of the Leisure Class* (2nd edn). New York: Shocken Books.

Macksey, R.A. (1982) Proust on the margins of Ruskin. In J.D. Hunt and F.M. Holland (eds) *The Ruskin Polygon: Essays on the Imagination of John Ruskin.* Manchester: Manchester University Press.

Mishan, E. (1969) *The Costs of Economic Growth.* Harmondsworth: Penguin.

Osborne, P.D. (2000) *Travelling Light: Photography, Travel and Visual Culture.* Manchester: MUP.

Parsons, N.T. (2007) *Worth the Detour: A History of the Guidebook.* Stroud: Sutton.

Proust, M. (1987) In J. Autret, W. Burford and P.J. Wolfe (eds) *On Reading Ruskin: Prefaces to* La Bible d'Amiens *and* Sésame et les Lys *with Selections from the Notes to the Translated Texts.* New Haven, CT: Yale University Press.

Ritzer, G. (2006) *McDonaldization: the Reader.* Thousand Oaks: Pine Forge Press.

Robinson, M. (1999) Cultural conflicts in tourism: Inevitability and inequality. In M. Robinson and P. Boniface (eds) *Tourism and Cultural Conflicts.* Oxford and New York: CABI Publications.

Sharpely, R. (1999) *Tourism, Tourists and Society* (2nd edn). Kings Ripton, Huntingdon: ELM Publications.

Urry, J. (2002a) *Consuming Places.* London: Routledge.

Urry, J. (2002b) *The Tourist Gaze* (2nd edn). London: Sage Publications.
Urry, J. (2005) The 'consuming' of place. In A. Jaworski and A. Pritchard (eds) *Discourse, Communication and Tourism*. Clevedon: Channel View Publications.
Walton, J.K. (2009a) Prospects in tourism history: Evolution, state of play and future developments. *Tourism Management* 30, 1–11.
Walton, J.K. (2009b) Histories of tourism. In T. Jamal and M. Robinson (eds) *The Sage Handbook of Tourism Studies*. London: Sage Publications.
Wiener, M.J. (1981) *English Culture and the Decline of the Industrial Spirit*. Cambridge: Cambridge University Press.
Wordsworth, W. (1984) In S. Gill (ed.) *William Wordsworth. The Oxford Authors*. Oxford: Oxford University Press.
Wordsworth, W. (2007) In S. Bushell, J.A. Butler, and M.C. Jaye, with the assistance of D. Garcia (eds) *The Excursion*. Ithaca and London: Cornell University Press.
Wright, S. (2002) Sun, sea, sand and self-expression. In H. Berghoff, B. Korte, R. Schneider and C. Harvie (eds) *The Making of Modern Tourism*. Basingstoke: Palgrave.

Chapter 2
The Ruskin Moment

This chapter attempts to provide comprehensive information about Ruskin's place in the history of British cultural tourism, and to answer the questions of where, when and how he did the travelling on which his culture criticism and guidebooks are based.

Historical Contexts

The European history of cultural tourism, in search of famous, pre-imagined sites, has religious origins, dating from the classical world of Greece and Rome as mapped in Homeric geography, where travellers made for such sacred centres as Delphi and Dodona seeking inspiration and guidance or to witness and participate in major ritualistic sporting events (Sigaux, 1966: 9–14). Medieval pilgrimage was directed to the Holy City of Jerusalem, once seen as lying at the centre of the world, which was the dominant destination from the 11th century until Catholic Rome began to establish itself from 1300, the first Holy Year, as the leading pilgrimage centre in Europe, while the shrine of St James of Compostella in northern Spain achieved a separate popularity. In the Renaissance, humanist learning and then other motivations entered in, as Nicholas T. Parsons writes in his history of the guidebook, *Worth the Detour*:

> In the mid-sixteenth century ... the emphasis began to shift from the purely scholarly traveller to the gentleman or young nobleman seeking to refine his manners and improve the governance of his country, for which purpose the Italian city-states were regarded by many as idealised models of *ratio gubernatoris*. (Parsons, 2007: 138)

Following the Reformation, a prohibition on travel to Rome for English travellers effectively began to be lifted in the second decade of the 17th century, and the Grand Tour, by which the heirs of the English governing classes established their elite rite of passage to political power by accessing the cultural experience of the classic lands of the Mediterranean, restored the status of Rome as the fount of Western culture, but now fully conceived as the cradle of the liberal arts rather than in religious terms (see Andrew, 2008).

The term 'Grand Tour' 'had first appeared in the early 17th century with reference to a tour of the French provinces, but had become associated with a more extensive European tour focused on Italy by Richard Lassels's guide, *The Voyage of Italy* (1670) which is considered 'the first true guide-book in the English language' (Parsons, 2007: 148). It was to be followed by many dedicated guides such as Thomas Nugent's highly popular *Grand Tour*, 1749, which was 'perhaps the most popular 18th-century guidebook for the Continent', though Lassels had importantly helped establish the explicitly aesthetic emphasis of the tour, 'using technical terms for works of art culled from his reading of Vasari' (Parsons: 151). Aesthetic experience and authority was located chiefly in Italy and the traveller acquired access to them by actual visits there: by the 17th century, 'traditional authority (usually Classical and literary)' was becoming rejected in favour of 'the truth of one's eyes' (Osborne, 2000: 9), which still involved validating and enhancing one's expected knowledge of the texts by seeing the places they referred to (see Hudson, 1993: 13). The landscape was not observed for itself, however, and 'In the accounts of grand tours made between 1640 and 1730 a pictorial view ... is exceptional' (Hussey, 1983: 84). The English cultural imagination was rather infused with the historical and literary associations which Joseph Addison saw in the Italian landscape described in his *Remarks on Several Parts of Italy* (1705): 'The greatest pleasure I took in my journey from Rome to Naples was in seeing the Fields, Towns and Rivers, that have been described by so many classic authors, and have been the scene of so many great Actions' (Parsons, 2007: 162–163). A sense of deference to Italian culture had been internalised by the time of the Restoration, so that William Aglionby's translation of Vasari's *Lives of the Artists* in his *Painting Illustrated in Three Dialogues*, attributed a national cultural deficit to the effects of the English revolution (Aglionby, 1685: 161). An appropriation could nevertheless be effected by patronage and connoisseurship. The Society of Dilettanti was formed in 1734 for the study of antiquities by noblemen who had been on the Grand Tour, and, as many publications fostered the fashion for collecting classical antiquities, it was laying the foundations of future scholarly specialisms. Overall, 'the tourist community' defined by these practices came to comprise in the 18th century what has been called 'the largest and most independent wandering "academy" that western civilisation has even known' (De Seta, 1996: 13).

Given Protestant undercurrents, the aesthetic was regularly under suspicion of becoming separated from the moral educational agenda of authors like John Evelyn, writing of *The State of France*, who commented in his diary: 'It is written of Ulysses, that he saw many cities indeed, but withal his remarks of mens manners and Customs, was ever preferred to his counting Steeples, and making Tours: It is this Ethicall and Morall part of Travel, which embellisheth a Gentleman' (Parsons: 138). But it could also represent the acquisition of an elevating liberal culture, as in Jonathan Richardson's *A Discourse on ... The Science of the Connoisseur* (1719): 'If gentlemen were Lovers of Painting, and Connoisseurs, this would help Reform Them, as their Example, and Influence would have the like Effect upon the Common People' (Richardson, 1719: 161). Thomas Nugent's *The Grand Tour* (1749) argued that travel made 'the complete gentleman', by exposing him to a different order of experiences, including the removal of prejudices, as the educative Renaissance programme shaded into Enlightenment patriotism. John Chetwode Eustace's book, *A Classical Tour Through Italy* (1813) (the seventh edition came out in 1841), was to be the last significant guide for the Grand Tourist addressed 'solely to persons of a liberal education' with the explicit aim of 'moral improvement': 'Nations, like individuals, have their characteristic qualities and present to the eye of the candid observer ... much to be imitated, and something to be avoided' (Eustace, 1813: 171).

The Grand Tour remained, necessarily, a minority and predominantly aristocratic interest throughout the 18th century, though the English travelled abroad more than other Europeans, due to their relative prosperity during the rise of an early consumer society that sucked in the middle ranks, competitively, and encouraged status enhancement or confirmation through the cultural capital of distant travel to prestigious places. Italy remained the chief destination, and when the peace after the Seven Years' War was declared in 1763 English people of the upper and middle classes crammed into Rome. According to Edward Gibbon, by 1785 'upwards of forty thousand English, masters and servants, are now absent on the continent' (Parsons, 2007: 155). If not to be taken literally, the claim indicates a perception that the exodus was numerous and on a novel scale. With the rise of French literature and polished manners, it became increasingly fashionable to prolong the stay in France on the way to Italy in order to sample a different taste, represented by public buildings and art collections. Despite its origins in pilgrimage and education, pleasure and amusement, which had never been absent, became more prominent, and Adam Smith in *The Wealth of Nations* (1776), representatively 'considered that a young man sent abroad to complete his studies, was apt to return more conceited, more unprincipled, more dissipated, and more incapable of any serious application than he could well have become in so short a time had he lived at home' (Maxwell, 1932: 2). The paths through the Swiss Alps and Savoy, however, emerged by the second half of the 18th century as themselves offering curious detours from the major route, and, as the educational benefits of nature were coming to the fore, a diversion, even an alternative destination, became established in order to accommodate the new vogue for mountains and glaciers that bore overtones of Protestant spirituality as well as proto-scientific curiosity.

The English approached their travels with an increasing sense of their superiority as Citizens of the World confident of their trade-based prosperity and political reputation for 'liberty', though they were drawn to the prestige of arts and letters abroad. They had, in their own Protestant minds, culturally colonised the Continent. But during the Napoleonic period this pattern was revolutionised by the military occupations of the French, and 'Once French troops entered [Rome] in 1798 the Grand Tour was in abeyance' (Andrew, 2008: 41) until its modified revival from 1815 onwards. Cut off from the Continent, cultural travel turned inward to explore the native beauty and history of mainland Britain, and domestic tourism, more immediately accessible to the rising middle classes, increased substantially. Following the Napoleonic Wars, the new and predominantly middle-class clientèle required the more detailed information and practical advice which featured in 'the prototype of the "bourgeois" guidebook' (Parsons, 2007: 139), Mariana Starke's *Letters from Italy* (1800), which was first into the new market. The cultivated middle classes also desired aesthetic direction, and expert opinions were provided, with exclamation marks classifying works of art in later works, eventually to be replaced by stars. Her *Travels on the Continent*, expanding the coverage of useful travel information, was published by John Murray and went through eight editions, and a composite of her earlier books entitled *Information and Direction for Travellers on the Continent*, published by Galignani, attempting to 'comprise, within the compass of One Portable Volume, all the information necessary for Travellers on the Continent of Europe, and the Island of Sicily', prefigured the great standard guides to come (see Buzard, 1993: 70).

Humanist and neo-classical aesthetic tourism had mutated into what Urry, after J. Towner, describes as 'the nineteenth-century "romantic Grand Tour" which saw the emergence of "scenic tourism" and a much more private and passionate experience of beauty and the sublime' (Urry, 1990: 4). Yet Romantic intensities were becoming generally available: Ruskin wrote:

> It is not possible to imagine, in any time of the world, a more blessed entrance into life, for a child of such a temperament as mine. True the temperament belonged to the age: a very few years, – within the hundred, – before that, no child could have been born to care for mountains, or for men that lived among them, in that way. Till Rousseau's time, there had been no 'sentimental' love of nature; and till Scott's, no such apprehensive love of "all sort and conditions of men" [from the *Book of Common Prayer*], not in the soul merely, but in the flesh. (35.115)

The proliferation of print culture disseminated images and descriptions and boosted the prestige of British art and letters themselves through the prints which featured the paintings of a succession of British Picturesque artists, and through the works of the Romantic writers (see The Ruskin

Gaze, Chapter 3). At the same time, similar scenes were popularised in galleries and exhibitions, dioramas, panoramas and other staged representations (see Altick, 1978: especially 99–116). Travelling became a prominent metaphor for individual development, represented by the picaresque novel and the *Bildungsroman*, so that 'By definition, the modern self was a journey' (Osborne, 2000: 9). Byron's poetic travelogues, *Childe Harold's Pilgrimage* (1812–1818), epitomised the age's collective desire for private fantasy, and the fantasy of individualism – he coined the word 'guidebook' in *Don Juan* (1823). It was Ruskin, however, steeped in both the picturesque artists whom he hailed as his 'modern painters', culminating in Turner, and in the writings of his early favourite authors, Wordsworth, Byron and Scott, who emerged as a crucial cultural guide for 19th-century Britain. He connected the high cultural tastes of Grand Tourism with the new tendencies of middle-class travel, reconciling its educational aspirations with the moral seriousness of the evangelical mind-set which predominated in early Victorian England. Furthermore, he was to attempt to extend its opportunities to the intelligent (in the Victorian sense of the word, connoting openness to and command of information) working class, as under his influence cultural tourism became a form of Protestant pilgrimage, directed to the exemplary monuments and communities of Christian Europe.

Situated chronologically and in hierarchical terms between the Grand Tour which had been 'very much the preserve of elites' (Urry, 2002: 4) and the approach of popular mass tourism, Ruskin's kind of cultural tourism – whether holidays for recreation and health, research visits, painterly and literary tours – was a distinctly middle-class practice which nonetheless sought to disregard or transcend economic divisions of class. Ruskin was reared in a devoutly evangelical family, in which even vacations were earnest: his mother in particular instilled expectations of workfulness and improvement, while his father, an affluent wine-merchant with serious aesthetic interests, introduced the field in which this discipline was to be expressed. The father shared in the broad characteristics of the 19th-century *Bildungsbürgertum*, or middle-class intellectuals, and their conscientious programme of self-improvement. Altogether, their habits and approaches presaged what would emerge, especially when influenced by Ruskin's own subsequent writings, as the pattern of '[h]olidays with a serious purpose', made by the kind of comfortably-off, 'earnest and extremely proper' middle-class Victorians who were to become, for example, Thomas Cook's continental tourists, 'with a Murray's guide or Baedeker in hand' (Thompson, 1968: 263).

Yet there were fundamental distinctions between the assumptions made by the principal contemporary guidebook published by Murray (Ruskin never mentions Baedeker), which was designed to marry useful practical advice for efficient travelling with cultural enlightenment, and Ruskin's own approaches.

He began touring before the first *Murray's Hand-book for Travellers in Holland, Belgium and North Germany* appeared in 1836, and wrote that the courier was 'a private Murray', before Murray was invented (35.109), but by 1848 the publisher was advertising more than 60 'Works for Travellers'. Successive editions, as the publishing dynasty came into the control of John Murray II and III, aimed to bring the possibilities of travel up-to-date as well as expanding and enhancing the cultural coverage. The firm updated the 14th edition of the *Handbook for Travellers in France* (1877), 'to take account of, *inter alia*, the great railway expansion that had occurred' since the first version 35 years earlier. It added a list of recommended reading to the *Handbook to Central Italy* comprising 'only such works as may be useful for reference, or in perpetuating the memory of those scenes which frequently survive all other recollections of the journey' (Parsons, 2007: 184). It incorporated information supplied by several new intellectual disciplines that were making advances – archaeology, Egyptology, geology, anthropology and the beginnings of art history as opposed to 18th-century connoisseurship. It aimed to offer everything the tourist might desire with objectivity, as none of the contributors and authors had their names on the title page of a 'Murray's Handbook'. The panoptic project was pursued even more methodically by Murray's continental twin, Karl Baedeker, who later commented on Ruskin's opinions in the *Stones of Venice*: 'The intelligent reader will temper Mr Ruskin's extreme and sometimes extraordinary statements with his own discretion' (Norwich, 2003: 110). Less overtly, Murray, who was more opinionated than Baedeker, and unlike him included many literary quotations from British Romantic authors, particularly Byron, which would affect the tourists' perception of place, purveyed a distinctly English ideology of common sense – a reassuring 'Made in England' guarantee of a tolerant '*Weltanschauung* that was even-handed (if a shade patronising) in its treatment of potentially contentious issues' (185). As time went by, Ruskin found he could not go along with what was happening. Though he had originally been happy to have his notes on works of art in Florence and Pisa included in the third, revised and improved edition of Murray's *Hand-book for Travellers in Northern Italy* (1847), based on his reputation as the author of the first two volumes of *Modern Painters* (1843 and 1846), a work which ironically and perhaps significantly Murray had declined to publish (see Clegg, 1981: 175–176, and Hilton, 1985: 95), and though he was himself heavily dependent on Murray's *Hand-book for Travellers in France* for his tour of 1848, he nevertheless developed a radical antagonism to Murray's influential attitudes and practices which he mocked for embracing and encouraging the haste and superficiality of the railway age.

Ruskin was actively involved in the revision of Murray's *Handbook for Travellers in Northern Italy*. The first edition was written by the classical scholar, Francis Palgrave, came out in 1842 and caused controversy. Ruskin criticised it for the unusual subjectiveness in its judgement and its evaluation of classical and Renaissance art, and it was heavily revised for the second edition of 1847. Ruskin made a number of contributions himself, on works of art in Florence and Pisa (see 28.326–330, Clegg, 1981: 175–176, and Hilton, 1985: 1, 95). There was an obvious overlap in his addressing the same educated Victorians who used Murray's guides assiduously to augment their knowledge of 'high culture'. Murray's ideal readers were the kind of dons and clergymen who frequently contributed to his publications, and like Ruskin, Murray was keen to take his readers to the actual sites which were the origins of the literary and historical associations he supplied. But to Ruskin the accumulation of ill-digested experiences was becoming an end in itself, and as MacCannell argues, the objects and places visited were turning into signs of cultural acquisition (MacCannell, 1976: 194).

As Palmowski explains, the guides both responded to and stimulated contemporary developments in cultural tourism: handbooks, and the practices they engendered, were formative of class attitudes, and affected trends in class and gender (Palmowski, 2002: 106). The shared cultural attitudes represented by the guidebook 'assisted in creating a national travelling culture which in turn contributed to a greater sense of national identity', and

> the growth of 'domestic' travel and the guidebook were crucial factors in the spread of the middle-class national identity which, in a century of peace with Britain's continental neighbours, served to highlight the communion of England, Scotland, and Wales, and their common distinctiveness *vis-a-vis* the continent. (Palmowski, 2002: 115; see also Hoppen, 1998: 513–520)

Barber argues that 'The years between 1830 and 1870 … represent the "high watermark of English tourism", as of "imperialism through tourism", when Switzerland became the "playground of Europe"…' (Barber, 1999: 179). Yet at the same time, during this period, the Romantic anti-capitalist tradition of such writers as Wordsworth and Southey became invigorated by the interventions of Carlyle and others to interrogate the sense of moral superiority in the Evangelical mission throughout the British Empire as it confronted an accompanying awareness of the narrowing provincialisation of the utilitarian/industrial character of economic dominance. Ruskin was positioned centrally in this critique (see Mendilow, 1986: 180–191).

Ruskin travelled from the perspective of that critical high ground. As he journeyed through 19th-century Europe, he became imaginatively possessed by the picturesque and sublime landscapes and the great monuments and artworks of a Christian civilization he saw with horror to be under urgent threat. Everywhere he saw that the economic and technical revolutions of capitalism were producing an unlovely society of competitive individualism, soulless mechanisation, ignoble warfare, cultural vandalism, moral and physical pollution of what he called 'the European death of the nineteenth century' (7.386). The predominant strategy of his various interventions became a passionate resistance to change, seen most distressingly in the destruction of cherished sites in Britain and all over the Europe he frequented. Ultimately, his travels amounted to a mission to save and recover the social and spiritual values still observable in Swiss and Savoyard pastoral communities in their Alpine settings, and in the buildings and paintings of the medieval and early Renaissance Italian city states, and of northern France in the High Middle Ages.

Clearly, the Continent was becoming re-opened to a range of diverse social experience which was gradually to encompass a programme of healthy activity and varied entertainment. Ruskin had begun his touring from the cultural and intellectual perspectives which extended from the Grand Tour into Murray's guides. His early Swiss tours, for example, had been mapped by foreign guidebooks which were translated into English after the conclusion of the Napoleonic Wars, including Reichard's *Itinerary of Italy* (1816) – Ruskin's edition was the enlarged one, n.d., and Ebel's *Switzerland* (1818) – Ruskin used his father's French edition, 1830–31, written 'for the learned tourist'. But when Thomas Cook started his travel business in 1841 with an excursion from Loughborough to Leicester, then branched out to lead a large touring party to Scotland and subsequently arranged for over 165,000 people to attend the Great Exhibition in London, a new phenomenon for a much wider and more heterogeneous clientèle had been born. In 1855 Cook mounted his first foreign excursion, to Calais, laying the first foundations for the 'circular tours' of Europe and the parties he was to conduct to Switzerland and Italy from the 1860s, and also to the United States and Egypt. His commercial motivations and standardised packages, which became more pronounced under the influence of his son John from 1866, prompted a superior attitude in the minds of some critics who considered them to be an uncomfortable 'mixture of idealism and business acumen' or 'philanthropy plus 5 per cent' (Brendon, 79–140; Parsons, 2007: 231). Yet some of Cook's motivations merged with Ruskin's, including the aim of increasing social access to previously excluded cultural experience, and a broad religious discourse shared by the Evangelical critic and the Low Church businessman connected with the uplifting and improving effect that both associated with informed exposure to travel, nature and culture. Ruskin himself was opposed to those who wished to exclude the working class from a real relation to art and widened cultural experience, but he was chary of the methods and motivations of those who appeared to be offering it. His writings appealed to many of Cook's tourists as much as to Murray's more independent travellers, and indeed both types were only, or seemed to be, different calibrations of the same middle-class professions, as Palmowski comments: 'Anecdotal evidence suggests that two groups availed themselves disproportionately of the opportunity to travel [on Cook's continental tours]: teachers and the clergy.' (Palmowski, 2002: 115)

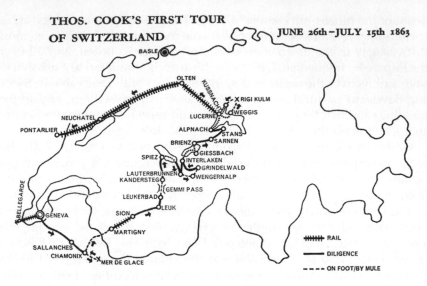

THOS. COOK'S FIRST TOUR OF SWITZERLAND

JUNE 26th–JULY 15th 1863

BASLE

OLTEN

KUSSNACHT

X RIGI KULM
WEGGIS
LUCERNE

NEUCHATEL

PONTARLIER

ALPNACH
STANS
SARNEN

BRIENZ

GIESSBACH
SPIEZ
INTERLAKEN
GRINDELWALD
LAUTERBRUNNEN
WENGERNALP
KANDERSTEG
GEMMI PASS
LEUKERBAD
LEUK

BELLEGARDE

GENEVA

SION

MARTIGNY

SALLANCHES
CHAMONIX
MER DE GLACE

╫╫╫╫ RAIL

───── DILIGENCE

─ ─ ─ ─ ON FOOT/BY MULE

2.1 Map of Thomas Cook's First Tour of Switzerland. In Jemima Morrell, *Miss Jemima's Swiss Journal: the First Conducted Tour of Switzerland.* The Thomas Cook Archive

The differences and similarities can be gauged from the account of Cook's first conducted tour to Switzerland in 1863 by one of the original tourists in *Miss Jemima's Swiss Journal*, which remained unpublished for 100 years. It describes the energetic attempts of a party of male and female family members and friends, partly accompanied by Cook himself, to wring every opportunity for climbing and sightseeing from the trip, with some modest anthropological and aesthetic gestures. They all had tremendous fun, and the enabling of cultural credibility which young women in

2.2 Unknown photographer. The Mer de Glace, Chamonix. From *Miss Jemima's Swiss Journal.* The Thomas Cook Archive

particular eagerly absorbed may be seen in operation. Ruskin, as in several of Cook's own *Tourist Handbooks*, is part of the menu being dutifully quoted at some length. 'Miss Jemima' agreed with Ruskin's descriptions, as of 20 miles of the River Rhône which she compared with her own observations (Morrell, 1963: 37), though she also found Murray's more accurate on occasion, and copied his description of the Geissbach word for word and allowed his version of the outlook from the Rigi Culm to saturate her view of the sunrise there. Similarly, one of Cook's first conducted tourists to northern Italy in 1864 studied his *Murray* carefully together with his companions, but 'When [he] arrived in Venice after parting with the group, he saw the city not only through Byron's, but also through Ruskin's eyes' (Palmowski, 2002: 113).

Cook actively endeavoured to undermine the grounds for the superior postures of what Buzard (1993) has termed 'anti-tourism', but by conformity rather than correction. Indeed, the firm's own offerings went upmarket following his son's taking over the business in 1878, when, as Buzard writes, 'egalitarianism shaded over into bourgeois respectability and exclusivity. His tourists in Italy, he points out, are *not* of the lower classes; they come from a higher social plane than that of his excursion-parties at home' (Buzard, 1993: 62). In particular, there was an attempt to create Cook's own niche for independent travel which had been a major differentiator for his critics: 'Cook's clients now had the choice of purchasing conducted tours or tickets for independent travel' (Buzard, 1993: 235), and from the 1870s the majority of Cook's tourists were actually individual travellers using the company's 'circular tickets'. Yet embedded in the tensions of the middle-class formation was the constant scrutiny of differentials which fundamentally involved deriding cultural access for the lower orders – however defined –who, it was felt, were encroaching on a domain to which they did not belong. Cook's 'cockney' tourists remained the constant butt of this snobbery, but so, from another viewpoint, were Murray's. There were shades of exclusivity, and in 1850 *The Times* had warned that it was Murray's handbooks which enabled 'the veriest cockney, the greenest school-boy, and the meekest country clergyman to travel to the European continent' (Pemble, 1988: 70–72). After all, as Henry James queried in his 'Swiss Notes', what *were* the differences when viewed from the high ground of the past era?

> I have even fancied that it is a sadly ineffectual pride that prevents us from buying one of Mr. Cook's bundles of tickets, and saving our percentage, whatever it is, of money and trouble; for I am sure that the poor bewildered and superannuated genius of the old Grand Tour ... wherever she may have buried her classic head, beyond hearing of the eternal telegraphic click bespeaking "rooms" on mountain-tops, confounds us all alike in one sweeping reprobation. (James, 1993: 629–630)

Even the grandest or most adventurous Victorian tourists became caught up in novel trends. Leslie Stephen, President of the Alpine Club (founded in 1858) in the 1860s, was irritated to find 'cockneys' and Cook's tourists at St Moritz. His disdain was involved in a respect for a fast-disappearing way of life, and he both rejoiced and lamented that, in discovering an unfamiliar view of the Weisshorn, 'it was hard to remember that we were within a short walk of the main post route and Mr. Cook's tourists' (Stephen, 1895: 91). He detested luxury hotels and retreated to untrodden peaks and hidden valleys in order to retain the sublime intimations and sense of traditional community he claimed to have derived from Ruskin himself, and yet he was, after all, chiefly an enthusiast for the mountaineering and winter sports which Ruskin loudly deplored.

Ruskin's views on aesthetic tourism continued to inform, both directly and indirectly, a distinctive tendency in cultural travel and leisure activities into the next century, as working hours were limited and holiday rights became law. The agenda and accessibility of popular tourism was later to be expanded, as we shall see, by workers' organisations such as the Toynbee Travellers' Club, associated with the workers' education centre at Toynbee Hall, founded by one of Ruskin's Oxford disciples, and the Cooperative Holidays Association. J.A.R. Pimlott evokes this new breed of serious tourists, who

> like the Grand Tourists before them, saw [foreign travel] as a means of self-improvement ... Middle-aged ladies who on winter evenings sat at the feet of the Christian Socialist lecturers might be found exploring the Louvre at the heels of a guide, and serious-minded young clerks from the Working Men's College might be seen in their summer vacations at the end of a rope on a Swiss glacier. (Parsons, 2007: 178)

Ruskin's Tours

Ruskin began his touring life with a sea voyage to Scotland in his third year, in 1822. The destination was to be a recurrent one throughout his life, regularly in his childhood as part of a wider northern expanse incorporating the Lake District and the Yorkshire Dales, accompanying his father's commercial travels and family visits to Perth. The earlier part of Ruskin's travelling days was based on the family home at Herne Hill, near London, where the family resided from 1823 to 1842, and the inland and continental tours mostly departed around the time of his father's birthday. They notably included one made in his 11th year, in 1831, when the Ruskins visited Wales and the Lake District, which produced his first appearance in print, a poem 'On Skiddaw and Derwent Water' for *The Spiritual Times* and a poetic account of the tour called *The Iteriad* of 1832. In the summers of 1837 and 1838 the Lakes and Scotland respectively were the culmination of his youthful domestic touring, and by then the educational pattern of visiting buildings and places of cultural importance and historical and aesthetic associations, together with early practice in a variety of scholarly researches (especially geology) and experimentation in poetry and drawing, linked to a programme of specialist instruction, was firmly established. It led, when Ruskin had become an Oxford undergraduate, to his first major project for publication based on the comparison of his British and European travels up to that point, *The Poetry of Architecture*, a series of articles published in the *Architectural Magazine* (1837–1838).

Altogether, his tours on the Continent spanned from 1825, when he was six, to 1888, in his 70th year. His father refers in his diary to the family's 'very first Continental journey' (1.xxv), when Ruskin was taken to Paris and some principal Belgian cities (Brussels, Ghent and Bruges). Momentously, for a 13th birthday present in 1832 Ruskin received a copy of Samuel Rogers's *Italy* (1830), where the associative landscape was illustrated in large part by engraved vignettes of Turner's drawings. This was one of the two most powerful incentives to his subsequent continental travels. The other was a copy of Samuel Prout's *Sketches in Flanders and Germany* (1833), a series of architectural lithographs, which the family acquired when it appeared in 1833, and which opened their gaze to continental buildings in such a way as to lead his mother to make the suggestion of following Prout's routes on their own travels, prolonging them in order to take in some Turner sites. Ruskin was 14 when this first comprehensive continental tour occurred, from May to September 1833, recounted in verse in the winter of 1833–1834 in the style of Rogers. Overall, it represented a life-determining experience which included his first sight of the Alps. The tour inspired various attempts at intellectual enquiry and artistic representation: his first prose work, 'Enquiries on the Causes of Colour in the Water of the Rhine' in Loudon's *Magazine of Natural History* (1834); the arrangement of his lessons in oil painting of 1836; and the poem, 'Salzburg', in *Friendship's Offering*, also that year. The tour of 1835 was a much more considered and significant undertaking, which effectively created the paradigm for Ruskin's future practices of cultural tourism – the stratification of scientific (especially geological), evangelical, historical and aesthetic discourses, as also the core map of the family's subsequent travels – the 'The Old Road', from Calais to Geneva, the Alps and Northern Italy, leading him to those landscapes and towns situated in Northern France, Western Switzerland and Savoy, and the Northern Italian States to which he repeatedly returned (see map 1, colour section). As Wolfgang Kemp points out: 'This route became canonical: Ruskin, who spent approximately half his life in travel, was to follow it twenty-six times in his life, with minor variations and abbreviations' (Kemp, 1990: 33). On the same journey, Ruskin made over 60 drawings.

Their early routes were guided principally by the example of English painters and writers in pursuit of aesthetic, historical and cultural associations, and partly by religious prejudice – in the early days, for example, they avoided the Catholic cantons whenever possible, while the changing political situations in revolutionary Europe also affected his movements from the later 1840s. Their agenda, as Ruskin acknowledged in *Praeterita*, was unconcerned with social encounters: 'we did not travel for adventures, nor for company, but to see with our eyes, and to measure with our hearts' (35.119). There were restrictions attached to the nature of family travel, as he did not travel without his parents until he was 26, and decided against the tantalising opportunity of travelling to Greece in 1852 as a result of his parents' fear of his taking the sea voyage. His destinations were selected for purposes of increasingly serious study, and the simply recreational aspect of touring was seldom prominent. The interdisciplinary agenda of his explorations and tireless observations is reflected in the series of diaries and notebooks which record his visits in media ranging from descriptive prose and verse to sketches and statistical data, while his constant drawing provided an archive of numerous illustrations for his books and lectures.

Like his domestic tours through the Romantic margins of Britain, Ruskin's continental atlas was to feature alternative topographies of 19th-century Europe. Their routes were determined by the usual consideration of health, the avoidance of wars and disease, and in the case of Switzerland by religious prejudices (see Towner, 1996 and Black, 1992). While the draw of cultural objects and remains was paramount, as Kemp comments: 'The Ruskins ... gravitated mainly to places devoid of the cultural and social attractions sought by the old-style traveller. In a sense, they filled in the gaps between other people's destinations, and journeyed to empty places on the map.' Though the Chamonix Valley was already becoming a tourist centre, it was hardly to be compared with the Riviera, and the family 'valued Lucca more than Florence and spent more time in Abbeville than in Paris' (Kemp, 1990: 38). Ruskin's France is provincial, deliberately skirting mushrooming conurbations. His Venice is distinctly *not* on the Path to Rome. Switzerland and Savoy are prized precisely for being off the map, relatively unfrequented and unspoilt by modern incursions. Superimposed on the actual journeys is a symbolic geography of Europe – encountering the territories of medieval Catholicism according to the discourse of northern Protestantism – which is memorably drawn in the verbally delineated map from the second volume of *The Stones of Venice*. There, he brings out the 'contrast in physical character which exists between Northern and Southern countries' and describes 'that variegated mosaic of the world's surface which a bird sees in its migration, that difference between the district of the gentian and of the olive which the stork and the swallow see far off, as they lean upon the sirocco wind.' The virtual view sweeps from the Mediterranean to 'a great peacefulness of light, Syria and Greece, Italy and Spain, laid like pieces of a golden pavement into the sea-blue', and looks gradually northwards, over 'a vast belt of rainy green, where the pastures of Switzerland, and poplar valleys of France, and dark forests of the Danube and Carpathians stretch', until it comes to 'leaden rock and heathy moor', 'irregular and grisly islands', and where 'at last, the wall of ice, durable like iron, sets, deathlike, its white teeth against us out of the polar twilight' (10.186). He next describes the variations of animal life and the works of northern man, 'instinct with work of an imagination as wild and wayward as the northern sea' (187), and defines 'wildness of thought, and roughness of work; this look of mountain brotherhood between the cathedral and the Alp' as 'an essential character of the existing architecture of the North' (188). This is 'The Nature of the Gothic' he maps in northern France and Switzerland, and even traces in Venice.

As an Oxford undergraduate he travelled in the then Romantic north of Britain, to the Lakes District, North Yorkshire and Scotland, deepening his picturesque eye and literary sensibilities. It was in 1836 that he first turned to the passionate defence and advocacy of Turner's painting – the family were to purchase their first Turner, *Richmond, Surrey*, in 1839, to be followed by 'Winchelsea' as his 21st birthday present in 1840. Later, in 1842, his father was to take a lease on a grander home at Denmark Hill, where their collection of almost a dozen Turners and other modern English painters was displayed. But in 1840, when, in line with his expertise in natural observations, he became a fellow of the Geological Society, he presented consumptive symptoms and was compelled to withdraw from Oxford. The consequence was another lengthy continental, mostly Italian, family tour from September 1840 to June 1841, which had a serious recuperative element.

The therapeutic aspect of the family travels was important from the start, when his mother encouraged his father to take time off from the pressures of the office, and sometimes to convalesce. The parents were always anxious about the health and physical well-being of their son, who as a mostly home-tutored child had missed the rough and tumble of school life and sporting activities. When he returned to their care after the Oxford diagnosis, they placed his health at the top of their concerns, above their cultural ambitions for him, and arranged for medical consultations which led to his visiting health spas such as Leamington, Matlock and Buxton. Anxieties about health remained a constant theme, and plans were often made with that concern in the foreground, as in the summer of 1847 when he revisited the Lakes and made a therapeutic journey round Scotland, followed by a visit to Folkestone. Seaside resorts figured largely in his holidaying in England, and in the year after the annulment of his marriage, 1855, he travelled to such seaside locations as Deal and Dover. Recuperating from cataloguing the Turner bequest, from May to October 1858, he took an unusually relaxing continental 'cure' in Switzerland and

Savoy. In 1861, he travelled to Boulogne in July–August for a few weeks' rest, and it was during a therapeutic visit to Matlock, when he was ill in 1871, that he determined to return to the recuperative power of the Lakes and establish his future home in that region. Seaports were the subject of some of Turner's most admired paintings, which Ruskin was eventually to describe in the *Harbours of England* (1856), and coastal areas remained favourite retreats to the end, and in 1886, amid mental collapse, he visited Heysham, later making expeditions along the Cumberland coast to several seaside villages. Following a temporary quarrel with his companion-cousin, he stayed for some time in Folkestone and Sandgate in 1887.

From 1841 what was to become the first volume of *Modern Painters*, 1843, which was an elaborate defence and exposition of Turner's truth to nature, was in gestation. In that year the family travelled to Genoa, Lucca, Pisa, Florence and Rome, and then on to Naples, Castellamare, Sorrento and Amalfi, returning via Naples to Rome and Albano. They returned via Florence, Venice, Lausanne and Calais. Throughout these travels, Ruskin kept detailed journals which fed into the coming book, which also was conceived as a comparative work between British and other European paintings, as its original full title indicates: *Modern Painters Their Superiority in the Art of Landscape Painting to the Ancient Masters.* The following year, 1842, after sitting for his degree, he made a wide-ranging journey with his family, from May to August, through northern France, Switzerland, the Low Countries, and back via Paris, keeping a journal, including drawings, throughout. Receiving lasting impressions, after passing through Rouen, they spent some days in Geneva and proceeded to Chamonix, where he made natural observations which found expression in the first volume of *Modern Painters*.

The year 1843, when he completed that work, was the only one in the decade in which he did not travel to the Continent. Thereafter, his travels became increasingly research driven and he began to study European art and culture more deeply, while he learned some Italian. Art, architecture and natural scenery were and remained interdependent interests. The family went off to the Continent again in May of 1844, making an important visit to Rouen, where Ruskin studied the stained glass, and in the summer he extended his travels to include a significant journey to Switzerland, where he was deeply impressed with his observations of nature, spending a week at Chamonix in July, and beginning his 30-year association with the Savoyard guide, Joseph Marie Couttet (see map 2, colour section). In August, he studied Italian artists in the Louvre, especially the Venetians, and wrote about them in his diaries.

1845 was the year of his first continental tour – of seven months – without his parents, and accompanied by his valet, John Hobbs chiefly to Italy (see map 3, colour section), via northern France and Geneva, and back via Paris. It was to be one of his most crucial cultural tours, and he wrote to his mother signalling a growing sense of authority – that he was, in a sense, now taking the lead: '. . . I think in other places you will find me a little more of the cicerone than I used to be, and perhaps something of a guide where I was formerly only an encumbrance' (4.xxvi). He was now determinedly deepening his encounter with European art and culture, opening his mind and eye to traditions which put his chauvinistic enthusiasms in their place, as he pursued the development of *Modern Painters*. His notebooks and letters home to his father are filled with information he was culling for this work, especially the second volume. The tomb of Ilaria di Caretto at Lucca turned him 'from the study of landscape to that of life' (28.146), and he was overwhelmed by the Campo Santo in Pisa. In August, he was studying Sismondi and the sites of Turner's drawing at Faido. In September, he began to pay much more attention to architecture, and at Venice was deploring the 'restoration' of St Mark's while absorbing the revelation of Tintoretto.

When Ruskin was married to Effie Gray in 1848 he became her cultural guide and mentor. With the stabilising of the European revolutions of that year, his marriage holiday took the form of an 11-week tour of northern France with his new bride (see map 4, colour section). At Rouen he deepened his notion of the symbolic witness of architecture, and of a service in the cathedral he commented that it 'has perhaps contributed more to my former ideas of the propriety of the splendour of music and architecture in religious service than any at which I have been present of the kind' (8.267n.5), while he wrote of Paris in the throes of revolution. In the winter 1848–1849 he composed the *Seven Lamps of Architecture*. He then focused on Venetian architecture, and in 1850 travelled with Effie to Venice, where they met the English local historian of Venice, Rawdon Brown, and where they stayed from November until March 1850. Ruskin filled his diaries with technical material and an account of his ramble among 'melancholy canals' between the Madonna dell'Orto and Sta Fosca. He was now working intensively on the first volume of the *Stones of Venice*, which was published in 1851, and returned to Venice with Effie in that year, travelling through France and Switzerland, including Chamonix, in August, and staying there from September until July 1852. It was an extraordinarily productive time as he brought forth the results of his labours. From September 1852 to February 1853, he worked constantly on the final two volumes of the *Stones of Venice*, which appeared in July and October respectively, and, following the delivery of the Edinburgh lectures, published as *Lectures on Architecture and Painting* in 1854, he brought out Part 1 of *Giotto and his Works in Padua* in November.

The world was changing fast. The scope and influence of his cultural interventions was broadening and developing towards more explicit social commentary. The Great Exhibition had opened in May 1851, and was met by his rejection of its industrial triumphalism, which eventually found expression in a denunciatory pamphlet, *The Opening of the Crystal Palace*, issued in 1854. His approbation, on the other hand, was extended to the Pre-Raphaelites, in support of whom he wrote two influential letters to the *Times*. Then, Turner died in December 1852, and by 1854 his marriage was in collapse.

Following his major excursions into European architecture, Ruskin turned back to the composition of *Modern Painters*, a work which had become challenged by other developing interests and the complication of his changing views. With the effective marital separation of April in the background, he travelled with his parents through France to Switzerland from May to October 1854, when he prepared many notes and drawings of Swiss mountainous scenery for *Modern Painters*: the third volume was to be published in January, and the fourth in April 1856. The greatest and most intense research project in the mid-50s, linking past and present, was his cataloguing of the Turner Bequest, which led to his *Notes on the Turner Gallery at Marlborough House 1856* and *A Catalogue of Turner Sketches in the National Gallery*, both published in 1857. It was exhausting work, and on a relaxing tour in Switzerland and Savoy in 1858 he prepared matter for the fifth volume of *Modern Painters*, which was to be published in 1860. From May to July 1859 he travelled on the last family tour with his parents, in Germany and Switzerland.

He addressed the developments in his personal and intellectual life (chiefly his anti-capitalism and the culmination of a gradual process, his 'un-conversion' from evangelical belief at Turin in 1858), by re-interrogating Swiss nature to draw out deeper meanings, and pursuing the social implications of his architectural analyses. These strands might have come together in the history of Switzerland which he now planned to write and illustrate, though, despite several attempts, it was never to be accomplished. In the mid-50s he wrote letters which represent an increased interest in social and intellectual issues, and in the autumn of 1854 he became involved with the Oxford Museum of Natural History, founded that year, and in the recently initiated Working Men's College in London, where he taught and evolved the lessons published as *The Elements of Drawing* in June (*The Elements of Perspective* was published in November 1859). The convictions behind all these enterprises found expression in July when he was writing *The Political Economy of Art* (*A Joy for Ever*, 1880). In the later 1850s, he delivered his northern anti-industrialist lectures: in 1857, he gave two lectures in Manchester; in 1858, he read a paper on 'Education in Art' to a Social Science Congress in Liverpool; in 1859, he gave the Manchester lecture, 'Unity of Art', and the Bradford lecture, 'Modern Manufacture and Design'. It was while in Switzerland in 1860 that he focused on his core critique of the market economy, writing the four articles, *Unto this Last*, mostly composed at Chamonix (first published in book form in 1862).

From the early 60s Ruskin began his search for a home which was only finally to be resolved with his purchase of Brantwood on Coniston Water in 1871. He travelled from May 1862 with his protégés, the painter Edward Burne-Jones and his wife in Italy, then alone to Switzerland in August, where he settled at Mornex, moving back and forth between there and London. In June he negotiated for a plot of land above Chamonix, intending to settle in the Haute Savoie, though negotiations broke down later in the year, and he returned to England. After his father died in 1864, his unsettled life became divided between a world of internal obsessions built around the much younger woman to whom he was to propose, Rose la Touche, and increased activities in the public sphere. He delivered his most famous lectures against the industrialisation of the arts, 'Traffic', in Bradford, and then two talks in Manchester which were to be published as *Sesame and Lilies* in 1865. He published two series of letter pamphlets, addressed to English working men: *Time and Tide, by Weare and Tyne*, 1869, and from 1871 to 78 *Fors Clavigera*, 87 letters, with nine later letters between 1880 and 1884. He also organised the Hinksey road-digging experiment for Oxford students to experience the virtues of manual work, and formed the St George's Fund, which was to become The Guild of St George.

Ruskin assumed a new role when in August 1869 he was elected Slade Professor of Fine Art at Oxford, and the following year he began his first lectures in that capacity, published that year as *Lectures on Art*, to be followed by three Oxford *Lectures on Landscape*. In 1871, he also began the series of lectures to be published as *Val d'Arno: Ten Lectures on Tuscan Art*, 1874. Characteristically, he wove in his renewed scientific interests in geology and in the mid-seventies delivered four lectures on 'Mountain Form in the Higher Alps', later included in *Deucalion*, 1875–1883. His intermittent breakdowns led to his resignation from the Slade Professorship, but in 1883 he was reinstated and delivered his first new lecture, 'Realistic Schools of Painting: D.G. Rossetti and W. Holman Hunt': the series delivered that year was collected in *The Art of England*. It was at this point, largely from the sense of educational duty which his new role entailed, that he embarked on the composition of what was to become a series of formal guidebooks, either new or adapted from previous works. In September 1874 he worked on *Mornings in Florence*, a guide 'for the English Respectable Tourist' (37.139), 'with which I hope to cut out Mr Murray a little this winter' (141), which was published in parts in 1875–1877. In 1876 he edited and provided a preface for a cultural guide to Italian and German art for 'The number of British and American travellers who take unaffected interest in the early art of Europe [which] is already large, and is daily increasing', and who were 'feeling themselves more and more in need of a guide-book containing as much trustworthy indication as they can use, of what they most rationally spend their time in examining'. Entitled *The Art Schools of Medieval*

Christendom, it was written to popularise Ruskin's opinions by Alice Owen, a former Oxford drawing student:

> The books of reference published by Mr Murray, though of extreme value to travellers, who make it their object to see (in his, and their sense of the word) whatever is to be seen, are of none whatever, or may perhaps be considered, justly, as even of quite the reverse value, to travellers who wish to see only what they may in simplicity understand, and with pleasure remember .... (34.129)

In May of 1877 he published the first part of *St Mark's Rest, The History of Venice, written for the help of the few travellers who still care for her monuments*, and sent off his *Guide to the Academy at Venice*.

His later continental tours were a matter of revisitings and new departures within former haunts. He returned to northern France in 1868 where his diaries are particularly observant around Abbeville, though he laments the 'desolation' (Ruskin, II: 651) and social fragmentation of France compared with a generation ago. In January 1869 he lectured on 'The Flamboyant Architecture of the Valley of the Somme' in London, and took up his early interest in northern French Gothic which was to find full late expression, when, after returning to Amiens in 1880, he published his final significant architectural work, *The Bible of Amiens* (1880–85), from which he also extracted a travellers' guidebook, written for 'the Intelligent Traveller'. Fresh enthusiasms were the discovery of Carpaccio in Venice from 1869 whose cycle of paintings on the legend of St Ursula were to become disturbingly associated with the dead Rose in 1877. He was able to confirm and deepen his attachment to Verona, which he now found 'unites all the things I have chiefly studied' (19.lii), on his Italian tour of 1869. Highlights which left lasting impressions on his writings were his visit to Assisi in 1874, where he stayed in the monastery, and a visit to the Sistine Chapel, further deepening his knowledge of, and antipathy to, High Renaissance art.

The Brantwood years enabled Ruskin to follow his interests in natural history and botany, and also to experiment with modest agricultural schemes on the estate which were intended to inform the running of the St George's farms and help reclaim wasteland abroad for productive purposes. But they were also riddled with sorrow following the death of his mother in 1871 and of Rose in 1875. From the start of that later year the black fogs and dark storms which he witnessed there are recorded unrelentingly and were to become the focus of two lectures delivered in 1884, 'The Storm-Cloud of the Nineteenth Century', in which he linked the moral corruption of industrial capitalism with natural pollution and decay. In this association he was following an established pattern of travellers' responses to industrial grime, especially London fog (see Porter, 1996: 34–35). In 1878, he became demented and entered a world of sporadic breakdown and withdrawal, which finally silenced him throughout his last decade. Before that, on medical advice, he made a continental tour to revisit northern France, first of all in the north: at Rheims ('confectioner's Gothic'), Avallon, Vézelay, where he considered Viollet-le-Duc's restoration 'very carefully vile' (33.xxxv), and Switzerland where he planned the last part of *Deucalion*, gathered material for his autobiography, *Praeterita*, and lamented the lost glory of Mont Blanc. He also passed through Italy, stopping at Turin, Pisa, Lucca and Florence.

From June to December 1888, he made his final continental journey, travelling through northern France (Beauvais, Dijon and Sallanches), Italy (Milan, Bassano and Venice) and Switzerland (Berne, Thun and Chamonix). He wrote the Epilogue to *Modern Painters* at Chamonix, and completed *Praeterita* on this tour, returning to Brantwood until his death in January 1900.

Ruskin's Cultural Travelling

Ruskin's earliest travels were family excursions, which took the conscious form of educational holidays, effectively promoting the precocious talents of an only and beloved son, and allowing his wealthy father to indulge and impart an enquiring connoisseurship in the arts and antiquities. Together with the subsequent continental tours, they became a domestication of the Grand Tour, superintended by the discipline of a strictly evangelical mother, who doted equally on husband and child. Her anxieties, coupled with the real and imagined delicacy of their son's health, meant that there was always a more or less valetudinarian aspect to their travel. As their journeys expanded from the insular, though widely ranged terrain of Britain to encompass favoured routes through mainland Europe, their experiences enabled the boy's attention to turn to a comparativist assessment of British and continental architecture and art influenced principally by picturesque drawing and Romantic literature.

In the shift away from the itinerary of classical humanism to inland British tourism, British painting and writing figured largely. Though primarily a critic, Ruskin was himself a practitioner of picturesque drawing and Romantic poetry and prose. He continued to compose derivative poetry until 1845, when, in the course of his continental tour, he finally renounced it with relief as unsuitable to his more discursive gifts. The most important influences on his early draughtsmanship were the vignettes of Turner's drawings for over half the engravings in Samuel Rogers's sub-Byronic poem, *Italy* (1830), a poetic journal with historical and narrative interludes in verse and prose, and then the lithographic plates for Samuel Prout's architectural *Sketches in Flanders and Germany* (1833), for which his father was a credited subscriber. Following their reading of the latter, the Ruskins decided to direct their annual tour to the

LIVERPOOL JOHN MOORES UNIVERSITY
LEARNING SERVICES

Continent in search of the places depicted, and in that way the precedent of the professional painter's 'tour', or the representation of a journey through particular towns and landscapes in a series of scenes, became a leading motif in the planning and experience of the family's travels.

The recording and representation of his travelling were to become its chief purpose over time, as part of his huge critical and educational programme. On the early continental tours Ruskin produced streams of Byronic verses and imitative sketches, and his emerging talents led to the appointment of a series of drawing masters who contributed to his technique and eye for the Picturesque. In 1834–1835, he took lessons from Anthony Vandyke Copley Fielding, the inaugural President of the Old Water-colour Society, and later, in 1841, from James Duffield Harding, on a less formal arrangement, though Harding helped to confirm Ruskin's predisposition to see in landscape a revelation of divine creation. Harding had been the student of Prout, who specialised in depicting continental towns, and whose work remained the dominant influence on Ruskin's own style into the early 1840s, in combination with the engravings of Turner's watercolour drawings for literary illustrations, and for his series *The Rivers of France* (1833–1835). Rogers himself, whom Ruskin visited as a young aspirant author, was an important model for Ruskin's continental touring. His travels came towards the close of the Grand Tour as it had been practised by the cognoscenti and dilettanti of the 18th century. From 1803, his seven rooms at 22 St James's Place became a considerable private museum with antique casts, curious collections, paintings, and engravings. A connoisseur, banker and patron of all the arts, he was able to fund handsomely illustrated gift books featuring state-of-the-art steel engravings. His own rather leaden verses in *Italy* confirmed the sense of place conveyed by Romantic association and historical allusion which fed into Ruskin's notion of the 'poetry of architecture'. Apart from in his adolescent poetry of love disappointment, Ruskin avoided the introspection of the hero of Byron's *Childe Harold's Pilgrimage* (1812–1818), in favour of examining the places themselves, though his encounter with other countries was generally steeped in literary associations: with Rousseau, Wordsworth, Shelley and Jeremias Gotthelf in the Alps, with Shakespeare, Dante, Byron and Shelley in Italy, and with Sir Walter Scott everywhere.

The next influence to modify his drawing style was that of David Roberts, the Scottish theatrical scene painter who became an immensely successful topographical artist. Ruskin first saw his work in the lithographs for *The Pilgrims of the Rhine* (1834), and *The Tourist in Spain* (1832–1833), by Thomas Roscoe, depicting scenes at Burgos, Granada and Seville, but it was his 'sketches in Egypt and the Holy Land', 1840, evidencing the 'faithful and laborious ... outlines from nature' with which to tackle a 'true portraiture of scenes of religious and historical interest'

2.3 Samuel Prout. *Abbeville*. Pencil. 14. facing 395. Photo by R. Martin Seddon

(35.262), which prompted Ruskin's greater consideration of balancing physical accuracy with other kinds of truthfulness.

The specialised instruction that fed into Ruskin's travelling practices was only one feature, though it was to lead to the chief outcome, of his privileged experience. He almost always travelled in company, and enjoyed the comfortable and leisurely style of a well-to-do family who were completely in control of their destinations and the time they would spend there. Originally the party, which usually favoured accommodation at old inns, included his former nurse, his older cousin, Mary, and a courier to facilitate transport, overcome language difficulties and arrange admission to special sites. Their unhurried regime typically involved a start from eight or nine, covering 40 to 50 miles a day, and then Ruskin 'sate down to dinner at four, – and [he] had done two hours of delicious exploring by [himself] in the evening; ordered in punctually at seven for tea, and finishing [his] sketches till half-past nine – bed-time' (35.111).

2.4 John Ruskin. *Casa Contarini* Fasan, 1841. Pencil. The Ruskin Library, Lancaster University

2.5 J.M.W. Turner. *Lake of Como*. Engraving by Edward Goodall. From Samuel Rogers, *Italy* (London: Printed for T. Cadell and E. Moxon, 1830), p. 32. Photo by R. Martin Seddon

The Jungfrau from Interlaken.
1833.

2.6 John Ruskin. *The Jungfrau from Interlaken*, 1833. Photogravure of pen draw-ing. From *The Poems of John Ruskin*, 2 vols., edited by W.G. Collingwood (Orpington and London: George Allen, 1891), Vol. 1, facing p. 140. Photo by R. Martin Seddon

2.7 David Roberts. *The Alhambra in Granada*. Lithograph. Frontispiece to *Picturesque Sketches of Spain* (London: Hodgson & Graves, 1837). Photo by R. Martin Seddon

2.8 F. Crawley. *Aiguilles*, *Chamonix*, 1854. Daguerreotype. The Ruskin Library,
Lancaster University

The family never travelled on Sundays, nor did Ruskin climb or sketch on
that day until late in life. The courier's tasks were later performed by his
personal servant of the time. That role was filled in 1841 by the 17-year-
old John Hobbs ('George'), who kept a detailed diary of the tours of 1846
and 1849 and also acted as amanuensis, providing the printer's copy of
Ruskin's writings and taking daguerreotypes, for which Ruskin was an
early enthusiast. Ruskin described him, 'indefatigably carrying his little
daguerreo-type box up everywhere and taking the first image of the
Matterhorn ever, as also of the aiguilles of Chamouni, drawn by the sun.
A thing to be proud of still' (35.453). In 1853, he was to be replaced by
Frederick Crawley, who also took daguerreotypes as directed, and made
fair copies of Ruskin's rough drafts. In 1844, Ruskin's father secured a
leading Alpine guide, Joseph Couttet, to direct and safeguard his son by
an arrangement which lasted many years: their final walks were in 1874.
During his marriage to Effie, Ruskin mostly travelled with his wife, either
alone or with his parents, and in later life with groups of friends and relations. He could also call upon members of an informal research team
staffed, at different times, by paid servants, semi-professionals, including
successive 'secretaries', and copyists commissioned to provide records of
artworks and buildings for his writings and lectures.

As the Romantic writer and artist developed into the Victorian social
critic, Ruskin had to operate within changing and ever more forceful economic pressures and social regulation. He worked both within and outside of established class positions at a time when his central discipline of
art criticism was beginning to become established as an academic and
intellectual discipline. Professionally, he had to create a new educational
role for himself to express his earnestness and dedication – the role of
cultural critic itself. His social outlook was poised between the cultural
connoisseurship and amateurism of the aristocratic grand tourist (his
father made him a Gentleman Commoner at Christ Church, Oxford, and
had a coat-of-arms painted on his own carriage) and his commitment

to enable cultural access to the workingmen he taught at the Working Men's College in London, and to whom he addressed several series of discursive letter sequences.

The approaches he had evolved and sought to communicate demanded the time and tranquil reflection which such travelling had afforded, enabling a respectful observation of cultural differences and acting out the philosophical base of empirical realism in protracted and carefully considered perception. Such experience demanded interactivity and interpretation, as part of a learning experience, and it found itself in critical relation to developments in the technologies of travel, involving road transport as well as the advent of steam by rail and sea, and the representations of travel, including his pioneering use of daguerreotypes and his carefully examined employment of early photography and various kinds of prints.

At first the family travelled solely by horse-driven vehicles, always Ruskin's preferred mode as he detested the rise of the railway which he argued undermined the traveller's ability to interact with the landscape. The private carriage loaned by Mr Ruskin's business partner, Henry Telford, was an example of the horse-drawn system which was on the verge of becoming old-fashioned in the later 1830s, as Bradshaw's railway timetable was introduced in 1839. It was conclusively overhauled in Britain in the early 1840s, when the famous coaches began to be replaced by trains, though the change took longer on the Continent. The steam engine and all that it initiated brought a revolution in transport and displaced the horse from the trunk stage-coach routes to other activities. A division was opening up between the new urban network being created and those areas relatively cut off from it which emphasised the town and country split. As Ruskin was later to complain from his uncompromising viewpoint: 'All vitality is concentrated through those throbbing arteries [the main lines] into the central cities; the country is passed over like a green sea by narrow bridges …'. (8.246)

Indeed, Ruskin thought the most 'profitable travelling' was on foot, and he described his own experience of trains to one correspondent in 1846 as the negation of travel as he had understood it:

> … the general effect of them is to render all the time that we pass in locomotion the same, except in feverishness, as that passed at home, and to enable us to get over ground which formerly conveyed to us a thousand various ideas, and the examination of which was fertile in lessons of the most interesting kind, while we read a page of the morning paper. (36.62)

He relished the mystique of hiring vehicles from Long Acre – their design, conveniences and luxuries, and fondly describes the experience of his youthful touring, '[i]n the olden days of travelling, now to return no more', moving on at a slow but informative pace from place to place, in a rhythm of anticipation and arrival, as

> from the top of the last hill he had surmounted, the traveller beheld the quiet village where he was to rest ... or, from the long hoped for turn in the dusty perspective of the causeway, saw, for the first time, the towers of some famed city, faint in the rays of sunset-hours of peaceful and thoughtful pleasure, for which the rush of the arrival in the railway station is perhaps not always, or to all men, an equivalent, – in those days, I say, ... there were few moments more fondly cherished by the traveller, than that which ... brought him within sight of Venice. (10.3–4)

The vantage point for vision was crucial for picturesque travelling, as Ruskin was keenly aware: '...the four large, admirably fitting and sliding windows...formed one large moving oriel, out of which one saw the country round, to the full half of the horizon. My own prospect was more extended still, for my seat was the little box containing my clothes ... and my horizon was the widest possible' (28.389). Equally important was the leisurely horse-drawn pace itself which enabled a constantly protracted visual intake: Ruskin later wrote that he was unsure whether one should use the expression to 'do' or 'see' a carriage-drive (see 16.336). The difference between the style of travelling described and that of the branch-line train may not have been as fundamental as Ruskin perceived it to be, certainly not to a later motor-driven age which now looks back with relative nostalgia to the rhythms of steam travel, but he especially bemoaned the effect of mechanical transport in destroying the quality of sensory perceptions which the 'jog-trot pace' of the hired post-chaise and pair provided, and the stable picture-like prospects available 'through the panoramic opening of the four windows ... .' (35.16)

Ruskin's advocacy of a travel experience centred on the possibilities of visual activity became embattled against mechanised transport, with the

2.9 Ruskin's double brougham. Photograph. The Brantwood Trust. In the roof basket is his travelling bath

consequences Carlyle bemoaned when describing 'touring expeditions which are now blinder than ever, and done by steam, without even eyesight, not to say intelligence' (Carlyle, 2: 181). Intelligence in the form of interactivity was threatened above all by the railway which, Ruskin wrote, 'transmutes a man from a traveller into a living parcel' (8.159), and 'Going by railroad I do not consider as travelling at all; it is merely being "sent" to a place, and very little different from becoming a parcel ...' (5.370). He derided the 'ferruginous temper' (8.66n) of the age, whereby 'every fool in Buxton can be in Bakewell in half-an-hour, and every fool in Bakewell in Buxton' (27.86), with grievous damage to the erstwhile tranquillity of Monsal Dale. Ruskin himself used trains and the cross-channel steamboat service which boosted continental tourism from 1820, but what he deprecated was the tendency of its unexamined effects, so that he scorned the 'doing' of Europe in a week which the railway was to make possible and which was, as Parsons points out, 'a tour that was actually on offer from Thomas Cook from 1862 onwards' (Parsons, 2007: 217):

> No changing of place at a hundred miles an hour ... will make us one whit stronger, happier, or wiser. There was always more in the world than men could see, walked they ever so slowly; they will see it no better for going fast ... The really precious things are thought and sight, not pace. (5.380–381)

Furthermore, the infrastucture was unsightly, disruptive and polluting. In 1864 he rebuked an audience of Mancunian industrialists for their association with the effects of railway enterprise:

> You have put a railway-bridge over the falls of Schaffhausen. You have tunnelled the cliffs of the Lake of Lucerne by Tell's chapel; you have destroyed the Clarens shore of the Lake of Geneva; there is not a

2.10 *Mornings in Florence.* Photo by R. Martin Seddon

2.11 Finely bound Ruskin Guidebooks. Photo by K. Hanley

quiet valley in England that you have not filled with bellowing fire . . . nor any foreign city in which the spread of your presence is not marked by a consuming white leprosy of new hotels and perfumers' shops. (18.89)

For him, those editions of the *Hand-book to Northern Italy* which described 'how to see all the remarkable objects in Venice in a single day', or, for 'the less hurried visitor . . . a week' (11.360), were part of the same ruinous trend of anti-aesthetic tourism. The moral and spiritual weight he attributed to the aesthetic experiences he pointed his followers towards is reflected in the presentation of the Travellers' Guides produced from the later 1870s: especially the two-volume edition of the *Stones of Venice* and *St Mark's Rest* he provided specifically for that market, *Mornings in Florence*, and the 'Intelligent Traveller's' section of *The Bible of Amiens*, 'Interpretations'. Contrasting with the serviceable red 'Handbooks' of Murray and Baedeker which were of a standard size and design to be held in the hand, were these precious volumes, often bound in leather and vellum, with rich tooling, and florally decorated inner linings, which resemble missals. Even the cheap Tauchnitz reprints from the Library of British and American Authors, familiar to the Anglophone travellers on the Continent, are often to be found with Italian stationers' labels elaborately presented in this way, and Ruskin's own printer-publisher, George Allen, produced the slender pamphlets of each single morning's walk in Florence, parts of his 'History of Venice', and his 'Interpretations' of Amiens Cathedral in dark red leather with golden lettering. Altogether, the precious and sacred overtones are designed to reflect the alternative values of his methods of sightseeing.

References

Addison, J. (1705) *Remarks on Several Parts of Italy*. London: J. Tonson.
Aglionby, W. (1685) *Painting Illustrated in Three Dialogues*. Printed by J. Gain, sold by W. Kettilby and J. Tonson.

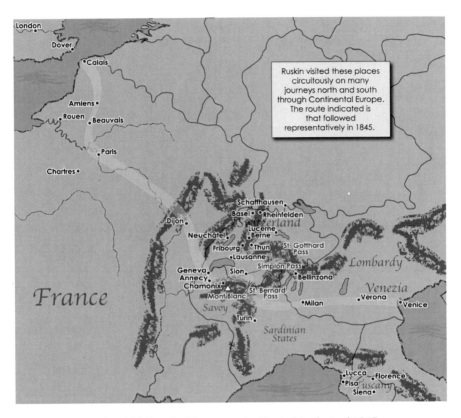

London
Dover
Calais
Amiens
Rouen
Beauvais
Paris
Chartres

Ruskin visited these places
circuitously on many
journeys north and south
through Continental Europe.
The route indicated is
that followed
representatively in 1845.

Schaffhausen
Basel Rheinfelden
Switzerland
Dijon
Lucerne
Neuchâtel
Berne
Fribourg Thun
St. Gotthard
Pass
Lausanne
Simplon Pass
Lombardy
Geneva Sion
Annecy Bellinzona
Chamonix
Mont Blanc St. Bernard
Pass
Venezia
Savoy Milan Verona
Venice
France
Turin
Sardinian
States

Lucca Florence
Pisa Tuscany
Siena

1 The Old Roads: The route indicated is that of 1845

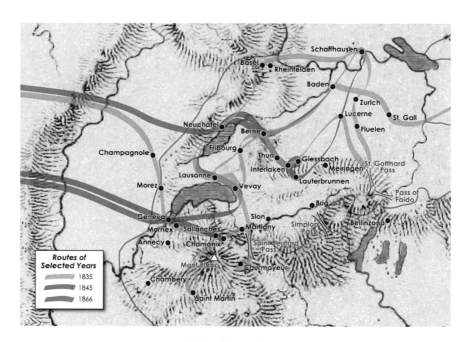

2 The Swiss Tours

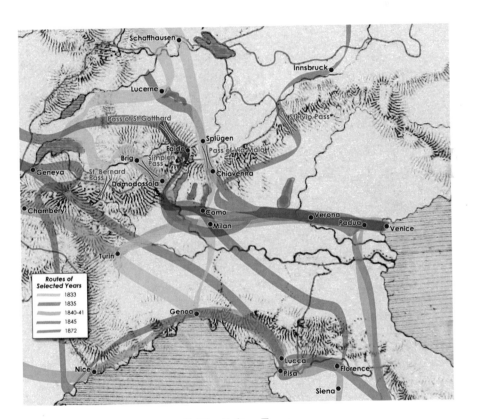

3 The Italian Tours

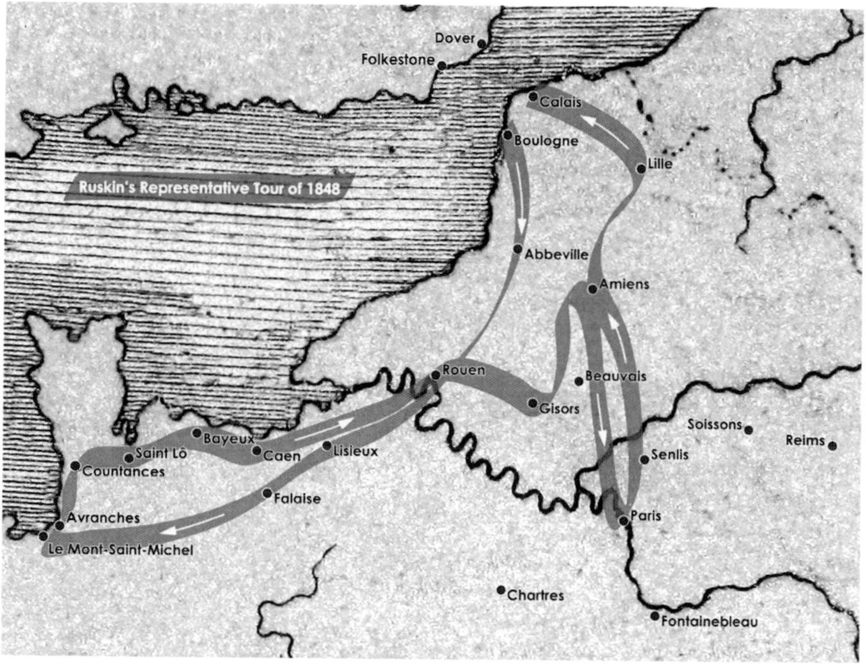
Ruskin's Representative Tour of 1848
Dover
Folkestone
Calais
Boulogne
Lille
Abbeville
Amiens
Rouen
Beauvais
Gisors
Soissons
Reims
Senlis
Paris
Bayeux
Saint Lô
Caen
Lisieux
Countances
Falaise
Avranches
Le Mont-Saint-Michel
Chartres
Fontainebleau

4 The French Tour of 1848

Altick, R.D. (1978) *The Shows of London*. Cambridge, MA: Belknap Press.

Andrew, P.R. (2008) The grand tour: An overview. In L. Borley (ed.) *The Grand Tour and its Influence on Architecture, Artistic Taste and Patronage*. Edinburgh: Europa Nostra.

Barber, G. (1999) The English-language Guidebook to Europe up to 1870. In R. Myers and M. Harris (eds) *Journeys Through the Market: Travel, Travellers and the Book Trade*. New Castle, DE and Folkestone.

Black, J. (1992) *Routes and Destinations, in his The British Abroad: the Grand Tour in the Eighteenth Century*. Stroud: Sutton Publishing.

Brendon, P. (1991) *Thomas Cook: 150 Years of Popular Tourism*. London: Secker and Warburg.

Buzard, J. (1993) *The Beaten Track: European Tourism, Literature, and the Ways to Culture 1800–1918*. Oxford: Clarendon Press.

Byron, G.G. (1812 –1818) *Childe Harold's Pilgrimage*. London: John Murray.

Carlyle, T. (1858–65) *The History of Frederick II of Prussia, Called Frederick the Great*. London: Chapman & Hall.

Clegg, J. (1981) *Ruskin and Venice*. London: Junction Books.

De Seta, C. (1996) Grand Tour: The lure of Italy in the eighteenth century. In A. Wilton and I. Bignami (eds) *Grand Tour: The Lure of Italy in the Eighteenth Century*. London: Tate Gallery Publishing.

Ebel, J.G. (1830–31) *Manuel du Voyageur en Suisse*. Paris: Audin.

Eustace, J.C. (1813) *A Classical Tour Through Italy*. London: J. Mawman.

Hilton, T. (1985) *John Ruskin: The Early Years*. New Haven and London: Yale University Press.

Hoppen, K.T. (1998) *The Mid-Victorian Generation, 1846–1886*. Oxford: Clarendon Press.

Hudson, R. (1993) (ed.) *The Grand Tour 1592–1796*. London: The Folio Society.

Hussey, C. (1983) *The Picturesque: Studies in a Point of View*. London: Frank Cass.

James, H. (1993) *Collected Travel Writings: The Continent*. New York: Literary Classics of the United States.

Kemp, W. (1990) *The Desire of My Eyes: The Life and Work of John Ruskin*. New York: Farrar, Straus and Giroux.

Lassels, R. (1670) *The Voyage of Italy*. London: J. Starkey.

MacCannell, D. (1976) *The Tourist: A New Theory of the Leisure Class*. New York: Schocken Books.

Maxwell, C. (1932) *The English Traveller in France, 1698–1815*. London: Routledge.

Mendilow, J. (1986) *The Romantic Tradition in British Political Thought*. Beckenham: Croom Helm.

Morrell, J. (1963) *Miss Jemima's Swiss Journal: The First Conducted Tour of Switzerland*. London: Putnam.

Murray, J. (1836) *Hand-book for Travellers in Holland, Belgium, and North Germany*. London: John Murray.

Murray, J. (1847) *Hand-book for Travellers in Northern Italy*. London: John Murray.

Murray, J. (1848) *Hand-book for Travellers in France*. London: John Murray.

Norwich, J.J. (2003) *Paradise of Cities: Venice in the 19th Century*. New York: Doubleday.

Nugent, T. (1749) *Grand Tour*. London: S. Birt.

Osborne, P.D. (2000) *Travelling Light: Photography, Travel and Visual Culture*. Manchester: Manchester University Press.

Palmowski, J. (2002) Travels with Baedeker—the guidebook and the middle classes in Victorian and Edwardian Britain. In R. Koshar (ed.) *Histories of Leisure*. Oxford, New York: Berg.

Parsons, N.T. (2007) *Worth the Detour: A History of the Guidebook*. Stroud: Sutton.

Pemble, J. (1988) *The Mediterranean Passion. Victorians and Edwardians in the South*. Oxford: Oxford University Press.

Porter, R. (1996) Visitors visions: Travellers' tales of Georgian London. In C. Chard. and H. Langdan (eds) *Transports: Travels, Pleasure, and Imaginative Geography, 1600–1830*. New Haven and London: Yale University Press.

Prout, S. (1833) *Sketches in Flanders and Germany: Facsimile of Studies Made in Flanders and Germany and Drawn on Stone*. London: C. Hullmandels.

Richardson, J. (1719) *A Discourse on ... The Science of the Connoisseur*.

Reichard, M. (n.d.) *Itinerary of Italy*. London: S. Leigh.

Rogers, S. (1830) *Italy, A Poem*. London: T. Cadell, Jennings and Chaplin E. Moxon.

Rogers, S. (1956) In J.R. Hale (ed.) *Italian Journals of Samuel Rogers*. London: Faber & Faber.

Ruskin, J. (1956–1959) In J. Evans and J. Howard Whitehouse (eds) *The Diaries of John Ruskin* (Vol. 2). Oxford: Clarendon Press.

Sigaux, G. (1966) *History of Tourism*. London and Geneva: Leisure Arts.

Smith, A. (1776) *The Wealth of Nations*. London: W. Strahan and T. Cadell.

Starke, M. (1800) *Letters from Italy*. London: R. Phillips.

Starke, M. (1820) *Travels on the Continent*; reissued as *Information and Directions for Travellers on the Continent of Europe*, 1824. London: R. Phillips.

Stephen, L. (1895) *The Playground of Europe*. London: Longmans.

Thompson, F.M.L. (1968) *The Rise of Respectable Society: A Social History of Victorian Britain 1830–1900*. Harmondsworth: Penguin.

Towner, J. (1996) Venturing Abroad: the European Grand Tour. In his *An Historical Geography of Recreation and Tourism in the Western World 1540–1940*. Chichester: John Wiley.

Turner, J.M.W. (1833–1835) *Turner's Annual Tour, The Rivers of France*. (Vol. 3). London: Charles Heath.

Urry, J. (2002) *The Tourist Gaze* (2nd edn). London: Sage Publications.

Chapter 3

Sightseeing with Ruskin

This chapter establishes the visual basis of Ruskin's travelling. Though it was part of an epochal shift from the early Grand Tourist's search for 'discourse', including foreign languages and conversations with eminent persons, to the emphasis on visual observation which Adler writes about, it aims at far more than the sightseeing enabled by an eye 'deliberately disciplined to emotionally detached, objectively accurate vision . . . ' (Adler, 1989: 18). It offered rather an interpretative scheme, extending from a focus on realist perception, which became the consistent method Ruskin followed in his cultural criticism and the travellers' guides he produced late in his career. Thereby he intended to counter the avoidance and neglect of serious aesthetic experience which characterised modern tourism, and also the superficiality which then and consistently in that industry, Urry claims, has become one of 'the implications that places are visually consumed' (Urry, 2005: 19).

Visual Representation

Ruskin's central role as an art critic made him a specialist in seeing. He came to judge that his early years, when his parents' supervisory regime had denied him a wide field of visual stimulus, had helped to produce his exceptional 'thirst for visible fact', and had developed 'that patience in looking, and precision in feeling, which afterwards, with due industry, formed [his] analytic power' (Ruskin, 1956–1959: 51). For him the primary medium is the visual, because, from his empiricist perspective, it is the hinge between sensation and idea, the material and the intellectual. His journals and notebooks all contain the mixed media of notes, descriptions, drawings and sketches, as his finished works of art and architectural criticism are illustrated with prints which are an integral part, indeed often the clearest expression, of their purpose. The chief original exemplar had been the composite text of Rogers's and Turner's *Italy*, but Ruskin was both writer and artist of his own works. They display an unusually complementary relation between the visual and written, inseparably bonded together like Blake's works. John Dixon Hunt writes about Ruskin's 'hesitations about the primacy of the visual over . . . the joint endeavours of the visual and verbal *tout simple*', and points out how his adult letters 'will often switch from sentence to sketch and back again to complete his meaning' (Hunt, 1978: 803; see Hunt, 1982: 5), but any uncertainty over this relationship concerns the successful transmission from the visual into the verbal. In *Praeterita* he even remarks on the advantages in his family's early travels of not understanding foreign languages so that they could take in more of their new experiences directly, 'and even in my own land, the things in which I have been least deceived are those which I have learned as their Spectator' (35.119).

Drawing, for example, provided him with, in his words, 'a power of notation and description greater in most instances than that of words' (16.143). He makes repeated statements like that in the third volume of *Modern Painters*: 'To see clearly is poetry, prophecy, and religion, – all in one' (5.333; see Hewison, 1976). For what he calls in the second volume of *Modern Painters*, 'The Theoretic Faculty', the mind's primary mode of contemplation, the eye provides a direct connection 'with the moral perception and appreciation of ideas of beauty' (4.35). Then, secondarily, the imagination is responsible for rearranging, in his words, 'the ideas it has received from external nature', performing 'the operations . . . which become in their turn objects of the theoretic faculty to other minds.' Ruskin writes that both primary and secondary modes offer what he defines as a 'true place for the intellectual lens and moral retina, by which, and on which, our informing thoughts are concentrated and represented' (Ruskin, 1956–1959: 36). The dialectic between the material and the moral is pictured as an eye, as Ruskin later elaborated in a lecture of 1877: '"Intellectual lens, and moral retina" – the lens faithfully and far collecting, the retina faithfully and inwardly receiving' (22.513), visual sensations becoming part of, and one with, the viewer's moral nature. His 'vision' is a moot term, but always visually grounded: 'All great men see what they paint before they paint it, – see it in a perfectly passive manner, – cannot help seeing it if they would; whether in their mind's eye, or in bodily fact, does not matter' (5.114).

The word 'landscape' is, of course, ambiguous. It means either a real natural scene *or* a visual representation of one, and Ruskin's theories on art point up the peculiar continuities between the material actuality and representations of it. For him, visual representation looks both ways – back to the original sensory perception, and forward to the communication of Ruskin's developing interpretation. It is crucial to recognise the realist claim, basic to Ruskin's vision, which guarantees its promise to open access to all his readers who may share it, as seers, prior to intellectual elaboration. As long as naturalism lies at its base, art also is capable of providing a *lingua franca*, as in medieval religious decoration, for all levels of society, even the illiterate, just as it made possible Ruskin's own ready assimilation of international cultural phenomena. The favoured medium of Ruskin's 'modern painters', watercolour drawing, had in particular opened the eyes of the middle classes to the real world it reflected, as Paul H. Walton comments, because it

> was based on an aesthetic of sensation, emotion, and associated ideas, an aesthetic of the common man, as opposed to the cult of 'high art' fostered by the Academy, which enabled the [water-colour] Society to encourage the new notion that 'taste' need no longer be the exclusive privilege of the aristocracy. (Walton, 1972: 21)

Ruskin's own architectural drawings and illustrations, especially for *The Seven Lamps of Architecture* (1849) and *The Stones of Venice* (1851–1853) established both his own critical perceptions and the imaginary guide to perception he was offering his readers. He sought to master the art of print illustration which became his pivotal vehicle of interpretation, and Alan Davis estimates that

> For *The Seven Lamps of Architecture, The Stones of Venice* and *Modern Painters* alone, he produced over 150 etched, engraved, and litho-graphed plates and more than 200 engravings on wood. He etched some of the finest plates by his own hand; [and] others were made in collaboration with professional engravers, under [his] careful super-vision. (Davis, 2003: 1)

He worked with the traditional skills of drawings, watercolours, wood cuts, copper-plate mezzotints, soft ground etchings, and lithographs, as well as newly invented techniques such as steel engraving, daguerreo-types, and other photographic techniques, and he frequently experimented with combined processes and a variety of representations of the same objects in several media. His openness to innovation is an important feature of his passion for visual mediation. Some illustrations are, in Turner's own term, 'translations' from one medium to another; others interactively interpret another artist's work. Throughout all his efforts to achieve the precise effects he aimed at, he was primarily concerned to enable his readers *to see* according to the extraordinary weight of content he attributed to that word, unfolding what Robert Hewison (1976) has described as 'The Argument of the Eye'. Such illustration involved selec-tive focus on significant detail; accuracy of representation; an area of expressiveness and symbolic power which had to be scrupulously and anxiously regulated by the values of moral realism he attached to strict material realism; and permanence of record, urgently at a time when the originals were under threat of destruction, or, what was for him the same thing, 'restoration'. Restoration was the grossest form of supposed reme-diation, which he detested for example when imposed on Venetian paintings for obliterating *'the real thing'*, still observable in 'Whatever is left of them, however fragmentary, however ruinous, however obscured and defiled ... there are no fresh readings ...' (10.437).

His theory and practice of book illustration relies on the intellectual use of the term 'illustration' as 'explaining', or serving to clarify. The original rhetorical sense, from Aristotle's *Enargeia* (vividness) to Quintilian's Latin equivalents of *illustratio* or *evidentia*, refers to an instrument of persuasion: putting something before the audience's eyes by highlighting it, a 'vivid representation'. Ruskin's book illustrations are specifically designed to shed light on the inherent laws, or Truth, of nature, which never entirely loses the trace of a pre-evolutionary sense of deist design coupled with an evangelical reading of Biblical typology. Because of his founding belief in Natural Theology – seeing the material world itself as, in Aquinas's term, God's created Second Book, the natural world for Ruskin is already pre-mediated, or textualised. In that way, for him nature itself has commenced the process of mediation, and all intellectual endeavour and cultural creativity of the artist or scientist or critic is, from Ruskin's viewpoint, a collaborative project of 'illustration', seen as a belated attempt at re-mediation and interpretation in which the written and visual components are similarly engaged. And seen in that light, all Ruskin's work may be described as 'illustration'.

Ruskin's illustrations have an inner history made up of the insights assembled over a lifetime's continuous travelling. He travelled from the early picturesque conventions through which he himself originally saw and represented his domestic and continental destinations to a deepening sense of his experience of places and art for which he developed experimentally the appropriate media to communicate it to his readers. He started out with the studio-based formulas imitated from his drawing master, Copley Fielding, though at the same time he was making more particularised architectural and geological sketches in his early notebooks from the age of 14, some of which turned into woodcut illustrations for scientific articles and for *The Poetry of Architecture* (1837–1838).

3.1 John Ruskin (after Anthony Vandyke Copley Fielding). *Loch Achray and Ben Venue*, 1834–1835. The Ruskin Library, Lancaster University

Like most of those who came to know Turner's work in the 19th century Ruskin encountered him through his engraved prints, in his case particularly in the exquisite vignettes of the 1830 edition of Samuel Rogers's *Italy*. Turner changed from copper-plate to steel engraving for this series to explore the possibilities that had been created by this newly advanced medium, in which the art of the engravers had been called upon to match Turner's painterly effects (which they in turn encouraged). Turner's contribution to the evolution of the vignette took the device from a largely ornamental function to become 'in miniature the "elevated pastoral" and the "historical landscape" of the great canvases' (Piggott, 1993: 97), and for Ruskin they were a revelation that trained his eye in both observing exact natural effects and ways of representing them. He was similarly captivated by the lithographic prints of the picturesque places and monuments of Europe in Samuel Prout's *Sketches in Flanders and Germany* (1833), and he copied and imitated the printed works of both artists studiously in pencil and pen and ink on all the tours he made in Britain and on the Continent throughout the 1830s. Later he described how their 'outline drawing applied to landscape' had concentrated his literalistic eye on what he described as the 'modern scientific process ... of a mathematically accurate and attentive summary of the facts of an entire landscape or street view, for the sake of those facts' (35.624), and how it determined his own method: '... always working resignedly at the thing under my hand till I could do it, and looking exclusively at the thing before my eyes till I could see it' (Ruskin, I: 217). But while he himself could attempt to replicate what he called Turner's 'microscopic touch' (Ruskin, I: 256) in his own drawn imitations, he became frustrated by many of the contemporary engravings which often failed to achieve it.

On the other hand, he gradually began to find the reductive technique of Prout's lithographic crayon equally inadequate for rendering architectural decoration, as he later wrote: 'I ... was as happy in the fifteenth century as in the tenth ... [and] used only such rude and confused lines as I had learned to imitate from Prout' (Ruskin, II: 623). He was becoming aware of a developing power of detailed observation which Turner's landscape prints reflected but which architectural drawing had not yet developed the techniques to convey, informed by what he described as his personal 'idiosyncrasy which extremely wise people do not share, – my love of all kinds of filigree and embroidery, from hoarfrost to high clouds' (Ruskin, 1956–1959: 157). In the later 1830s he mostly abandoned Prout's signature 'acicular precision of sharp black line ending with a dot' (Ruskin, II: 623). He was coming to view his skill in picture-making as increasingly subsidiary to his study of the power of art to reveal the created world.

The 'truthfulness' at which he aimed had a specific Romantic and religious content, which at first he loosely called 'poetry'. Prout's Picturesque, for example, featuring crumbling domestic and historical buildings, merged easily with Wordsworthian naturalism, the sense of natural scenery blending with human constructions. It was a perception he had derived from Wordsworth's poetry and from the 1835 edition of *Wordsworth's Guide to the Lakes*, which repeatedly draws attention to the aesthetic of organicism:

> These humble dwellings remind the contemplative spectator of a production of Nature, and may (using a strong expression) rather be said to have grown than to have been erected; the houses rise by an instinct of their own, out of the native rock. (Wordsworth, 1977: 62)

It was confirmed by his own observations on his Lake District visits, especially the tour of 1837 which he recorded in a series of drawings (see Hanley, 2007). Ruskin defined a crucial stage in his own perception of the external world when studying an aspen tree at Fontainebleau in 1842, and noticed the principle of 'natural composition', as natural objects '"composed" themselves, by finer laws than any known of men' (3.xxi–xxii). It marked a recurrence of an insight he remembered having first experienced when out walking as a student he observed an ivy-wreathed tree, with graceful trails of clinging foliage which he decided to sketch. Trying to transfer the natural object to paper in line and shadow made him aware that this endeavour to copy nature was the right work of the artist, and it became the principle of 'truth to nature', and the perception that 'Precisely the same faculties of eye and mind are concerned in the analysis of natural and pictorial forms' (6.xx), which became the grand theme of *Modern Painters*. Despite what Ruskin later called the 'wretched conventionalism'

3.2 John Ruskin, *Troutbeck*, 1837. Pencil. The Ruskin Library, Lancaster University

3.3 John Ruskin. *Trees and Rocks*, 1845. Watercolour. The Ruskin Library, Lancaster University

of his early Proutism, it was Prout's work which had helped fasten historical architecture in his imagination, in ways which fed into the consideration of landscape and building he was theorising at the same time for *The Poetry of Architecture* as an extension of Wordsworthian organicism. The domestic architecture in this work is Proutian, while the historical villas are Turnerian.

3.4 John Ruskin. *Cottage near Altdorf.* Woodcut. From *The Poetry of Architecture.* (1.35) Photo by R. Martin Seddon

3.5 John Ruskin. *Villa, Sommariva, Cadenabbia.* From the *Architectural Magazine*,
No. 3, *The Villa*, June 1838, p. 247. Photo by R. Martin Seddon

Radically, what bound cultural associations and the landscape together for
Ruskin was his sense of their shared moral organisation.

Remarkably, although *Modern Painters* was the culmination of Ruskin's
analysis of landscape art, particularly Turner's, the first two volumes of
that work, 1843 and 1846, were not illustrated, because Ruskin had not
yet prepared any media which could begin to do justice to Turner's original art. The third volume of *Modern Painters* (1856), was the first to contain engraved illustrations, for which the page-size had to be enlarged.
His ambition thereafter to have his own exacting intentions realised
eventually led to his employing his own engraver, later to become his
publisher, George Allen. In the meantime, between 1845 when he made
his first solo visit to the Continent and 1860, by when he had completed his
major illustrated books on landscape and architecture, Ruskin had transformed his approach to drawing, and with it his approach to visual illustration in general. He conscientiously moved away from what he called the
'outward delightfulness' of picturesque conventions to realise his own

3.6 Unknown photographer. *St Mark's and Clock Tower*, Venice. Daguerreotype.
The Ruskin Library, Lancaster University

3.7 Unknown photographer. *Detail of S. Denis and Angels, Rheims Cathedral.* Daguerreotype. The Ruskin Library, Lancaster University

interpretative gaze on landscape, art and architecture in what he referred to as a 'comprehension of the pathos of character beneath' (6.15–16). He describes the dispassionate approach he sought: '. . .it entirely refuses emotion. The work must be done with the patience of an accountant, and records only the realities of the scene – not the effects on them' (35.624).

Besides a new appreciation of Italian painting, the 1845 tour brought him another momentous discovery in the daguerreotype, which appealed at once to his desire for exactitude. Ruskin referred to it as 'the sun's drawing', and wrote: 'It is very nearly the same thing as carrying off the palace itself; every chip of stone and stain is there, and of course there is no mistake about proportions' (3.210). He bought his own apparatus and began his collection this year, which probably added up to considerably more than the 233 he lists, acquiring some in Italy and France up to 1852, and others in

3.8 Unknown photographer and John Ruskin. *Maria della Spina, Lucca.* Daguerreotype (left) and Drawing (right). The Ruskin Library, Lancaster University and Sheffield Galleries and Museums Trust

Switzerland from 1854 to 1858, by which time they had become outmoded (Wildman, 2006: 1). As he became appalled by the ruin of Venetian architecture, he wrote that the invention had arrived 'just in time to save some evidence from the great public of wreckers' (3.210). He set himself the task of preserving images of Gothic decoration in Italy and France, particularly his 'pet bits' (3.10), which were in process of disintegration.

In employing and mastering all the new techniques he attempted scrupulously to apply them to his priorities, including, for example, preserving the image of what was becoming lost, rather than the economics of inexpensive replication. Of engraving he insisted: '*Permanence*, you observe, is the object, not multiplicity' (22.320). While daguerreotypes succeeded in avoiding the soullessness of the simply mechanical, as each image was unique, and though he eagerly began to base his architectural drawings on them, their sharpness and precision did not after all fully realise the character he tried to express in his own drawings. This entailed a deepening of perception, which he owed to his new exposure to Italian painting and architectural decoration and his resulting response to what he was to call in the second volume of *The Stones of Venice* 'The Nature of Gothic'. The perception of what he viewed as natural and spiritual *life* depended on it. From his new exposure to Venetian painting, especially Tintoretto, Ruskin began to learn the dramatic and expressive power of local colours balanced with chiaroscuro. The newly felt depth of cutting and the shaped materiality of Gothic decorative sculpture, which he admired on his 1848 French tour, similarly demanded a fresh approach to representation.

The method of copper-plate mezzotinting which Turner had employed for the series of prints collected in his *Liber Studiorum* (1807–1809) had been abandoned after Turner's first visit to Italy in 1819–1820 as incapable of registering the finer effects and details he had come to demand and which he found could be depicted on steel plates. But Ruskin now returned to the more expressive qualities which had been reproduced from the pen and sepia drawings on which Turner's plates had been based and to

3.9 J.M.W. Turner, *Near Blair Athol, Scotland*. Etching and mezzotint. Plate XLVII, *Liber Studiorum* (London: George Newnes; New York: Charles Scribner, n.d.). Photo by K. Hanley

3.10 John Ruskin, *Shoot of Spanish Chestnut at Carrara*. Watercolour facing 15.114.
Photo by K. Hanley

which the artist had added etched outlines. Ruskin began to draw in a similar manner, and to develop more expressive media, based on daguerre-otypes but aiming for fuller character, including what would appear as his own mezzotint illustrations for *The Stones of Venice*. A more immediate departure was the soft ground etching for *The Seven Lamps of Architecture* (1849). Soft ground etching, which Ruskin described as 'a kind of mixture of mezzotint – etching – and lithograph' (8.16), was old-fashioned when he chose it as the medium for the highly textured architectural images in the first edition of *The Seven Lamps of Architecture*. He was proud that they were,' as he wrote, 'not only, every line of them, by my own hand, but bitten also ... by myself, with savage carelessness' (8.15). 'Savageness' was

3.11 John Ruskin. *Study of Portal and Carved Pinnacles, Cathedral of St Lô, Normandy*, from *The Seven Lamps of Architecture*, 1848. Etching. Photo by R. Martin Seddon

3.12 John Ruskin. *Ornaments from Rouen, St Lô, and Venice,* from *The Seven Lamps of Architecture,* 1848. Etching. Photo by R. Martin Seddon

one of the essential characteristics of his 'Nature of Gothic', and they were considered crude by contemporary critics. Their roughness afforded a more impressive version of the organicism of the architecture, and of one plate he wrote: 'it was meant to show the greater beauty of the natural weeds than of the carved crockets, and the tender harmony of both' (8.82). But he aimed for what he called the 'Rembrandtism' of chiaroscuro, 'that is to say ... the sacrifice of details in the shadowed parts in order that greater depth of tone might be afforded on the lights' (11.311–312). Ruskin considered his etchings 'by far the most sternly faithful records of the portions of architecture they represent which had ever yet been published; and I am persuaded that in the course of time, this severe truth will give them a value far higher than that which is at present set upon plates of more delicate execution' (8.276–277).

Having spent what he referred to as 'two long winters ... in drawing of details on the spot', his demands for the illustrations to *The Stones of Venice* were great: 'Nothing is so rare in art, as far as my experience goes, as a fair illustration of architecture; *perfect* illustration of it does not exist' (10.114). By the time he had come to coordinate his theories and experiments he employed a variety of mixed media, as he wrote in the preface, he used

> any kind of engraving which seemed suited to the subjects – line and mezzotint, on steel, with mixed lithographs and woodcuts, at considerable loss to uniformity in the appearance of the volume, but, I hope, with advantage, in rendering the character of the architecture it describes. (9.9)

He also produced an additional folio volume in three parts, *Examples of the Architecture of Venice, Selected and Drawn to Measurement from the Edifices,* because he found it impossible to reduce his architectural drawings to the scale necessary for inclusion in *The Stones* without losing accuracy of

3.13 John Ruskin. *Temperance and Intemperance in Curvature.* Plate 1, *The Stones of Venice*, volume 3, (Smith, Elder and Co., 1853). Photo by R. Martin Seddon

detail. This series of prints are at full scale of the original drawings, and Ruskin took the opportunity of using chromolithography to create printed pages in colour.

The perceptions Ruskin was anxious to convey to his readership finally amounted to a diagnosis of the moral significance of the various styles and periods, contrasting the life-enhancing epoch of the Gothic with the fall into Renaissance selfishness. He separated these features out in the two principal buildings of St Mark's and the Ducal Palace. A full visual interpretation involved intense observation informed by historical research brought to the point of moral discrimination, which then have all to find adequate and expressive representation if they are to be successfully communicated to his readers. A representative plate compares the nobility and 'reserve of resource' of early Gothic decoration with the 'confused wantonness' and 'failing invention' of later work. The moral reading which it illustrates in this particular work is that 'the safeguard of highest beauty, in all visible work, is exactly that which is also the safeguard of conduct in the soul, – Temperance, in the broadest sense'.

The Ruskin Gaze

Ruskin had a way of, to use his own word, 'watching' things until he became absorbed in their externality. A friend described a day he had spent in the Lake District: 'Since early morning Ruskin had lain and wandered in the folds and hollows of the hills; and he came back, grave as from a solemn service, from "day-long gazing on the heather and the blue"' (Cook, 1912: 125). It is the kind of looking and renewed looking which he wrote to his father he directed at Fra Angelico's dancing angels in the Uffizi for 'an hour and a half', until he could see 'how *they* do it' (4.332). Whenever he achieved these heightened experiences of vision he believed he had perceived some commanding truth, which he felt called upon to help his readers to share. His endeavour was to bring, in Jacques Lacan's terms, all the discourses which make up visuality, and which constitute a 'screen' between the subject and the world, into line with the fullest imaginable act of vision: the screen which he managed was aimed at deconstructing the dominance of mediation itself (see Bryson, 1988: 91). His travels are effectively a search for these configurations: for the possibility of *seeing* the Truth, which for him extends from sensory perception of the real, to its accumulated cultural associations, to their moral significance. Whenever that construction breaks down – and that is mostly – he is ready to try to explain why and to denounce the art and society responsible, but readers who have been willing to travel in his footsteps have acknowledged the gift of a new way of seeing, whether or not they share its ultimate claims. Charlotte Brontë, for example, wrote, when she first read the first volume of *Modern Painters*: 'Hitherto I have only had instinct to guide me in judging art; I feel now as if I had been walking blindfold – this book seems to give me eyes' (see Hilton, 1985: 73). Proust elegised Ruskin's passing as that of a continuing tradition of seeing: 'Dead, he continues to enlighten us, like those dead stars whose light reaches us still, and one may say of him what he said on the occasion of Turner's death, "Through those eyes, now filled with dust, generations yet unborn will learn to behold the light of nature"' (Proust, 1987: 49).

Ruskin's evangelical and realist predispositions in constructing this gaze involved him in a critique of established aesthetic and literary frameworks for representing natural forms, leading to what he came to view as 'the Turnerian Picturesque' in the fourth volume of *Modern Painters* and the articulation of his own version of the Romantic creative imagination, which evolved from the terminological conversation he held with Wordsworth and Coleridge over Imagination and Fancy, in both their poetry and critical writings, in the second volume. It was from the Romantic poets that Ruskin absorbed an instinctive attachment to the tradition of Locke's empirical realism and its refinement in the associationist psychology of David Hartley, which remained the basis of Ruskin's philosophical intuitions even throughout his later study of Plato (see Collingwood, 1971 and Wilmer, 1996). The crux lay in the artist's claims for altering and re-creating actual natural experience, and because the specific area of his analysis was the visual arts he was able to scrutinise and gauge it in materially observable ways. As a young student of the Picturesque, Ruskin learned from his drawing masters how to compose natural scenes into pictures. Christopher Newall points out that his first instructor, Charles Runciman,

> [encouraged] Ruskin to compose landscape subjects from his imagination, according to the conventions of the Picturesque movement – which provided rules about how the elements of landscape should stand in relation to one another and dictated to what degree they should be generalized and harmonized. Always loath to invent, Ruskin swiftly learned how to lift parts from existing landscape drawings and patch them together into credible compositions 'with extreme industry, and an independence of mind, quite distinct from originality – that is to say, I borrowed or imitated just what pleased myself.' (Newall, 1993: 82)

Indeterminacies between inherent and imposed formal arrangement were a feature of picturesque theory and practice. William Gilpin, the original theorist, distinguishes between Beauty, which pleases in its natural state, and the Picturesque, which is susceptible to being illustrated by art, in his essay 'On Picturesque Beauty' (Andrews, 1989: 57). Whereas a *'scene of mountains'* may be 'a chaotic huddle of mountains' which the painter has to compose by *'imaginary combinations'*, a *'mountain scene'* 'is one in which Nature herself has made these beautiful combinations' (Gilpin, 2001: 174). Yet Gilpin also sometimes hints at a broad and implicit kind of authenticity attached to his rearrangements, as when he writes of his Scottish works that they were not meant to be topographical records, but rather to give *'the character of the country'* (Gilpin, 2001: 222; italicised phrases are Gilpin's). But Ruskin's feeling for natural theology and his adherence to empirical realism led him to insist on a reverence for the exact appreciation of divine creation and for the virtues of fidelity to its revelation, which resulted in a fundamental demand for literalism. In the first volume of *Modern Painters* he examined landscape art intensively for its observation of what could actually be perceived in the natural world. His most famous critical enquiry into what he called 'the pathetic fallacy' in the third volume of *Modern Painters* represents his critical rejection of the dangerous distortions of subjective projection into the real world. The hazards had been memorably satirised in Thomas Rowlandson's prints for William Combes's *Dr Syntax in Search of the Picturesque* which send up the impractical abstractions of an aesthetic which comically fails to come to terms with reality. Yet at the same time Ruskin saw the pressure towards literalism which, for example, the daguerreotype placed on art as likely to diminish another kind of representational potential. While he refers to the daguerreotype to criticise the comparative inexactitude of Claude, Poussin and Canaletto, he is also anxious that photographic realism may go too far in '[making] the eye too fastidious to accept mere handling' (3.210): '[William Henry] Hunt, I think, fails in foliage ... as the daguerreotype does, from over-fidelity' (Ruskin, 1956–1959: 603). Ruskin's attempt to reconcile the contradictory demands of the particular and the generalised resulted in the extraction of actual, highly representative details from their literal context which he increasingly adopted after 1846, as described by his father: 'fragments of everything ... in such bits that it is to the common eye a mass of Hieroglyphics – all true – truth itself, but Truth in mosaic' (8.xxiii).

Out of his experimentation in reconciling a faithful attention to real things with the effects of active and intense interpretation Ruskin developed a distinctively critical gaze which mirrored the visionary art of Turner and the literary formulations of the Romantics (see Dickinson & Hanley, 2008: xiv–xx). Turner was, as ever, the test case. When picturesque manipulations modulated into the Sublime much was at stake in inventive representation as it came to be read typologically, as scriptural and spiritual discourse (see Finley, 1980: 28). Piggott writes of how Turner created emblems or symbols in his vignettes: 'through the eye, the mind is "dilated" and "exalted" – these are the terms used by the engraver John Landseer, lecturing to the Royal Institution in 1807, to describe the operation of the sublime in expressing a metaphysical meaning through images' (Piggott, 1993: 17). In the first volume of *Modern Painters*, Ruskin argues

3.14 Thomas Rowlandson. *Dr Syntax Tumbling into the Water*. Drawn and coloured after the original. From *Doctor Syntax in Search of the Picturesque*, in *Doctor Syntax's Three Tours etc* (London: John Camden Hotten, n.d.), facing p. 31. Photo by K. Hanley

how Turner's landscapes may represent the divine typology of infinity, as distant views seem to dematerialise, and Piggott points out how 'Philip Hamerton wrote in 1879 of the way in which in Turner's vignettes the objects come out of nothingness into being, and Turner avoids too much materialism in his treatment of them until he gets well towards the centre' (Piggott, 1993: 18). Yet after Turner's 1840 tour to Italy, when his drawing became less outlined and light forms prevailed, even Ruskin became uncomfortable with their immateriality.

Ruskin knew intimately how freely Turner used the sketches for his completed works and how he often altered the image he had originally drawn quite radically in the course of the engraving process. As Ruskin's instinct was for exactitude on moral grounds, he was compelled to come to terms with the creative significance of Turner's adaptations. A constant feature was the use of juxtaposition to evoke underlying or inherent truths. The traditional technique for covering the visual field of a scene was that described in William Sanderson's *Graphice* (1658), instructing the draught-sman to adopt a raised viewpoint and then

> score your *Tablet into three divisions* downwards, from the top to the bottom, set your face directly opposite to the midst of your *Horizon*, and keeping your body fixed, observe what is comprehended directly before your eyes, and draw that into form upon your *Tablet* in the middle-*Division*. Then turning your head only (not your body) to the right hand, draw likewise what is presented to your *sight*.... (Andrews, 1989: 78–79)

But Turner's art characteristically assembled views from various view-points in the same work (see Finley, 1980: 104, 120 and 161), and Ruskin used his own illustrations to monitor and approve Turner's revisionary art. In two cases he went to great lengths to determine the range of Turner's creative alterations to the literal shape of the landscape – for *The Falls of the Rhine at Schaffhausen* (1831–1832), in the fifth volume of *Modern Painters*, and *The Pass of Faido* in the fourth. He produced a sequence of representations, based on a close scrutiny of Turner's art and his own actual observations of the same scenes, including Ruskin's own drawings of the original site, various details from Turner's versions, as well as sche-matic analyses of his own and Turner's drawings. The comparative examination of these stages of mediation led Ruskin to what he consid-ered a legitimising account of what in the third volume of *Modern Painters* he described as the 'Moral of the Landscape' applied to 'Turnerian Topography' (see Hanley, 2007: 258–267).

In Turner's original *Pass of Faido* (1843), Ruskin writes that literal topo-graphy is mastered by other effects in the 'dream-vision' (6.41) of a great artist to assemble what he defined as 'a perfect summary of Alpine truth' (6.380). With difficulty, Ruskin identified the original scene on his 1845

3.15 John Ruskin. *The Pass of Faido*, 1845. Pencil, bodycolour and watercolour.
The Ruskin Library, Lancaster University

continental journey, and made at least two sketches of it himself. From that time, he became intrigued by the different kinds of accuracy he could attribute to Turner's art, as he wrote to his father: 'The Stones, road, and bridge are all true, but the mountains, compared with Turner's colossal conception, look pigmy and poor. Nevertheless, Turner has given their actual, not their apparent size' (5.xvi). He probably visited the scene on three more occasions, and on one of his visits he obtained a daguerreotype of a distant view. When he came to assemble his materials for discussion in the fourth volume of *Modern Painters* he etched a 'topographical outline' from his own sketches and a similar outline based on Turner's 1843 drawing in order to contrast the two. He copied details from Turner's original several times, focusing on different effects, as in his etching of the top left of Turner's drawing, urging his reader to trace over it, 'and with his pen to follow some of the lines of it as carefully as he can, until he feels their complexity, and the redundance of the imaginative power which amplified the simple theme, furnished by the natural scene, with such detail . . . ' (6.270). Overall, Ruskin's scrupulous re-presentation of Turner's art aims to bring out the strict interplay between his literalism and his visual imagination. He

3.16 J.M.W. Turner. *Simple Topography* (left) and *Turnerian Topography* (right).
Engraved by John Ruskin. 6.34/35. Photo by K. Hanley

3.17 J.M.W. Turner. *Crests of the Slaty Crystallines.* Engraved by John Ruskin. 6.269. Photo by K. Hanley

considers, for example, his own 'topographical outline' of what he calls 'the *real* scene', which demonstrates, by comparison, Turner's 'modification of the view in the ravine' by introducing 'a passage from among the higher peaks ... to convey the general impression of their character'; as that character 'could not be taken from the great central aiguilles, for none such exist near Faido; it could only be an expression of what Turner considered the noblest attributes of the hills next to these in elevation' (6.269).

The multiple realism of Ruskin's 'mosaic' approach generated some of his own finest drawings, which are made up of separate sheets on which the different parts of a building or panorama are drawn, like a more or less angled jigsaw. For example, the composite, or 'fragmented vision' (Walton, 2006: 109), of the large view of the Castelbarco Tomb, Verona, which is constructed from a number of sketch-book pages, registers movement within the gaze. The optical effect goes beyond that achieved by simply copying photographic images such as daguerreotypes, or the reflections shown by the camera lucida which he also used (see Milbank, 2006: 98–99), or the projections of the camera obscura, producing 'aspects or views without a static or single viewer – [which] record the observations of a spectator moving through actual space' (Alpers, 1989: 51–52). Such an 'aggregate of views made possible by a mobile eye' (27) emphasises the terms of a new encounter with the external world in 17th-century Dutch art, one which foregrounded the dialectics of empiricism in 'an opening up of perception and representation to the effects of an objective material reality. In this formal sense it was an art of travelling' (Osborne, 2000: 7). But for Ruskin the locus of reality and the mobilities of perception were never subjectivised. The shifting aspects represent an interpretative interactivity which is consistently subdued to the objects of perception in the belief that his gaze might penetrate to 'laws' which were materially and discursively unifying.

The principle of composition was associative, and he developed his ideas on the representation of mountain character so as to account for it. He believed that Turner's 'first conceptions of mountain scenery seem to have been taken from Yorkshire; and its rounded hills, far-winding rivers, and broken limestone scars', and that they had 'formed a type in his mind to which he sought, as far as might be, to obtain some correspondent imagery in all other landscape'. One striking result was that Turner 'almost always preferred to have a precipice *low down* on the hillside, rather than near the top' (6.300), and, though the reverse is true of the cliff ranges in western Switzerland and Savoy, Ruskin observes that Turner instinctively sought out or created the impression of landscape structures derived from his 'early affection' (302) and memories of Yorkshire, formed prior to his first Continental tour of 1802. The result was what Ruskin termed a 'variance' in Turner's mind which informs his English and French drawings between the 'two great instincts' of his Yorkshire 'affections' for 'humble scenery, and gentle wildness of pastoral life' and his Swiss 'admiration' for 'largeness of scale' (303), so that

> as in Switzerland he chose rounded Alps for the love of Yorkshire, so in Yorkshire he exaggerated scale, in memory of Switzerland, and gave to Ingleborough, seen from Hornby Castle, in great part the expression of cloudy majesty and height which he had seen in the Alps from Grenoble. (304)

Ruskin had concerned himself over many years with technical issues related to this principle of combination in his own art. Even as a child, he had been aware of the problems of representing what was more or less out of sight, and he later wrote that he was 'delighted' when his first drawing master 'inquired for my colour box ... because I think that there is a power in painting, whether oil or water that drawing is not possessed of, drawing does well for near scenes, analyses of foliage, or large trees, but not for distance ...' (Hilton, 1985: 24). The *complexity* of reconciling generalisation and particularisation was a prominent consideration in picturesque practice which was facilitated by the Claude Glass, a small, dark, convex mirror in which the artist or tourist could view the reduced proportions of a landscape scene and simultaneously focus on foreground and distance, as Gilpin described: ' ... in the minute exhibitions of the convex-mirror, composition, forms, and colours are brought closer together; and the eye examines the general effect, the forms of the objects, and the beauty of the tints, in one complex view' (see Andrews, 1989: 69). In a youthful paper on 'The Conversion of Perpendiculars' Ruskin had begun to describe effects of 'finishing' pictures which critics have seen as an anticipation of the theory of impressionism (see Cook, 1912: 88), when the artist more actively selects

> [o]ne locality ... as chiefly worthy of the eye's attention; to that locality he directs it almost exclusively, supposing only such partial distribution of sight over the rest of the drawing, as may obtain a vague idea of

the tones and forms which set off and relieve the leading feature. Accordingly, as he recedes from this locality, his tones become fainter, his drawing more undecided, his lights less defined, in order that the spectator may not find any point disputing for authority with the leading idea. (1.239)

His own art was to specialise in directing attention to localities within an overall view, according to the tendency towards a closer reading of the landscape which Wordsworth's *Guide to the Lakes* promoted: 'The rejection of "pictorialism" was shared by those, painters as well as writers, who turned away similarly from the prospect or panorama towards the close-up view or the telescopically isolated distance' (*The Discovery*, 1984: 94). Pre-Raphaelite detailism, often defying the actual focusing of the eye, was both influenced by Ruskin's writing and influential on his own draughtsmanship, especially in Millais' work (see Walton, 1972: 81). Ruskin's 1845 watercolour drawing of the Ca' d'Oro, Venice, for example, characteristically depicts from a far-away standpoint what he wished to bring out – 'the capitals of the windows in the upper story, most glorious sculpture of the fourteenth century' and '[t]he fantastic window traceries' (11.371) – with an intricacy which could only be observed from close up. The logic of his gaze was to result in very many seemingly unfinished works such as this which nevertheless depict selected local features in a resolved state of high elaboration. It also found characteristic expression in details of natural specimens and decorative fragments. Inflected in the almost preternatural accuracy which he enjoined on his drawing students was expanding significance, achieved by a focus which was intellectual as well as visual. Accordingly,

3.18 John Ruskin. *Ca' d'Oro, Venice*, 1845. Pencil, watercolour and bodycolour. The Ruskin Library, Lancaster University

he encouraged his drawing students to copy his own rendering of the Spina Chapel at Pisa (see above, illustration 3.8):

> ... try merely the bead moulding with its dentils, in the flat arch over the three small ones, lowest on the left. Then examine those three small ones themselves. You think I have drawn them distorted, carelessly, I suppose. No. That distortion is essential to the Gothic of the Pisan school; and I measured every one of the curves of those cusps on the spot, to the tenth of an inch. (28.408)

The representational field was metonymically continuous, as the detail stood for implied real contexts. Sometimes the context was simply the rest of the scene or the building, and sometimes it evoked a wider visual circumambience, for example all Tintoretto's Biblical sequences in the Scuola di San Rocco, or the overall redemptive scheme of the 'Bible' of the West Front of Amiens Cathedral. Beyond those lay the cultural geography of the cities, regions and nations which had gone into the making. The interpretative gaze effected the unpeeling of those layers of signification which all art, for good or ill, symptomatised. The successful artist managed his medium so as to deepen that significance. John 'Warwick' Smith, for example, described how ideas were generated from physical manipulation: 'Turner has no settled process but drives the colours about till he has expressed the idea in his mind' (Andrews, 1989: 38), and the intellectualisation of colour was indeed decisive for the transformation of Turner's art:

> ... unlike John Constable's colour sense, Turner's was developed not so much from studying natural effects as from reflecting on them. From 1810, however, one is struck by a growing penchant in Turner's work for more intense colours, and specifically for the three primaries: red, yellow, and blue. (Finley, 1992: 46)

Ruskin was acutely sensitive to Turner's colour symbolism. He points out, for example, that 'Turner saw deeper crimson than others in the clouds of Goldau' (34.326), the Alpine village where 457 people were buried in a mountain slide. Material traces signalled trains of historical and cultural resonances for Turner to match Scott's and Byron's textual reading of landscape and monumental remains. Aided by Turner's suggestiveness, Ruskin sees stages in the shift from the actual to the metonymic which retain an originating physical reference. As he writes in the section on 'The Use of Pictures' in the third volume of *Modern Painters*: 'The duty of the artist is not only to address and to awaken, but to guide the imagination; and there is no safe guidance but that of concurrence with fact' (5.179). He responds, for example, to the visual linking in Turner's *A Vision. Voyage of Columbus*, where 'the level flake of evening cloud ... [is] admirably true to the natural form, and yet how suggestive of a battlement' (4.299). Once the cultural imagination is in play, there is a hierarchy of association attached to actual experience, as Ruskin's discriminating response to Byron's descriptions demonstrates. Whereas for Murray all Byronic associations simply outweighed any others, so that, as Buzard writes of the *Handbook for Travellers in Switzerland*, 'Byron's handling of the legend of Bonnivard gave the English poet, in Murray's estimation – not the imprisoned Swiss patriot – the better claim to be taken as the place's presiding spirit' (Buzard, 1993: 126), in *Praeterita* Ruskin considers Rogers a 'dilettante' compared with Byron because he makes no distinction between his evocation of what Ruskin considers the historical Tell and the purely fictional St Preux (see Watson, 2006: 148): 'Even Shakespeare's Venice was visionary; and Portia as impossible as Miranda. But Byron told me of, and reanimated for me, the real people whose feet had worn the marble I trod on' (35.151). Nevertheless, the literary imagination, always prompted by the same real scene, also substantiates a cultural materialism of its own. In viewing Turner's vignette of Clarens Ruskin can associate his own references with the composite aesthetic gaze mediated in sequence by Turner from Rogers's poem and from Rousseau's *La Nouvelle Heloïse*:

> Here would I dwell, forgetting and forgot;
> And oft methinks, (of such strange potency
> The spells that Genius scatters where he will)
> Oft should I wander forth like one in search,
> And say, half-dreaming, "Here ST. PREUX has stood!"
> Then turn and gaze on CLARENS. (Rogers, 1830: 6)

Yet Ruskin feels most responsive when fictional imagination is united with historical sense of place, as in Turner's illustrations to Scott, for example his panoramic engraving of *Edinburgh, from St Anthony's Chapel*, 'the scene in the Heart of Midlothian – (scene in the moonlight, where Jeannie goes alone)' (13.465).

In the end, for all its elaborations, Ruskin's gaze is seeking an encounter with something already actually there – something resistant and powerful enough to gaze back at him, the 'perceptibility' of Benjamin's 'aura' as it stares back over space and time at the viewer with its cultural otherness (see Benjamin, 1973: 184). It is the 'stony stare' which James describes in his essay, 'Venice: an Early Impression', in the statues in the cathedral of Torcello, '[seeming] to wait for ever vainly for some visible renewal of primitive orthodoxy, and one may well wonder whether it finds much beguilement in [seeing only] idly gazing troops of western heretics – passionless even in their heresy' (James, 1993: 340). Ruskin experienced the full and intensifying sensation of that stare in what he called the 'most precious "historical picture" in the world' (24.296), appropriately a mosaic 'on the west of the south transept' in St Mark's, representing 'the Priests, the Clergy, the Doge, and the people of Venice' at the highpoint of Christian civilisation, 'an abstract … or epitome of those personages, as they were, and felt themselves to be in those days' (295).

LIVERPOOL JOHN MOORES UNIVERSITY
LEARNING SERVICES

3.19 J.M.W. Turner. *Edinburgh, from St Anthony's Chapel*. Engraved by W. Miller
Frontispiece to *Tales of a Grandfather*, 1836. From *Scott's Prose works*, 24 vols.
(Edinburgh: Robert Cadell, 1834–36), Vol. 22. Photo by K. Hanley

Ruskin as Guide

It was not until late in his writing career, from the mid-1870s to the
mid-1880s, that Ruskin decided to formalise the travel guidance which
had been either overt or implicit in the pages of all his best known

3.20 *Pontifices. Clerus. Populus. Dux Mente Serenus*. Mosaic. South transept of
St Mark's. Photogravure from a drawing by Charles Fairfax Murray, 24. facing
296. Photo by R. Martin Seddon

writings. By that time the tendencies to cultural decline and the loss of imaginative perception accompanying it which he had bemoaned in them all had become critical. When he was called to the Slade Professorship of Fine Arts at Oxford in 1874 he felt a new sense of responsibility as an educator of public taste in all matters of aesthetics: after all, his own works, particularly those concerning Venice and Switzerland, had helped to foster cultural tourism to those places, and yet he was suspicious of the actual effects of the practices which he saw promoted by the publishing and tourist industries. In particular, he was keen to distinguish his own agenda and methods from those of contemporary guidebooks, above all those issued by Murray, who aimed to incorporate and subsume Ruskinian aesthetics as optional and specialised. In his diary note written in Florence for 31st August 1874 he wrote: 'Lay long awake dividing days, and planning attack on Mr Murray's guides' (Ruskin, 1959: 808). Now Ruskin set himself the project of alluring Murray's tourists into his own ways of seeing, as he explained in the Preface to the first edition of *Mornings in Florence: being Simple Studies of Christian Art, for English Travellers* (1875–1877) his initial contribution to the sequence of short guidebooks, either specially written or cheaper and abbreviated editions of larger studies arranged for this audience. For this work he used a series of unpublished Oxford lectures on 'The Aesthetic and Mathematic Schools of Art in Florence': 'It seems to me that the real duty involved in my Oxford professorship cannot be completely done by giving lectures in Oxford only, but that I ought also to give what guidance I may to travellers in Italy' (23.293). To follow were *Guide to the Principal Pictures in the Academy of Fine Arts at Venice* (1877), *St. Mark's Rest. The History of Venice Written for the help of the few travellers who still care for her monuments* (1877–1884), the Travellers' Edition of *Stones of Venice* (1879–1881), arranged and edited for use by students and tourists, with a new index to buildings for on-the-spot consultation, and 'Interpretations', his Travellers' Guide to Amiens Cathedral, available separately or as part of his comprehensive description of *The Bible of Amiens* (1880–1885).

A leading feature of his guides is the recurrent satirical dialectic with Murray, whom he derided for a consistent appreciation of 'judicious restoration' (27.315), which Ruskin saw as negating the workings of memory and the expressive creativity of human imperfection:

> When, indeed, Mr Murray's Guide tells you that a building has been 'magnificently restored', you may pass the building by in resigned despair; for that means that every bit of the old sculpture has been destroyed, and modern vulgar copies put up in its place. (23.355)

He also opposed Murray's uncritical attitude to modernisation, such as his celebratory two-column account in the *Handbook for Travellers in Northern Italy* of the Austrians' 'great work' in constructing the railway bridge across the lagoon from Mestre so as to get to Venice 'in 8½ minutes' (Murray, 1847: 311) from the mainland. For Ruskin, the instructive difference from the past was being destroyed: the bridge looked just like 'the Greenwich railway', the city 'as nearly as possible like Liverpool' (4.40–41n4). Along with the fabric and natural environments of the past the capacity *to see* them was disappearing, and Ruskin was endeavouring both to preserve the real objects and to recuperate the perceptual powers they represented. Contemporary tourism was dulling, or negating, the quality of individual personal experience which was the basis of his recommended cultural travel and which required above all sufficient time to register the evolution of thought from sensation. Indeed, his exacting approach shared the reader's anxiety about ever *completing* a visit (see Damien, 2010: 25–26). He offers his reader 'one piece of practical advice' – 'If you can afford it, pay your custode or sacristan well' (23.293). The idea is that by winning the affability of the guide he will allow you sufficient time and enable you to see everything properly. In the third volume of *Modern Painters* he described the pace and expanding awarenesses of his favoured approach on a 10 to 12 mile walk along a country road:

> ... every yard of the changeful ground becomes precious and piquant; and the continual increase of hope, and of surrounding beauty, affords one of the most exquisite enjoyments possible to the healthy mind; besides that real knowledge is acquired of whatever it is the object of travelling to learn, and a certain sublimity given to all places, so attained, by the true sense of the spaces of earth that separate them. A man who really loves travelling would as soon consent to pack a day of such happiness into an hour of railroad, as one who loved eating would agree ... to concentrate his dinner into a pill. (5.371)

One well-known reception of Ruskin's *Mornings in Florence* was E.M. Forster's *A Room with a View* (1908), where it is considered 'invaluable and exasperating' (see Buzard, 1993: 288). Because Forster's target at this point in his novel about breaking down life-denying conventions, the chapter 'In Santa Croce', was cultural tourism in general, he does not radically distinguish between Ruskin's approach and that of the standard guidebooks, here represented by the 1906 Baedeker's *Handbook to Northern Italy*, and he memorably, but misleadingly, conflates the two. Though the original sketches of the Lucy Novels, from which the published novel emerged, describe the difference of method – while Ruskin plans his visit precisely to elicit individual response from personal experience by focusing on epitomising objects, the standard guidebook demands a distractingly general programme of study – both schemes are coercive and come between the viewer and her spontaneous perceptions:

> Those who trusted to Baedeker began in an orderly manner with the right aisle, worked up it into the right transept, where they disappeared into a door leading to the sacristy and ... chapel, to emerge presently & inspect in turn the chapels to the right of the choir, the choir, the chapels to the left of the choir, the left transept and finally came down the left aisle and departed exhausted and frozen into the warmer air outside. A Baedeker transit lasted any time between two hours and a half and ten minutes, and as Lucy was sitting in the left aisle, she was near the end of it and the objects of interest near her ... received less than their due proportion of attention. But those who trusted to Ruskin's *Mornings in Florence* visited her early, for the tomb of Carlo Marsuppi, under which she sat, was ... selected by the great purist as a foil to the excellencies of the sepulchral slab near the door. (Quoted in Buzard, 1993: 288–289)

Forster catches Ruskin's comically magisterial tone: 'She began by finding a sepulchral slab, the book informing her that if she did not like it, she was to leave Florence at once' (Forster, 1908: 288). He also tellingly suggests how even the self-approving interpretative experience of earnest visitors, endeavouring to follow the Ruskinian method, can easily become detached from the real things: Lucy thinks she has found the slab in question, and likes it, but has actually got the wrong one!

Despite his anxieties and ironies, Ruskin was solicitous for, even pragmatic about, the predicament of the individual tourist. Instead of the formidably compendious guidebook, he introduced the format he was to employ in subsequent guides, supplying his reader with a digestible, pamphlet-size commentary, here on six separate walks, priced tenpence each, which might be collected into a volume, or not: Ruskin himself issued this work in book form from 1885. (A seventh part was also supplied by R. Caird at Ruskin's request, describing the fresco of 'The Visible Church' in the Spanish Chapel, and eventually published in 1906.) He subsequently issued a series of photographs to illustrate the bas-reliefs on 'The Shepherd's Tower', Giotto's Campanile, part six, while an *Illustrated Edition* with photographs was issued by The Brothers Alinari. Indeed, his methods attracted a popular following, and by the third edition, 1889–1891, up to 8000 copies of each part were printed, while the complete volume editions were electrotyped, reaching the 'Nineteenth Thousand' in the early 1900s, as well as foreign language and many unauthorised American editions. Cook writes that it became 'as familiar a companion to the tourist in Florence as Baedeker itself' (Cook, 1912: 26.225), and it is worth reflecting that, recommended by Baedeker and many other guides, these publications 'contributed considerably to his reputation' (Damien, 2010: 27).

Though Ruskin was willing to make helpful concessions to the practical possibilities of contemporary travel, unlike the impersonal guidebook he addressed the lack of time as a dilemma which he offered in his preface to manage as productively as possible to achieve real and worthwhile experience: 'The following letters are written as I would write to any of my friends who asked me what they ought preferably to study in limited time; and I hope they may be found of use if read in the places which they describe, or before the pictures to which they refer' (23.293). His Travellers' Edition of *The Stones of Venice* most of the material on architectural practicalities, and even the central section on 'The Nature of Gothic', adding more pin-pointing footnotes. In future guides he made a virtue of necessary selection and concentration by employing his epitomising method of focusing his readers' attention intensively on the most symptomatic objects and details. In order to draw out the trains of legitimate cultural and moral associations a full reading entailed, he had to filter and organise the blocks of background information supplied by Murray. Place and text had to be connected if the guidebook was not to substitute for the experience of travel, so that, as Ruskin wrote, 'Many people go to real places, and never see them' (18.212). It was a recognition echoed by the youthful James in his essay on 'Venice': 'Venice has been painted and described many thousands of times, and of all the cities of the world it is the easiest to visit without going there' (James, 1993: 287). That was the condition James Bryce noted in Italy in 1865 of tourists seeming 'to see the sights for no purpose but that of verifying their Murray...' (Pemble, 1987: 72).

Ruskin's alternative, personal and pinpointing tour is structured around a mounting promise of imaginative insight. The first walk in *Mornings in Florence*, for example, performs an actual guided tour of Santa Croce, conducted as a kind of dramatic monologue, implying the responsive presence of the reader/tourist consistently addressed as 'you'. He cajoles the reader to construct with him the desire to see the epitomising object, choosing Giotto as the most significant painter to be viewed, then the kind of fresco to focus on: 'You would surely like, and it would certainly be wise, to see him first in his strong and earnest work, – to see a painting by him, if possible, of large size, and wrought with his full strength, and of a subject pleasing to him' (23.295). His best pictures reflect the perfected art of the time he designed the Campanile of the Duomo, and St Louis turns out to be the optimal subject, the 'best king', himself a Franciscan when the order was at the heart of the best period of Florentine culture, the 13th century:

> So if one wanted to find anything of [Giotto's] to begin with, specially, and could choose what it should be, one would say, 'A fresco, life size, with campanile architecture behind it, painted in an important

place: and if one might choose one's subject, perhaps the most interesting saint of all saints – for *him* to do for us – would be St. Louis.' (296)

The ploy is to create a dialogue between the emergent aspiration of the reader and the more (deeply) experienced knowledge of the guide/writer, who can meet it while accommodating, though actually revising, the mainstream tourist approach to the church – with an opera-glass and Murray, even directing you 'to the chapel on the right of the choir ('k' in your Murray's Guide)' – and leading you circuitously, but inevitably, towards the visual epiphany. But when you arrive at the fresco of St Louis of Toulouse what you are given is not simply the anticipated image but a critical gaze at it: 'It is St. Louis, under campanile architecture, painted by – Giotto? or the last Florentine painter who wanted a job – over Giotto? That is the first question you have to determine ...' (297). In order to be able to enter into that consideration which lies at the roots of realist perception Ruskin opens the all-encompassing implications, starting with that of 'restoration'. The immediate context is the chapel of the Bardi della Liberta where the frescos cover the walls, and Ruskin proceeds to rattle off the dry historical data from Murray, which, as he recognises, might be off-putting; but he wants to be very specific:

> Under such recommendation, the frescos are not likely to be much sought after; and, accordingly, as I was at work in the chapel this morning, Sunday, 6th September, 1874, two nice-looking Englishmen, under guard of their valet de place, passed the chapel without so much as looking in.
>
> You will perhaps stay a little longer in it with me, good reader, and find out gradually where you are. Namely, in the most interesting and perfect little Gothic chapel in all Italy – so far as I know or can hear. There is no other of the great time which has all its frescos in their place .... (297–298)

His tone becomes more animated as he reveals that the imaginary party have arrived at the founding sight/site – the one which will most richly repay associative scrutiny – and he broadens the imaginative context, unfolding the religious topography:

> ... think where you are, and what you have got to look at.
>
> You are in the chapel next the high altar of the great Franciscan church of Florence. A few hundred yards west of you, within ten minutes' walk, is the Baptistery of Florence. And five minutes' walk west of that, is the great Dominican church of Florence, Santa Maria Novella.
>
> Get this little bit of geography, and architectural fact, well in your mind. There is the little octagon Baptistery in the middle; here, ten minutes walk east of it, the Franciscan church of the Holy Cross; there, five minutes walk west of it, the Dominican church of St. Mary. (298)

Next Ruskin unpacks the historical leaps contained within that cultural geography: 'Now, that little octagon Baptistery stood where it now stands ... in the eighth century. It is the central building of Etrurian Christianity, – of European Christianity', and four centuries later when Saints Francis and Dominic re-empowered medieval Christianity they were 'the effectual builders' of their orders' 'churches of Holy Cross and St. Mary' (298). Thereafter, 'the immediate sign in Florence' of their renewed inspiration 'was that she resolved to have a fine new cross-shaped cathedral instead of her quaint old little octagonal one; and a tower beside it that should beat Babel: which two buildings you have also within sight' (298–299). The 'preaching and teaching' of the religious orders then generated the efflorescence of the arts in Florence: 'She burst out into Christian poetry and architecture, of which you have heard much talk: – burst into bloom of Arnolfo, Giotto, Dante, Orcagna, and the like persons, whose works you profess to have come to Florence that you may see and understand' (299).

Ruskin has told us what we have come for – something substantial and more than we had originally imagined. What he is after all instructing us in is not the whole historical manifold itself so much as the ability to see it in the concrete details of the church, as he gradually imparts the method of his gaze. He redirects our gaze back to the chapel and quizzes us on various features and datings, having raised the issues involved: 'I will ask you to think a while, until you are interested; and then I will try to satisfy your curiosity' (301). He leads us back into the nave, and asks us to look about 'and see what sort of a church Santa Croce is', and then supposes we will find that it 'is, somehow, the ugliest Gothic church you ever were in'. There are no vaultings, it looks like a barn and has hardly any apse. It is 'not beautiful by any means; but deserving, nevertheless, our thoughtfullest examination' (303). The T-shaped church represented the cross as a gibbet, a place of suffering, and the large nave was functional, especially for a preaching order. This is one kind of worthy Christian message which the old church conveyed, but it has been 'defaced by Vasari, by Michael Angelo, and by modern Florence'. Their influence is represented by the huge and expensive tombs at the sides of the aisles, and Ruskin asks us to restore Arnolfo's original Gothic in our minds: 'Tear them all down in your imagination ...' (305). And so we come to 'Lucy's' sepulchral slabs at the west end. The first, 'one of the most beautiful pieces of fourteenth-century sculpture in the world' (306), is that of an ancestor of Galileo – Ruskin had a photograph made of a drawing of it, which he put on sale to illustrate this work. He draws our attention to the 'falling drapery of his cap [which is] in its few lines, faultless, and subtle beyond description', and says that if you can appreciate 'its ornamental relations of line' then

> you can understand Giotto's drawing, and Botticelli's; – Donatello's carving, and Luca's ... And if you will kneel down and look long at

Sepulchral Slab of Galileus de Galileis
in Santa Croce

3.21 *Sepulchral Slab of Galileus de Galileis Santa Croce, Florence.* Photogravure of Drawing by A.H. Mackmurdo. 23. facing 308. Photo by R. Martin Seddon

the tassles of the cushion under the head, and the way they fill the angles of the stone, you will – or may – know, from this example alone, what noble decorative sculpture is, and was, and must be, from the days of earliest Greece to those of latest Italy. (308)

As we move back to Giotto's chapel, he points to 'the much-celebrated tomb of C. Marsuppini, by Desiderio of Settignano', where 'the drapery is chiefly done to cheat you, and chased delicately to show how finely the sculptor could chisel it' (310). Like other such evidence of display in Renaissance artistry in sepulchral carving, it is a kind of 'mechanical man-ufacture' (309).

Of course, Ruskin realised that some, indeed many, of his readers were imaginary travellers for whom he was presenting, especially by way of his illustrations, only an approximation to the benefits of real travel; but the force of argument led him to prioritise the position of his reader-travellers, as in 'The Schools of Art in Florence': 'And now I must tell you quickly what will be useful to you in visiting Assisi – my staying-at-home hearers must be patient with me, for it is really necessary now to give travellers some clue better than their Murray's Guide' (205). The reward of real travel was what Ruskin promised his readers in the preface to 'Art Schools of Medieval Christendom' as an experience 'they may in simplicity understand, and with pleasure remember' (34.129), one that is both directly assimilated and invested with recollection. Relying on reviving the cultural memory of the past by tracing the associative links which places and objects represent, the effect resonated with the romantic myth of restoring a lost childhood, the pristine sensations of Wordsworth's childhood vision, as Rogers claimed:

> No sooner do [men] enter the world, than they lose that taste for natural and simple pleasures, so remarkable in early life ... Now travel, and foreign travel more particularly, restores to us in a great degree what we have lost ... All is new and strange. We surrender ourselves, and feel once again as children. (Rogers, 1830: 170–171)

In his travelogue, *Pictures from Italy*, Dickens appealed to 'the liveliest impressions of novelty and freshness' (Dickens, 1846: 2) as an antidote to his belatedness, revitalising clichéd destinations with new sensations. Clearly traditional canons are themselves boosted if and when the effect comes off, as Buzard describes how Rogers 'recharges the classical and Shakespearean associations of Italy with the energy of his own overwhelming delight at being there' (Buzard, 1993: 105):

> Am I in Italy? Is this the Mincius?
> Are those the distant turrets of Verona?
> And shall I sup where Juliet at the Masque
> Saw her beloved Montague, and now sleeps by him?
> Such questions hourly do I ask myself;
> And not a finger-post by the road-side
> 'To Mantua'– 'To Ferrara' – but excites
> Surprise and doubt, and self-congratulation. (Rogers, 1830: 41)

But for Ruskin what excited pleasure and delivered a sense of satisfaction was the realisation of a more specific sense of arrival, when the accumulation of associations was brought back into eye-opening relation with immediate perception, and the associative circle fused imagination and reality. Sometimes the imaginative representation was inadequate, and the place called for a greater effort in living up to its actual beauty, as when in the first volume of *Modern Painters* Ruskin ran through a number of artists who had depicted Venice – Canaletto, to whom 'we look ... in vain', Prout ('No, Mr Prout, it is not quite Venice yet'), Clarkson Stanfield ('No, Mr Stanfield, it is scarcely Venice yet') – before coming to Turner's work ('Yes, Mr Turner, we are in Venice now'.) (3.256–257). At other times it required imaginative exertion to draw out the potential of a place, as at Blonay in 1849, when a beautiful scene seemed less than delightful until Ruskin repeated 'I am in *Switzerland*' to himself 'over and over again, till the name brought back the true group of associations – and I felt I had a soul ...' (Ruskin, II: 381–382).

The bonding of signifier and signified, when anticipation, constituted by literary and artistic representation, is met with the experience of realisation, is a leading motivation of cultural travel. If the picturesque traveller had pursued an idealised image of natural scenery or the historical past, the Romantic traveller was in quest of identifying with a writer's personal response to those scenes. For the early 19th-century travelling imagination Byron was central, and Ruskin felt in particular that his Venice, 'like Turner's, had been chiefly created for us by Byron' (35.295). When the pleasures and prestige of the imagination are confirmed by actual and originating sensation a deep experience of renewal is accomplished, as the shock of the old creates an aesthetics of revelation. Bringing personal experience within the range of recognised cultural power is far more richly self-enhancing than the mere acquisition of information on the one hand and literary day-dreaming on the other. It offers a sense of deeply satisfying recognition, very different from that kind of 'imaginative geography' by which, for example, 'the traveller is able to claim possession of the Grand Tour as the source of pleasurable alterity …' (Chard, 1999: 14). Here again, Ruskin was keen to discriminate between marketised cultural experience and sharing in his integrating interpretative gaze. Buzard notes that Byron's texts

> were also quickly supported by subsidiary texts designed to help readers and tourists to follow in the pilgrim's footsteps. The poet himself had supplied some notes for *Childe Harold*, but his friend Hobhouse gave the world a book-length guide to the work's Italian references …. (Buzard, 1993: 119)

3.22 J.M.W. Turner. *Kirby-Lonsdale Church Yard*. Engraved by C. Heath. Plate 4 *Views in Lancashire and Yorkshire, from original drawings* (London: Bickers & Son, 1872). Photo by K. Hanley

Murray 'produced a pocket-sized Lord Byron's Poetry, so as to enable Travellers to carry it with their other HANDBOOKS ...', and William Whetmore Story wrote: 'Every Englishman [abroad] carries a Murray for information, and a Byron for sentiment, and finds out by them what he is to know and feel at every step' (120). But the negotiations involved in Ruskin's gaze were precarious. Disappointment with a destination was just as likely an upshot, and whenever the associative circle was broken and there was a disconnection between a pre-mediated imagination of a place and the reality, there Ruskin was deflated. Worst of all, the general breakdown in the culturally informed gaze was leading to the unchecked destruction of definitive places, objects and monuments through misconceived restoration, industrial exploitation or sheer neglect. He was, for example, outraged and pained by the pollution and mechanisation of the Lune Valley at Kirkby Lonsdale in 1875, a scene deeply implanted in Ruskin's visual memory by Turner's watercolour drawing, *Kirkby Lonsdale Churchyard*, and a cluster of literary associations nearby (see Hanley, 1995). The search for a fulfilling correspondence of representation became the logic of his critical judgements and the agenda of his cultural guiding and its selective focusing. It structured the continuous history of his interpretation of places.

References

Adler, J. (1989) 'Origins of Sightseeing'. *Annals of Tourism Research* 16, 7–29.
Alpers, S. (1989) *The Art of Describing: Dutch Art in the Seventeenth Century*. Harmondsworth: Penguin.
Andrews, M. (1989) *The Search for the Picturesque: Landscape Aesthetics and Tourism in Britain, 1760–1800*. Aldershot: Scolar Press.
Baedeker, K. (1906) *Handbook to Northern Italy* (13th edn). Leipzig: Karl Baedeker.
Benjamin, W. (1973) On some motifs in Baudelaire. In H. Zohn (ed.) *Illuminations*. London: Fontana.
Bryson, N. (1988) The gaze in the expanded field. In H. Foster (ed.) *Vision and Visuality*. Seattle: Bay Press.
Buzard, J. (1993) *The Beaten Track: European Tourism, Literature, and the Ways to Culture 1800–1918*. Oxford: Clarendon Press.
Chard, C. (1999) *Pleasure and Guilt on the Grand Tour: Travel Writing and Imaginative Geography 1600–1830*. Manchester: Manchester University Press.
Collingwood, R.G. (1971) *Ruskin's Philosophy* [reprint of 'An Address delivered at the Ruskin Centenary Conference, Coniston, August 8th, 1919']. Chichester: Quentin Nelson.
Cook, E.T. (1912) *The Life of John Ruskin* (Vol. 2). London: George Allen.
Damien, E. (2010) Ruskin and Murray's handbooks: Battles for tourist guidance in mid-19th century Italy. In R. Dickinson and E. Sdegno (eds) *Special Issue on Nineteenth Century Travel and Cultural Education, Nineteenth Century Contexts* 32 (1), 19–30.
Davis, A. (2003) *'A Pen of Iron': Ruskin and Printmaking*. Exhibition catalogue. Lancaster: Ruskin Library.
Dickens, C. (1846) *Pictures from Italy*. London: Bradbury and Evans.

Dickinson, R. and Hanley, K. (eds) (2008) Introduction. In *Ruskin's Struggle for Coherence: Self-Representation through Art, Place and Society*. Newcastle Upon Tyne: Cambridge Scholars Publishing.

Finley, C.S. (1992) *Nature's Covenant: Figures of Landscape in Ruskin*. University Park, VA: Pennsylvania State University Press.

Finley, G. (1980) *Landscapes of Memory: Turner as Illustrator to Scott*. London: Scolar Press.

Forster, E.M. (1908) *A Room with a View*. London: Edward Arnold.

Forster, E.M. (1977) In O. Stallybrass (ed.) *The Lucy Novels: Early Sketches for A Room with a View*. London: Edward Arnold.

Gilpin, W. (2001) *Picturesque Travel*. Introduced by Gavin Budge. Bristol: Thoemmes Press.

Hanley, K. (1995) The discourse of natural beauty. In M. Wheeler (ed.) *Ruskin and Environment: The Storm-Cloud of the Nineteenth Century*. Manchester: Manchester University Press.

Hanley, K. (2007) *John Ruskin's Northern Tours 1837–1838: Travelling North*. Lampeter: Edwin Mellen.

Hewison, R. (1976) *John Ruskin: The Argument of the Eye*. London: Thames and Hudson.

Hilton, T. (1985) *John Ruskin: The Early Years*. New Haven, CT: Yale University Press.

Hunt, J.D. (1978) "'Ut Pictura Poesis.' The Picturesque, and John Ruskin". *Modern Language Notes* 93, 794–818.

Hunt, J.D. (1982) Oeuvre and footnote. In J.D. Hunt and F.M. Holland (eds) *The Ruskin Polygon: Essays on the Imagination of John Ruskin*. Manchester: Manchester UP.

James, H. (1893) *Transatlantic Sketches*. Boston: Houghton, Mifflin.

James, H. (1993) *Collected Travel Writings: The Continent*. New York: Literary Classics of the United States.

Milbank, A. (2006) A fine grotesque or a pathetic fallacy?: The role of objects in the autobiographical writing of Ruskin and Proust. In R. Dickinson and K. Hanley (eds) *Ruskin's Struggle for Coherence: Self-Representation through Art, Place and Society*. Newcastle: Cambridge Scolars Press.

Mulvey, C. (1983) *Anglo-American Landscapes: A Study of Nineteenth-Century Anglo-American Travel Literature*. Cambridge: Cambridge University Press.

Murray, J. (1838) *Handbook for Travellers in Switzerland*. London: John Murray.

Murray, J. (1847) *Handbook for Travellers in Northern Italy*. London: John Murray.

Newall, C. (1993) John Ruskin and the art of drawing. In H. Welchel (ed.) *John Ruskin and the Victorian Eye*. New York: Harry N. Abrams, in association with the Phoenix Art Museum.

Osborne, P.D. (2000) *Travelling Light: Photography, Travel and Visual Culture*. Manchester: Manchester University Press.

Pemble, J. (1987) *The Mediterranean Passion: Victorians and Edwardians in the South*. Oxford: Oxford University Press.

Piggott, J. (1993) *Turner's Vignettes*. London: Tate Gallery Publications.

Proust, M. (1987) In J. Autret, W. Burford and P.J. Wolfe (eds) *On Reading Ruskin: Prefaces to La Bible d'Amiens and Sésame et les Lys with Selections from the Notes to the Translated Texts*. New Haven, CT: Yale University Press.

Prout, S. (1833) *Facsimiles of Sketches Made in Flanders and Germany and Drawn on Stone by Samuel Prout F.S.A.* London: C. Hullmandels.

Rogers, S. (1830) *Italy, A Poem*. London: T. Cadell, Jennings and Chaplin E. Moxon.

Rousseau, J-J. (1761) *Julie, Ou La Nouvelle Héloise*. Amsterdam: Rey.

Ruskin, J. (1956–1959) In J. Evans and J.H. Whitehouse (eds) *The Diaries of John Ruskin*. (Vols. 1–2). Oxford: Clarendon Press.

Scott, Walter (1818) *The Heart of Midlothian*. Edinburgh: Constable.

Sternberger, D. (1977) *Panorama of the Nineteenth Century*. New York: Urizen Books.

The Discovery of the Lake District: A Northern Arcadia and its Uses. (1984). London: The Victoria and Albert Museum.

Turner, J.M.W. (n.d.) *Liber Studiorum*. London: George Newnes; New York: Charles Scribner.

Urry, J. (2002) *The Tourist Gaze* (2nd edn). London: Sage Publications.

Walton, P.H. (1972) *The Drawings of John Ruskin*. London: Oxford University Press.

Watson, N. (2006) *The Literary Tourist; Readers and Places in Romantic and Victorian Britain*. Houndmills: Palgrave.

Wildman, S. (2006) *Ruskin and the Daguerreotype. Exhibition catalogue*. Lancaster: Ruskin Library.

Wilmer, C. (1996) Was Ruskin a materialist? In M. Wheeler (ed.) *Time and Tide*: *Ruskin and Science*. London: Pilkington Press.

Wordsworth, W. (1977) In E. de Selincourt (ed.) *Wordsworth's Guide to the Lakes* (5th edn). Oxford: Oxford University Press.

Chapter 4
The Interpretation of Places

The destinations described in this chapter which were constantly revisited by Ruskin represent his three chief interests: Swiss mountain scenery and the agrarian community of the Alps of Western Switzerland and Savoy; early Venetian Renaissance painting, leading him to the study of Gothic and Byzantine architecture; and Northern French Gothic architecture. The aim is to unpack what he saw in them, as his interpretative gaze penetrated through aesthetic mediations to their cultural, social and moral significance. The layered meanings of all three locations were generated by his changing autobiographical encounter with their historical and cultural pre-existences over more than four decades. Overall, they constitute a paradigm of Ruskin's travelling from a Romantic paradise, through personal and historical trauma, to his many-faceted version of Restoration.

These places are separated because they are principal sites he revisited repeatedly and they came to represent his most elaborated interpretations. The historical model of Swiss pastoral nationalism at first merged with the original promise of the Romantic British north up to the early 1840s; Venice presented the first major contradiction to his relatively naïve reading of the *Modern Painters'* Picturesque in its revelation of early Renaissance painting, prompting a deeper social analysis and eventual religious crisis, the effects of which dominated Ruskin's writings from the mid-40s to the end; and Northern France was the territory whose earlier aesthetic pleasures he came to recuperate in the 1880s for his resistance to the assaults of modernism, reaffirming a discourse of religious traditionalism. But this narrative of conflicted development actually took place within each location, as Ruskin travelled to them all recurrently throughout his life. The Alps, Venice and Northern France, therefore, chiefly represent in turn one thematic emphasis in distinct sections below, but each also fits into the whole story of a life of travel.

The Alps: Western Switzerland and Savoy: Nature's Lost Eden

The world Ruskin encountered in his childhood and youth had mirrored the representations of Romantic literature and picturesque art, especially Wordsworth and Turner. Together, they invoked a deeply desirable harmony between the purposes of Man and Nature which he formulated as the leading aesthetic principle in his first serious work, *The Poetry of Architecture* (1837–1838), based on the early continental tours of 1833 and 1835 compared with his undergraduate inland tours of the Lake District and Scotland, in 1837 and 1838 respectively. It was an apprehension and belief which found culminating expression in his early celebration of Turner, who to Ruskin's eyes depicted a divinely created landscape beauty, in volume one of *Modern Painters* (1843). To some extent, that Edenic construction depended on the repression of his deep and permanent consciousness of the Fall, which casts an Evangelical gloom throughout his juvenile poetry and even the happiest scenery and found some resolution in his doctrine of the expressive values of imperfection. But what he found irrefutable was the destruction of the physical scenery and the society it had nurtured through commercial and industrial advancement, in particular as they emanated from Britain, and especially as they became spread for example through the development of the Swiss tourist industry (see 6.454–456). As the world of his childhood and youth was lost and progressively disappeared, his need for retaining its promise intensified, and his attachment to the works which he believed had immortalised it grew. His travels became an anxious and often painful search for the remnants of Turner's landscapes, Scott's feudalism and the arts of pre-Renaissance Christendom.

Ruskin was introduced to the natural paradise of Switzerland by the scenes Turner depicted for Rogers's *Italy* (1830). In May–June 1833 the family journeyed via Schaffhausen to the Italian Lakes and Milan, returning over the Simplon Pass to Sion, Lausanne, Fribourg, Thun, Lucerne and Zurich. The next tour of 1835, from July to September, during a six month continental tour of France, Switzerland and Italy – from Geneva to Chamonix, Courmayeur, Vevay, Basel, Zurich, St Gotthard, Thun, Lausanne, Baden and St Gall – familiarised them with areas which Ruskin would constantly revisit over the years. He recorded the journey in a dedicated journal, a long poetic narrative and an extensive series of drawings, as well as pursuing a serious interest in geology. Altogether, it was a fertile manifestation of the mindset established in 1833, 'science mixed with feeling' (35.116). The *Voyages dans les Alpes*, 1779–1796, by the botanist and geologist, Horace Bénédict de Saussure, was his guide at this point at least as much as Turner's drawings, and his scientific investigations led to two of the articles published in 1834, when he was 14, on the colour of the water of the Rhine and the geological strata of Mont Blanc and the Swiss Alps, illustrated with engravings after his own sketches. His emotional response to his first glimpse of the Alps 'high above the Rhine' at Schaffhausen in 1833 was to the sacred sublime, a displacement of Biblical paradisal geography:

> They were clear as crystal, sharp on the pure horizon sky, and already tinged with rose by the sinking sun. Infinitely beyond all that we had ever thought or dreamed, – the seen walls of lost Eden could not have been more beautiful to us; not more awful, round heaven, the walls of sacred Death. (35.115)

In 1835 they summoned him to 'the Holy Land of my future work and true home in this world' (35.167). Later, several tours were to focus on Chamonix, where he made many drawings and developed his highly involved treatment of 'mountain beauty' for volumes four and five of *Modern Painters*, 1856, 1860 respectively.

His revisitings of Chamonix and the drawings he made there epitomise his relations with Alpine scenery and 'Swiss' communities: it is actually situated in what was then the Italian kingdom of Savoy, but shared the cultural identity of western Switzerland. From his first tours there in 1833 and 1835 the region became an extension of the Romantic, distinctly northern culture of the English Lake District and Scotland and, in line with Romantic literature and painting, was seen as the natural and social embodiment of the undisturbed organicism of 'old times'. The comparative European aesthetics of this construction provided the bedrock of his engagement with art and society as Ruskin returned to interrogate the origins of his convictions in the light of the encroachments of industrial capitalism. These came to include the horror of its spreading corruptions among the Alps themselves – Mont Blanc, the 'great mountain, which one thought so eternal, faded like a white rose' (23.li) in 1874, and its north-western slopes were affected by the brown 'plague-cloud' (34.70) in 1882 – and his travels there challenged his gaze to re-establish the residual promise of remembered images from his first experiences and earlier mediations by Turner and others.

Ruskin became expert in Alpine knowledge. His delight in climbing and wandering in the Alps in addition to his knowledge of the flora and rocks, was significantly supported by the Savoyard guide, Joseph Couttet, who accompanied him on many continental journeys from the mid-40s. He enjoyed the physical experience, and though he did not like the wind and his feet tended to tire, he particularly enjoyed 'strolling' in the Jura, especially among cloud formations: 'The mere power of familiarity with the clouds, of walking with them and above them, alters and renders clear our whole conception of the baseless architecture of the sky' (6.424). He was exhilarated by light effects: 'I don't know anything more wonderful in the Alps than this feeling of insufferable sunshine, with all the crevices

4.1 John Ruskin. *State of Snow on Mont Blanc*, 1849. Pencil and ink. The Ruskin
Library, Lancaster University

in the snow about one filled with icicles' (5.xxxi). His main aim in climbing, however, was for the views, arguing that mountains are best observed
from below rather than from their tops: 'The real beauty of the Alps is to
be seen, and seen only, where all may see it, the child, the cripple, and the
man of grey hairs' (18.25). In his attempt to capture admired scenes, he
became a pioneering enthusiast for photography, claiming that 'the first
sun-portrait ever taken of the Matterhorn (and as far as I know of any
Swiss mountain whatever) was taken by me in 1849' (26.97).

Ruskin's picturesque and Romantic encounter with Alpine scenery is
depicted in his early works. The vignette below is clearly influenced
by Turner's engravings in Rogers's *Italy* (1830). It was engraved for
Friendship's Offering (1844), an annual 'gift book', where it accompanied
Ruskin's poem, 'A Walk in Chamouni', opening: 'Together on the valley,
white and sweet,/The dew and silence of the morning lay:/Only the tread
of my disturbing feet/Did break, with printed shade and patient beat,/
The crispèd stillness of the meadow way' (2.222). Most of Turner's completed Alpine subjects, like that illustrated below, were commissioned by
Walter Fawkes of Farnley Hall near Otley in Yorkshire, which Ruskin later
visited to view the Turner collection, and he was himself to commission
Alpine scenes. His own perceptions of favoured locations such as
Chamonix were shaped by his love for Turner, and a diary entry from 1844
demonstrates how he measured the real against Turner's representations:

Chamouni, June, 23. – 9 o'clock, morning. There is a strange effect on
Mont Blanc. The Pavillon hills are green and clear, with the pearly
clearness that foretells rain; the sky above is fretted with spray of
white compact textured cloud which looks like flakes of dead arbores-
cent silver. Over the snow, this is concentrated into a cumulus of the
Turner character, not heaped, but laid sloping on the mountain, silver
white at its edge, pale grey in interior; the whole of the snow is cast

4.2 John Ruskin. *Le Glacier des Bois, Chamonix* 1843–1844. Pencil, ink and
watercolour. The Ruskin Library, Lancaster University

into shadow by it, and comes dark against it, especially the lower
curve of the Aiguille du Goûter. (3.xxvi)

It is difficult to separate his descriptions of the actual scene and Turner's
depictions, as he reminisces, for example, about visual impressions of

the lake, in the whole breadth of it from Lausanne to Meillerie, for
Turnerian mist effects of morning, and Turnerian sunsets at evening;
and moonlights, – as if the moon were one radiant glacier of frozen
gold. (35.518)

Ruskin, however, prized his vision of the Swiss way of life as much as the
Romantic sublime. He saw the Protestant pastoralism of a remote and still
medieval world as offering the concrete fulfilment of the kind of organicism
in which his architectural and social thought was rooted. Ruskin's acquaintance with the Giessbach Falls near the Lake of Brienz, for example, had
been enabled by their discovery by several 18th- and 19th-century painters.
They were made accessible to visitors by creating paths from the lake shore
to the top, and in 1832 the first hotel-restaurant was opened, to be followed
by three increasingly large establishments in the course of the 19th century.

4.3 Unknown artist. *The Giessbach Falls 1816*. Pencil, sepia wash and bodycolour. Private Collection. Photo by R. Martin Seddon

It was to develop exactly in the way he abhorred. By the 1880s, the hotel
was to offer modern lighting, playgrounds, a skittle alley, daily concerts,
tennis courts, and therma and electro-baths. Ruskin wrote of the beauty
and uniqueness of the falls, but when the family visited them in 1833,
Ruskin particularly admired the simple songs performed by the Swiss
family at the inn which impressed him with the importance of folk music
in peasant education and later urged it as a model for schooling in the
Lake District.

Integral to Ruskin's Alps were the literary and religious associations he
recognised there. An example of the deepened gaze occurs in 'The Lamp
of Memory' section in *The Seven Lamps of Architecture*. Amid the pastoral of
spring in the lower Alps, 'near the time of sunset, among the broken
masses of pine forest ... above the village of Champagnole, in the Jura'
(8.221), his memory is disturbed by a postlapsarian shadow of violence:

> ... on the opposite side of the valley, walled all along as it was by grey
> cliffs of limestone, there was a hawk sailing slowly off their brow,
> touching them nearly with its wings, and with the shadows of the
> pines flickering upon his plumage from above; but with the fall of a
> hundred fathoms under his breast, and the curling pools of the green
> river gliding and glittering dizzily beneath him .... (8.223)

The hawk, with its predatory threats and a consciousness of the tooth and
claw, its snake-like 'flickering', the reflection in the snake-like 'curling',
gliding and glittering pools, and the theology of its *falling* shadow, is
ambiguous. With it comes a deepening realisation that the fall of nature is
the inception of human history, and the fear it prompts turns out to be as
much of the loss of human presence – of a non-European place without
human association – as of its contamination:

> ... the writer well remembers the sudden blankness and chill which
> were cast upon it when he endeavoured, in order more strictly to

arrive at the sources of its impressiveness, to imagine it, for a moment, a scene in some aboriginal forest of the New Continent. The flowers in an instant lost their light, the river its music; the hills became oppressively desolate; a heaviness in the boughs of the darkened forest showed how much of their former power had been dependent upon a life which was not theirs, how much of the glory of the imperishable, or continually renewed, creation is reflected from things more precious in their memories than it, in its renewing. (8.223)

The meaning of the scene was over-determined for Ruskin by other literary associations. '[T]he writer well remembers' recalls Wordsworth's 'I well remember that . . .' from 'Tintern Abbey', and Turner's vignettes in Rogers's *Italy* had saturated Alpine landscape with European history. 'The Lake of Geneva', Rogers's opening poem, evokes

> The pine-clad heights of JURA.
>
>   . . .
>
> And on the edge of some o'erhanging cliff,
> That dungeon-fortress never to be named,
> Where, like a lion taken in the toils,
> Toussaint breathed out his brave and generous spirit. (Rogers, 1830: 4)

Toussaint L'Ouverture was the leader of the African slaves who resisted Napoleon's edict re-establishing slavery in San Domingo, and died after 10 months' imprisonment in the Castle of Joux, near Besançon in April 1803. His struggle was the subject of one of Wordsworth's best-known sonnets among the 'Poems Dedicated to National Independence and Liberty', 'To Toussaint L'Ouverture', in which Wordsworth promises that his fall will be restored by inhabiting an unusually humanised reading of nature: 'Though fallen thyself, never to rise again,/Live, and take comfort. Thou hast left behind/Powers that will work for thee; air, earth, and skies' (ll. 8–12; 112). Ruskin's evening glow, catching the castle's walls, is tinged with revolutionary red and the deep knowledge of *human* sacrifice, spreading also to Granson on the Lake of Neuchâtel, the scene of the defeat of Charles the Bold by the Swiss in 1476 as described in Chapter 32 of Scott's *Anne of Geierstein*:

> Those ever springing flowers and ever flowing streams had been dyed by the deep colours of human endurance, valour, and virtue; and the crests of the stable hills that rose against the evening sky received a deeper worship, because their far shadows fell eastward over the iron walls of Joux, and the four-square keep of Granson. (8.223–224)

The Ruskin family were conscientiously alive to the religious demarcations within Switzerland, and on their tours made sure as far as possible to stick to the Protestant cantons. Though the religious boundaries were an historical and geographical patchwork, as late as 1846 sectarian divisions almost caused a civil war. Ruskin at first joined in a tradition of English prejudice dating from the 17th century and influentially articulated by Archdeacon William Coxe, who commented in his standard guidebook on 'uncleanliness ... disgusting beyond expression' (Coxe quoted in Green, 1789: 116) in the Valais, pointing to the prevalence of goitres and cretinism which he preposterously related to their attachment to Catholicism. The chapters 'Mountain Glory' and 'Mountain Gloom' in the fourth volume of *Modern Painters*, for example, contain a strained sectarian geography, which Ruskin later recanted, proclaiming the spiritually beneficent effect of 'Mountain Glory' on Swiss Protestants, opposed to the alternative 'unspeakable horror', which darkens the lives of mountaineers with 'the shadow of death' (6.396), or 'Mountain Gloom', among Roman Catholic Savoyards.

Nevertheless, 'Mountain Glory' does register powerfully his faith in the edifying power of the relation between man and nature whenever it is enabled. While he realised that it would not necessarily operate – 'various institutions have been founded among [the mountains] by the banditti of Calabria as well as by St Bruno' (6.432) – yet he makes a resilient claim, for example, that the cultural achievements of the Greeks and Italians derived from 'their mountain scenery' (6.426). He suggests an educational experiment to prove his point: 'The matter could only be *tested* by placing for half a century the British universities at Keswick and Beddgelert, and making Grenoble the capital of France' (6.439). The idea that what he saw as a natural environment, freed from the destructive effects of industrialisation and economic competitiveness, would provide not only the best context for a system of national education, but also part of the programme was initiating a new environmentalist discourse with which to counter the uprooted entrepreneurial energies of the day. The position of Swiss culture was critical, and the social extensions of the nature-based Alpine community remained fundamental to his developing theories. After signing off on the proofs of the fifth volume of *Modern Painters* in May 1860, he travelled to his beloved Chamonix for a rest, spending much of his time that summer climbing with the American artist, W.J. Stillman, and stopping to draw alpine roses and sketch the scenery. At the same time, he stayed at the Old Union Inn and wrote *Unto this Last*, turning from writing on art and architecture to political economy.

The tourism which was progressively encouraged by the Romantic fashionability of the Alps, influenced by the trend-setting transports in the Valais narrated in Rousseau's *Julie, ou la nouvelle Héloïse* (1761), breached the Arcadian way of life shielded by the mountains. By 1851, a casino was opened at Chamonix, and Ruskin was to bemoan the gradual inroads of

industrialised modernity and commercialisation on the thereto undisturbed seasonal rhythms of a simple agrarian society. What had remained
untouched and seemed inviolable was conquered and tracked. When he
lay sketching the Matterhorn in August 1849 no one had come near to
climbing it – nor was to for another 16 years when Edward Whymper
made the first ascent. The summit of the Rigi was at last conquered in
1873, to be followed by the railway two years later. Tunnelling spread the
railway, and he was outraged when a bridge was constructed over the
falls of Schaffhausen and mindless pastimes caught on: 'The Alps themselves, which your own poets used to love so reverently, you look upon as
soaped poles in a bear-garden, which you set yourselves to climb and slide
down again, with "shrieks of delight"' (18.89–90). He scorns the English in
particular for teaching the Swiss 'the foulness of the modern lust of
wealth. . .' (18.29). Although he frankly enjoyed taking a party of friends to
the newly developed holiday centres – Neuchâtel, Interlaken, Giessbach,
and Lucerne, he predictably found later that the luxurious hotel life was
undermining his serious attention to the mountains. Ironically, however,
his own drawings of the Matterhorn and the Chamonix Aiguilles were
indirectly enthusing a rising generation of climbers. The conflicted upshot
of his Swiss travels was reflected in his ambiguous relations with members of the Alpine Club – he was himself one – including several painters.
One of the earliest presidents, Leslie Stephen, acknowledged Ruskin's
writings as a chief spur to the vogue for Alpine mountaineering, though
Ruskin himself deplored it.

For several years in the mid to later 1850s he was preparing a book on
Swiss history, in which the Lake of Lucerne was to figure prominently: 'a
complete centre of the history of Europe, in politics and religion ... as
Venice is a centre of the history of Art' (7.xxxii). But though he completed
many drawings in illustration, sometimes 'in illustration of Turner's
sketches at those places' (35.484–485), including Thun, Sion, Chamonix,
Fribourg, Geneva, Basle, Baden, Schaffhausen and Rheinfelden, he never
wrote it (see Hayman, 1990: 10). Ruskin's aims were, in fact, not merely to
recommend and represent the objects of aesthetic or even spiritual epiph-
anies, but were also practical: 'all the investigations undertaken by me at
this time were connected in my own mind with the practical hope of
arousing the attention of the Swiss and Italian peasantry to an intelligent
administration of the natural treasures of their woods and streams'
(26.339). Indeed, he bought a field at Chamonix and later planned to live
first at Mornex and then on the Brezon above Bonneville in 1863, though
these ideas were abandoned as he returned to live at Brantwood on
Coniston Water in the Lake District, where the views reminded him of
Switzerland. Later, he promoted and introduced the English translation of
Jeremias Gotthelf's *Ulric the Farm Servant: A Study of the Bernese Lowlands*

(1888), as a pattern for the kind of agrarian community based on the self-sufficiency of the small-holder which the Guild of St George was seeking to promote in Britain.

Venice: The Fall of Art

Between his first continental visit of 1833 and his last of 1888, Ruskin made numerous significant visits to Venice of varying duration. Until 1845 his Romantic encounter had been filtered through the lenses of Byron, Rogers and Turner, benefiting from the increased prominence of Venice on the tourist map, partly owing to Byron's stay there in 1817, following the dissolution of the Napoleonic empire in 1815. He had cut his teeth as the defender of Turner's accuracy in his depiction of St Mark's place, the basilica and the Ducal Palace in an unpublished essay of 1836, but he came to recognise the crucial importance of his visit of 1845 for his changed and developing understanding of the relationship between art and society. By then he had ceased to be a tourist and become an expert critical commentator, researching the second volume of *Modern Painters*. The change is an important one as it illustrates the possibilities inherent in travel for access to cultural authority, reaching the point when the traveller becomes the guide. Travelling there repeatedly thereafter – he devoted his most sustained study to it between 1849 and 1853, and even resided there from September 1851 to June 1852 – he came more and more to see the cultural and moral history of European civilisation inflected in the art and architecture of what he viewed as the 'central' city of European civilisation.

The chauvinistic proposition of the very Ruskinian subtitle of *Modern Painters* – that the English painters of his own day were 'superior', both morally and technically, 'in the art of landscape painting to the ancient masters' – met with a severe check when, travelling throughout northern Italy to examine religious art in 1845, he was suddenly exposed to a different and bewildering vision in the paintings of Jacopo Robusti, 'Tintoretto', in Venice. The Venetian school was not established in British taste, and Parsons writes that 'In 1722 Jonathan Richardson had published (with his son) *An Account of Some of the Statues, bas-reliefs, Drawings and Pictures in Italy, Etc. with Remarks*, which was as much a treatise as a guide' and which '[discarded] the entire Venetian school of painting on the grounds that the 'people [of Titian, Tintoretto and Veronese] neither look nor act with that grace and dignity as those of Raffaele, Michelangelo, Giulio [Romano], Correggio, Guido [Reni] and so on.' (Parsons, 2007: 161). But, Ruskin's encounter with quattrocento and early Renaissance 'primitive' painting from May 1843, now confirmed at Pisa on this tour, opened out new directions for his critical gaze, diverging from the established 18th-century orthodoxy of Sir Joshua Reynolds which placed Raphael and Michelangelo at the pinnacle of taste. His future Italian tours followed this fresh path, taking him back to Venice, as well as on related routes, to Verona and Sienna, and through his writings drawing serious-minded middle-class cultural tourists in his wake.

Ruskin describes the life-changing jolt to his sensibilities when, travelling with the artist, James Duffield Harding, 'in the spare hour of one sunny but luckless day, the fancy took us to look into the Scuola di san Rocco', the grandiose building of a charitable guild:

> Tintoret swept me away at once into the 'mare maggiore' of the schools of painting which crowned the power and perished in the fall of Venice; so forcing me into the study of the history of Venice herself; and through that into what else I have traced or told of the laws of national strength and virtue. (35.372)

It was a disturbing experience which caused a troublesome detour from the writing of *Modern Painters* in mid-career to *The Stones of Venice*, but which was also the hinge into a matured worldview. He had now seen Venice 'with man's eyes' (4.352):

> ... and when we had got through the upper gallery, and into the room of the Crucifixion, we both sate down and looked – not at it – but at each other, – literally the strength so taken out of us that we could not stand! When we came away, Harding said that he felt like a whipped schoolboy. I ... felt only that a new world was opened to me, that I had seen that day the Art of Man in its full majesty for the first time .... (354)

Tintoretto's art was absorbing in its tension between materiality and transcendence, and even his *Paradiso* in the Ducal Palace, Ruskin wrote,

4.4 John Ruskin. *Detail from Tintoretto's 'Adoration of the Magi': Magi and Cherubs*, 1852. Pencil and ink wash. The Ruskin Library, Lancaster University

'conceives his Paradise as existing now, not as in the future' (22.106). Tintoretto became a leading cultural guide, a 'compromise' early Renaissance figure, between 'the modest and faithful religion' (22.81) of the quattrocento, for him best exemplified in Venice by Giovanni Bellini and Vittore Carpaccio, and the period ending with Tintoretto's death in 1594, after which he judged decline set in with the worldly show of Michelangelo, especially, and Titian and Raphael: he 'stands up for a last fight; for Venice, and the old time' (83). Bellini had achieved an independent style, still in contact with Ruskin's then most approved Purist style of the primitives, especially Fra Angelico, who had fascinated him in Florence on the same tour, even imparting metaphysical intimations, and whom he holds up as the supreme artist at the end of the second volume of *Modern Painters* (1846), writing to his father: 'I spent an hour and a half before a Fra Angelico ... and I saw *angels* dancing to-day, and so I know how *they* do it' (4.332). As he writes in the Preface to *St Mark's Rest*: '... at a glance (when we have learned to read), we know the religion of Angelico to be sincere, and of Titian, assumed' (24.203). Whereas Michelangelo delights in the body for its own sake, for example, Ruskin writes that Tintoretto works 'as if, through his human body, were working the great forces of nature' (22.87). In the Scuola, Ruskin focused on *The Crucifixion* for the summation of Tintoretto's conflicted imaginative revelation, between soul and body, epitomised by the fact that 'the broad and sun like glory about the head of the Redeemer has become wan, *and of the colour of ashes*' (4.271). Ruskin was coming to recognise the extension of his governing aesthetic principle – the necessary relation between the real world and moral significance – into a clear-cut historiography of European art which was informed by the narrative of the moral and artistic Fall of Venice, dated from the deaths of two noble doges in the early 15th century, and which found full expression in *The Stones of Venice* (1851–1853).

4.5 Louise Virenda Blandy. *Copy of Fra Angelico*. Watercolour. Collection of the Guild of St George, Sheffield Galleries & Museums Trust

4.6 John Ruskin. *Copy of the central part of Tintoretto's 'Crucifixion'*, 1845. Pencil, chalk, black ink, ink wash and bodycolour. The Ruskin Library, Lancaster University

The 'Paradise of cities' (1.453) may have fallen, Ruskin argued, and the chief consequence of his researches was to hold it up to contemporary Britain as a parallel and a warning, but it could still be viewed as an inspiration. His conclusion was that 'Venice is superficially and apparently commercial; – at heart passionately heroic and religious; precisely the reverse of modern England' (9.25), and 'that the decline of her political prosperity was exactly coincident with that of domestic and individual religion' (23). His new perceptions led him to discriminate between the moral content of Gothic and Renaissance art and architecture and to date the degeneration of Christian civilisation exactly according to the ethos of the different periods in *The Stones of Venice*. From its aesthetic record, Ruskin inferred a Venetian history in which he beheld a moral paradigm for the whole of European civilisation up to the present.

After the 'witness of Painting' (30), Ruskin turned to the evidence of Venetian Gothic architecture. Entering northern Italy from the Riviera, Ruskin had travelled through several towns where he had admired the churches, but what was to grow into his serious study of architecture probably began with the life-lasting impressions of Jacopo della Quercia's sculpted tomb of Ilaria di Caretto in the cathedral at Lucca and the buildings he encountered at Pisa (see Bradley, 1987: 18). In Venice he found a style which he was to discover had evolved from 'the refinement and spiritualisation of Northern [Lombardic] work under [the influence of the southern Arabic]' (40) and attained its highpoint 'from the middle of the thirteenth to the beginning of the fifteenth century', coinciding with 'the central epoch of the life of Venice' (43–44). What followed was the 'rationalistic art' of the Renaissance, 'marked by a return to pagan systems ... ' (45). What had resulted from commerce and wars was an interaction between Christian Lombard (Frankish) and Byzantine-Moorish architecture, which collided centrally in Venice, and it was in defining the common characteristics of northern Gothic and the Venetian transformations that Ruskin arrived at his abstracted notions of Gothicism as cultural and moral principles.

He diagnosed the moral significance of the various styles and periods which he separated out in the two principal buildings of St Mark's and the Ducal Palace. St Mark's is a combination of Gothic structural features and Byzantine 'decoration over vast plain surfaces' (10.124). Ruskin recreates the traveller's gaze as it approaches the precious basilica, suddenly presented with the 'vision [rising] out of the earth', described in one of his greatest prose passages: '...and all the great square seems to have opened from it in a kind of awe ... a multitude of pillars and white domes, clustered into a long low pyramid of coloured light; a treasure-heap it seems' (82). He was particularly susceptible to the Byzantine influence, claiming that it was responsible for '[w]hatever in St Mark's arrests the eye, or affects the feelings' (78), and he admired the frescos and Greek-inspired mosaics. This was the element which distinguished Ruskin's re-education of the traveller's eye: as has been pointed out, he 'was perhaps the first western European to champion Byzantine art and architectuire, and ... the Byzantine art of mosaic ...' (Norwich, 2003: 114). Characteristically, he

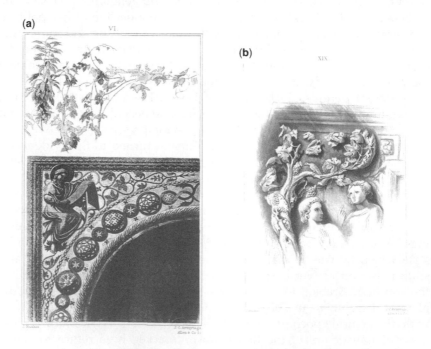

4.7 (a) John Ruskin. *The Vine. Free, and in Service*. Photogravure. Facing 10.115. (b) John Ruskin. *Leafage in the Vine Angle*. Photogravure. Facing 10.115 and 360. Photos by R. Martin Seddon

inferred a series of 'Laws' for incrustation – cladding with decorative sheets of marble and other stonework – to inform the traveller's discrimination of the principles of 'justice' underlying the ornamentation. For example, he describes three different relations between 'fact and design' (218) in the representation of a vine which he considers justified:

> [A, top] represents a spray of vine with a bough of a cherry tree, which I have outlined from nature as accurately as I could ... there is no attempt at design in it. [B] represents a branch of vine used to decorate the angle of the Ducal Palace. It is faithful as a representation of vine, and yet so designed that every leaf serves an architectural purpose ... [A, bottom] is a spandril from St Mark's, in which the forms of the vine are dimly suggested, the object of the design being merely to obtain graceful lines, and well-proportioned masses upon the gold ground ... Now the work is, in all three cases, perfectly healthy. (218)

He examines the principal Byzantine capitals in great detail, especially the lily capitals, the northern one of which he took immense care in drawing. He is delighted with the intricate braided work which for him finally reveals 'some dim feeling of the setting forth ... of the intricacy, and alternate rise and fall, subjection and supremacy, of human fortune' (163). Similarly, Ruskin's eye was delighted by the Byzantine and Gothic palazzi, with their beautiful marble incrustation riveted to the brickwork: 'while the burghers and barons of the North were building their dark streets and grisly castles of oak and sandstone, the merchants of Venice were covering their palaces with porphyry and gold' (10.98). But he was correspondingly offended by the Renaissance palazzo, painfully devoid of decoration.

The Ducal Palace is 'the central building of the world' (9.38), because it contains the three elements of the Roman, Lombard, and Arab in exactly

4.8 John Ruskin. *Lily Capital, St Mark's*. From *The Stones of Venice*, volume 2 (London: Smith. Elder and Co., 1853), facing p. 136. Photo by R. Martin Seddon

equal proportions. Applying his characteristic evaluation, he maintains that the decorated angles of the capitals manifest the difference between the Gothic's 'frank confession of its own weakness' and the 'firm confidence in its own wisdom' (10.359) of the Renaissance. Accordingly, the subject of the Gothic sculptures on the Fig tree angle is the Fall of Man and on the Vine angle the Drunkenness of Noah, while the Renaissance angle displays the Judgement of Solomon. In both the Gothic sculptures, 'the tree, which forms the chiefly decorative portion of the sculpture ... was a necessary adjunct' (360), whereas the Judgement of Solomon 'is of immeasurably inferior spirit in the workmanship; the leaves of the tree, though far more studiously varied in flow than those of the fig-tree from which they are partially copied, have none of its truth to nature' (363).

Ruskin's notebooks and related sketches show him painstakingly measuring and recording Venetian artefacts: 'It became necessary for me to examine not only every one of the older palaces, stone by stone, but every fragment throughout the city which afforded any clue to the formation of its styles' (9.4). But, his overall interpretative procedure is to move from the real scene or object to the associative history it narrates, and to see further the moral implications which that history, once it has been opened out, also represents. The beginning of *St Mark's Rest*, which was designed particularly to point up the moral lessons, establishes his method by reading the two pillars in the Piazzetta for all they are worth: 'Your Murray

4.9 Unknown photographer. *Adam and Eve and Fig Tree, the Ducal Palace, c. 1880.* Albumen print. Private collection. Photo by R. Martin Seddon

4.10 John Ruskin. *The Vine Angle, the Ducal Palace*. Photogravure. 10. facing 362.
Photo by R. Martin Seddon

tells you that they are "famous," ... It does not, however, tell you why, or
for what the pillars are "famous"' (24.207). He continues to evoke their
significance by dividing the aspirations which lay behind such splendid
statements from contemporary materialism – a distinction lost on 'Another
of Mr Murray's publications', *Sketches from Venetian History* (1831–1832),
which '[suggested] ... that the Venetians had as little piety as we have
ourselves, and were as fond of money', whereas, Ruskin argues, the reality is that Venice was 'not covetous merely for money. She was covetous,
first, of fame; secondly, of kingdom; thirdly, of pillars of marble and gran-
ite, such as these that you see; lastly, and quite principally, of the relics of
good people [i.e. 'the dead bodies of St Donato and St Isadore', as well as
of St Mark himself]. Such an "appetite," glib-tongued cockney friend, is
not wholly commercial' (24.209–210). In explanation, Ruskin tells the
exploits of Doge Dominico Michiel, who conquered Tyre and Byzantium
and brought the pillars back as spoils, concluding with the inscription
from his tomb: 'here lies the Terror of the Greeks' and 'WHOSOEVER
THOU ART, WHO COMEST TO BEHOLD THIS TOMB OF HIS, BOW
THYSELF DOWN BEFORE GOD, BECAUSE OF HIM' (217).

4.11 Unknown photographer. *The Judgement of Solomon, the Ducal Palace, c. 1880.* Albumen print. Private collection. Photo by R. Martin Seddon

4.12 Unknown photographer. *The columns of San Marco and San Teodoro, the piazzetta, near St. Mark's Square,* c. 1880. Albumen print. Private collection. Photo by R. Martin Seddon

In the next chapter he proceeds to interpret the art of the pillars themselves starting with their design from base to capital, and commencing the kind of dense virtuoso reading which extends from detail to huge historical and cultural extrapolation. He has his reader/traveller cutting cubes of Gruyère cheese in order to appreciate the change in carving which occurs in the 14th century and which leads to the down-playing of decoration and urges that 'there is infinitude of history in that solid angle [in the upper arcade], prevailing over light Greek leaf':

> Here is, indeed Norman temper, prevailing over Byzantine; and it means ... western for eastern life, in the mind of Venice. It implies her fellowship with the western chivalry; her triumph in the Crusades, – triumph over her own foster nurse, Byzantium. (24.224)

His procedure, by this stage, had become more freakish and bizarre, exaggerating the Ruskinian signature of the highly personal, idiosyncratic, and intemperate. Nonetheless it still offers enormous syntheses and insights into western cultural history. As Jeanne Clegg has pointed out, however, Ruskin's imaginative account of Venetian history is structured around his focus on specific historical moments, and, indeed, he 'created havoc with the sequence of political events' (Clegg, 1981: 86–87).

In the next chapter, which Ruskin mischievously entitles 'St Theodore the Chair-Seller', in allusion to the furniture store where he eventually comes upon an image of 'the Protector of the Republic' (24.207), he delivers an exemplary lesson on the decline of religious sincerity which starts in front of St Mark's, beginning with the delicate carving of a lamb on the bas-relief in the left-hand arch, the reverent work of 'a Christian man' (242), in a symbolism of belief. Ruskin then moves on to a 'panel on the left side of the central arch, in front' depicting St George which is 'no more a symbolical sculpture, but one quite distinctly pictorial, and laboriously ardent to express, though in very low relief, a curly-haired personage, handsome, and something like George the Fourth, dressed in richest Roman armour ...' (243). 'Thus far has

4.13 *Bas-relief of the Apostles and the Lamb, St. Mark's.* Woodcut by H.S. Uhlrich. 24.242. Photo by R. Martin Seddon

4.14 *St. George*. Woodcut by H.S. Uhlrich from the sculpture on the west front
of St. Mark's. 24. facing 244. Photo by R. Martin Seddon

Venice got in her art schools of the early thirteenth century', writes Ruskin,
'the legend kept, in faith yet; but the symbol become natural; a real armed
knight ...' (245). The walk then continues back through the Merceria to the
Ponte de' Baratteri, 'Rogue's Bridge', where Ruskin writes 'you may stop to
look back at the house immediately above the bridge' observing 'a horizon-
tal panel of bas-relief' (245). There may be seen another St George, this time
with the dragon, which Ruskin describes as 'Venetian fifteenth century
work of finest style': 'it is now a symbol consisting in the most literal realiza-
tion possible of natural facts. That is the way, if you care to see it, that a
young knight rode, in 1480, or thereabouts' (246). Moreover, its formal skills
are intended to invite close examination: 'see how studious the whole thing
is of beauty in every part, – how it expects *you* also to be studious' (247). The
real change in this art relates to the quality of belief, '[h]alf way to infidelity',
which it represents:

> But the fifteenth century sculptor *does*, partly, mean to assert that St.
> George did in that manner kill a dragon: does not clearly know

4.15 *St. George and the Dragon*. Photogravure from a house in Venice. 24. facing
246. Photo by R. Martin Seddon

whether he did or not; does not care very much whether he did or not
… but is more bent, in the heart of him, on making a pretty bas-relief
than on anything else. (24.248)

The walk proceeds to 'the piazza of St Salvador, with a building in front
of you, now occupied as a furniture store, which you will please to look at
with attention' (248), observing what he describes as a 'solidly rich front of
Ionic pillars, with the four angels on the top, rapturously directing your
attention, by the gracefullest gesticulation, to the higher figure in the
centre!' (249). Ruskin announces: 'You have advanced another hundred
and fifty years, and are in mid seventeenth century' and are beholding
'Raphaelesque art of the finest', featuring set poses, dramatic expression
and drapery 'arranged in "sublime masses"… ' (249). The upshot is that
'To this type the Venetians have now brought their symbol of divine life in
man. For this is also – St. Theodore!' He continues, however: 'Nevertheless,
through all this decline in power and idea, there is yet … some wreck of
Christian intention, some feeble colouring of Christian faith' (250). Fifty
years later, the traveller is next led to observe what has happened in the
'last manner of Venetian sculpture' by comparing the sculptured ornaments on the arches of both sides of the Ponte delle Guglie over the
Cannaregio under the Palazzo Labia designed by Michelangelo and wit-
nessing 'the last imaginations of her polluted heart, before death': 'her
intellectual death precedes her political one by about a century…' (251).

On the basis of his generalised observations Ruskin's scheme of Venetian political history – the chief concern of British historians – simplifies. In the following chapter, 'The Shadow on the Dial', he evokes boldly what he sees as the 'four quite distinct periods' which according to him are fundamentally shaped by the state's religious and moral life. The first seven hundred years, 'from the fifth to the eleventh century', marking the 'process of growth and mental formation', that is 'Christianity from the Greeks, chivalry from the Normans, and the laws of human life and toil from the ocean' (254). The second period, during the 12th and 13th centuries, 'is that of her great deeds of war, and of the establishment of her reign of justice and truth', 'chiefly characterised by the religious passion of the Crusades' (254). The third period, which includes 'the fourteenth and fifteenth centuries, and twenty years more', to 1520, is one of 'religious meditation', and was that in which Venice established 'schools of kindly civil order' and its most thoughtful arts, so that 'The entire body of her noble art-work belongs to this time'. The fourth period of luxury and display lasts for just 80 years, 'and terminates, strictly, with the death of Tintoret, in 1594; we will say 1600' (255). This is the grand narrative which informs subsequent chapters on the lives of representative Doges and on the interior decoration of St Mark's.

Ruskin's cultural critique of Venice epitomised the judgements which he extended to all his travels in northern Italy: in Venetia generally, especially at Verona; at Florence, Lucca, Pisa, Siena and throughout the rest of Tuscany (see Clegg & Tucker, 1992); and in Umbria, at Assisi and Padua. As he turned his attention to other places, his views on art were to contradict themselves and develop in what he later referred to as 'oscillations of temper, and progressions of discovery' (7.9) under the pressure of new insights and fresh enthusiasms. These transformations may be represented by a series of three very different marriages. The first appeared on his visit to the Gallery of Turin in the summer of 1858. It proved a turning point, occasioned chiefly by his response to the art of Paulo Veronese, and particularly to his *The Queen of Sheba and Solomon*, which Ruskin declared led to his becoming 'conclusively *un*-converted' (29.89) from the narrowing Evangelicalism in which he had been reared. The Titians which he subsequently saw in the German galleries confirmed his revision of what he had formerly dismissed as worldly and sensual in the Renaissance Venetian painters but now viewed as 'Worldly visible Truth' (89), a 'nobility' which was shared even by Michelangelo. The purist pietism he had once valued supremely now seemed surprisingly weak – even in Fra Angelico, while he now responded to a 'strong and frank' and 'magnificent Animality' (7.xl).

At Assisi in 1874, however, he was to examine his reappraisals once more, leading him to renounce 'the fallacy that Religious artists were weaker than Irreligious' (23.xlv). Since 1858, he had believed that the worship of visionary truth by sacred artists like Giotto and Fra Angelico had undermined the effectiveness of their art, making them produce

4.16 Paulo Veronese. *The Queen of Sheba and Solomon*. Photogravure (16. facing 186). Photo by R. Martin Seddon

less perfect work. Now he reassessed his responses to two Florentine painters – Giotto and Botticelli. Writing of the latter's combination of the Heathen and Christian, and the bodily and spiritual, he now revised his estimate of his Madonnas in the Uffizi, 'and was more crushed than ever by art since I lay down on the floor of the Scuola di San Rocco before the Crucifixion' (23.xlix). It was another marriage scene, very different from Veronese's, which clinched the change. While drawing Giotto's fresco of *The Marriage of Poverty and Francis* above the high altar in the Lower

4.17 Giotto. *The Marriage of St Francis and Poverty*. Photogravure of fresco (28. facing 164). Photo by R. Martin Seddon

Church at Assisi he saw that what were 'merely absences of material science' (xlv) (laws of perspective, shading and composition) did not detract from the power of what he had always recognised to be Giotto's sanity, sincerity and visual drama. The values he then drew from the Franciscan order more generally sowed some of the seeds which were to germinate into the quasi-medieval Guild of St George.

Thereafter, the symbolic content of religious art became increasingly personalised. Ruskin had already discovered for himself an enthusiasm for Carpaccio in 1869, but it was in the autumn and winter of 1876–1877 that he became gradually obsessed with his cycle of eight paintings in the Accademia at Venice illustrating the life of St Ursula, and particularly that of *The Dream of St Ursula*, about the saint's vision of her coming martyrdom during her betrothal to a pagan prince. Ruskin's own fantasy of a spiritual marriage with his adored Rose La Touche, who had died in 1875, became disturbingly associated with the saint and her fate, so that the third marriage resulted in sublimation.

4.18 Vittore Carpaccio. *The Dream of St Ursula*. Chromolithograph from photograph coloured after Ruskin's drawing. 27. 8, facing 344

The themes of the chapters included in *St Mark's Rest* on the Carpaccios in San Giorgio de Schiavoni, 'The Shrine of the Slaves' and James Reddie Anderson's account edited by Ruskin as 'The Place of Dragons', were originally intended to make up a separate companion pamphlet to his *Guide to the Principal Pictures in the Academy of Fine Arts at Venice* (1877). In the latter, Ruskin considers the gallery's great works according to his moral and historical system, but with more detailed and complicating attention. He begins by pointing to the three 'severe Gothic' sculptures over the entrance door which '[indicate] the beginning of [Venice's] Christian life ...', particularly the Madonna in the centre which, with the infant '[sprawling] on her knee in an ungainly manner' and her own 'quiet maiden dignity ... in no manner of sentimental adoration', represents 'Venetian naturalism', or the 'steady desire to represent things as they really (according to the workman's notions) might have existed. The new tendency is different from the 'Byzantine formalism' (24.149) and other earlier Greek influences, and derives from Giotto in Florence influencing the Gothic of Padua and so arriving in Venice. All the important paintings in the Academy are subsequent to these sculptures of the late 14th century, and so date from the following 200 years.

His individual perceptions involve mind changes and contradictions which show the history of his looking. Titian's 'Assumption', for example, with chairs placed in front, 'everybody being expected to sit down, and for once, without asking what o'clock it is at the railroad station, reposefully admire' (152). While Ruskin presumably supports this concentrated attention, he nevertheless takes the opportunity to qualify the established reputation of this work as the gallery's accepted leading masterpiece, quoting himself from 25 years previously: 'The Traveller is generally too much struck by [it] to be able to pay proper attention to the other works in this gallery' (11.361). But he has partly changed his mind, and now praises the 'composition' and other representational skills as 'unsurpassable' (24.153). Nevertheless, he distinguishes it from the Madonnas of Vivarini and Bellini which are symbols by which 'they conceived the presence with them of a real Goddess', whereas Titian's Virgin does not 'symbolize any Virgin here with us', so that 'he does not in the least believe his own representation, nor expect anybody else to believe it. He does not, in his heart, believe the Assumption ever took place at all' (153). His lack of belief casts a melancholy over his work, 'a strange gloom', dark colours and 'great spaces of brown, and crimson passing into black' (154).

Later, Ruskin focuses on the three distinct epochs he defines, and fixes on the best examples. The first is 'the Vivarini epoch' ('bright, innocent, more or less elementary, entirely religious art'), from 1400 to 1480; the second is 'the Carpaccian epoch' ('sometimes classic and mythic as well as religious'), from 1480 to 1520; the third is 'the Tintoret epoch' ('supremely powerful art corrupted by taint of death'), from 1520 to 1600. He tries to reduce them for the assimilation of his readers, to whom he is giving an easily acquired but powerful framework: 'if you fasten these firmly in your mind, – 80, 40, 80, – you will find you have an immense advantage and easy grip of the whole history of Venetian art' (155–156).

He works his way round the gallery to achieve the climax of his new enthusiasm for Carpaccio's visionary art. To illustrate the first epoch, he points to Nicolo Semitecolo's *Ascension* 'painted in real belief that the Ascension *did* take place; and its sincerity ought to be pleasant to you, after Titian's pretence'. The next picture is Mantegna's St George, meant to illustrate the second epoch, repaying a microscopic inspection: 'To which, give ten minutes quietly, and examine it with a magnifying glass of considerable power'. It is minutely produced with a considered touch, but after all to be considered 'only as a piece of workmanship' (156). Several paintings later he arrives at two pictures which are very different: 'make up your mind for a long stand'. One is Veronese's 'The Annunciation', 'of the most instructive and noble kind', and the other 'the best picture in the Academy of Venice, Carpaccio's "Presentation"'. The Veronese is a mixture of 'the infection of his aera' and 'his own quietest and best virtues' (158). Then he turns to the Carpaccio, which is a summation of all the Venetian virtues: 'You may measure yourself, outside and in, – your religion, our taste, your knowledge of art, your knowledge of men and things, – by the quantity of admiration which honestly, after due time given, you can feel for this picture'. 'This is essentially Venetian, – prosaic, matter of fact, – retaining its supreme common sense through all enthusiasm'. It is admirable in colour 'precisely because it is not the best piece of colour there; – because the great

4.19 Viltore Carpaccio. *Presentation in the Temple*. 24.xlv. Photo by R. Martin Seddon

master has subdued his own main passion, and restrained his colour-faculty, though the best in Venice ... Carpaccio ... does not want you to think of *his* colour, but of *your* Christ' (159).

Northern France: Restoration in Architecture

Ruskin's serious touring in Northern France began as a pilgrimage in the footsteps of Samuel Prout's *Sketches*. It was a favourite terrain for picturesque painters such as Richard Parkes Bonington, David Roberts, David Cox and T. S. Boys, and popularised in books such as Thomas Roscoe's *The Tourist in France* (1834), illustrated with engravings after Harding's drawings. Ruskin admired the physical beauty of the landscape, which he believed Turner had discovered: 'Lowland France, Picardy and Normandy, the valleys of the Loire and Seine, and even the district ... traversed between Calais and Dijon; of which there is not a single valley but is full of the most lovely pictures' (3.238). Proust noted that in one of Ruskin's drawings of Amiens, 'Ruskin did not separate the beauty of the cathedrals from the charm of the regions from which they sprang' (Proust, 1999: 42). When combined with the Gothic architecture, which Ruskin believed showed the French nation to have been the greatest in the world of the twelfth and thirteenth centuries when it was invented, 'The whole of Northern France (except Champagne)' presented to him 'a perpetual Paradise' (6.419).

4.20 John Ruskin. *Amiens from the river ('Jour des Trépassés')*. Engraved by George Allen. 33.facing 25. Photo by R. Martin Seddon

The established British reception of French culture had formed in the 18th century when, as French literature and manners became central to European culture, it became fashionable to linger in France on the way to Italy. Social polish was to be obtained in Paris. The French taste for the fine arts was increasingly admired by the middle classes after the Revolution, increasing the interest in public buildings and art collections. Ruskin was directing his own gaze at Picardy and Normandy, regions which had long been relatively accessible continental ground for the English aesthetic tourist. Buzard records that Smollett 'refused to provide details of Abbeville, Amiens, or St Denis in his *Travels through France and Italy* (1776) on the grounds that "all these particulars are mentioned in twenty different books of tours, travels, and directions ..."' (Smollett, 1776: 158). Though Northern France was not on the main agenda for the Paris-bound Victorians, its provinciality was part of its distinctive charm, and part of the historical arrest which so appealed to Ruskin. It is rich in interesting village churches, castles, and chateaux which attracted 19th-century English tourists especially to Picardy – Amiens, Abbeville and Beauvais – both en route to the south and for itself, with its antique monuments and picturesque landscapes.

In Picardy and Normandy he repeatedly revisited the places where he could still observe the presence of the medieval Christian society and its arts which he wished his contemporaries to see as a continuing model. He had a relish for the worn histories of these towns, especially Abbeville, to which he responded with a sense of warm familiarity:

> For cheerful, unalloyed, unwearying pleasure, the getting in sight of Abbeville on a fine summer afternoon, jumping out in the courtyard of the Hotel de l'Europe, and rushing down the street to see [St Wulfran's Collegial Church] again before the sun was off the towers, are things to cherish the past for, – to the end. (35.127)

He experienced the life of a holistic community there: 'For here I saw that art (of its local kind), religion, and present human life, were yet in perfect harmony. There were no dead six days and dismal seventh in those sculptured churches' (35.156), and observed the workings of its pre-capitalist economy: 'The commercial square, with the main street of traverse, consisted of uncompetitive shops, such as were needful, of the native wares' (157).

His interests came to centre on the northern Gothic cathedrals. Following the Abbé Suger's architectural innovation at St Denis, between 1140 and 1220 new cathedrals were begun on an ever-growing scale and French Gothic reached its zenith in the late 13th century, with its classifying features of the pointed arch, the flying buttress, the rib-vault, and the invention of tracery. Characteristically, Ruskin's essentialising approach challenged period boundaries to accommodate the 'vital sculpture' (19.251) of the 15th-century Gothic he described in his lecture, 'The Flamboyant Architecture of the Valley of the Somme' (1869) the kind of Gothic referred to in English as 'perpendicular'. The narrative of the later Gothic flowering follows that of his Venetian historiography, simplified into the foundation by a king-led warrior class; the development of domestic arts; the achievement of the cultural peak; and finally the fall into luxury.

His researches into the mostly 15th-century St Wulfran's and other medieval buildings at Abbeville were only 'the preface and interpretation of Rouen' (35.156), which he calls '*the* place of north Europe as Venice is of the South'. (Links, 1968: 45). At Rouen too he encountered the social inclusivity which was to become the basis of his critique of contemporary Britain, and which was an imaginative lesson the British could acquire from travel. The old town

> Gathered itself, and nestled under the buttresses like a brood beneath the mother's wings [while] the quiet, uninjurious aristocracy of the newer town opened into silent streets, between self-possessed and hidden dignities of dwelling, each with its own courtyard and richly trellised garden. (35.156–157)

4.21 John Ruskin. St. *Wulfran, Abbeville*, 1868. Pencil, watercolour, bodycolour and ink. The Ruskin Library, Lancaster University

In 1844, he visited Rouen Cathedral to study the stained glass for his own design for the new east window of St Giles's, Camberwell. On his three-month tour of northern France in 1848, when political events in Venice deflected him from his aesthetic researches there, it became the chief object of investigation for *The Seven Lamps of Architecture* (1849), evidencing key Gothic virtues of workfulness: 'The delight with which we look on the fretted front of Rouen Cathedral depends in no small degree on the simple perception of time employed and labour expended in its production' (3.94), and expressiveness: 'in all this ornament there is not one cusp, one finial, that is useless – not a stroke of a chisel is in vain ...' (8.52). In many manifestations, he celebrated the kind of naturalism which he describes in the tympanum over the west door of the Church of St Maclou at Rouen:

> The Gothic inventor ... makes the fire as like real fire as he can; and in the porch of St Maclou at Rouen the sculptured flames burst out of the

Hades gate, and flicker up, in writhing tongues of stones, through
the interstices of the niches, as if the church itself were on fire.
(10.232–233)

4.22 *The Last Judgement Tympanum of St Maclou, Rouen.* Photo by K. Hanley

Illustrating the 'noble vitality in the art of the time', he selects one of the
grotesque quatrefoils surrounding the Bookseller's Doorway on the north
side of Rouen Cathedral, pointing to the expression of 'gloomy and angry
brooding' on one tiny prone figure: '. . . the fellow is vexed and puzzled in
his malice; and his hand is pressed hard on his cheek bone, and the flesh
is *wrinkled* under the eye by the pressure' (8.217). Proust was drawn to
follow Ruskin's steps to Rouen in pursuit of this description, and he found
in the carving a promise of communal survival, through art communicating shared feelings over time: from the long-dead mason, to the recently
dead Ruskin, to his own living, but equally passing, response. Ruskin has
many criticisms of the later, decadent instances of Gothic, in the cathedral
and the church of St Ouen.

His distinctive and influential discourse of restoration, which was to
become acute in Venice from the 1850s, became explicitly more ideologically anti-revolutionary from 1848 as a result of his tour around Northern
French Gothic, and it found memorable expression in the 'Lamp of
Memory' in *The Seven Lamps of Architecture* (1849). In *The Bible of Amiens*
(1880–85), his contribution to the Anglo-French debates on restoration
finds its fullest articulation, invoking the enduring European Christian
community in the West Front of Amiens Cathedral, which, founded in the
region where Gothic art had been born, in the nearby Aisne and Oise
valleys at the beginning of the 12th century, had withstood the revolutionary period of the 1790s and 1848. The aesthetic values which Ruskin by

4.23 John Ruskin. *Sculptures for Bas-reliefs of the North Door of the Cathedral of Rouen*. Engraved by R.P. Cuff. From *The Seven Lamps of Architecture*. 8. facing 216. The figure described is at the bottom right. Photo by R. Martin Seddon

now demanded far exceeded the pleasures of the Picturesque. When he visited the Amiens district in 1854 he was distressed in exploring the waterways by the signs of decay and human messiness which depressed him with their social implications:

> All exquisitely picturesque, and as miserable as picturesque. We delight in seeing the figures in the boats pushing them about the bits of blue water in Prout's drawings, but, as I looked today at the unhealthy face and melancholy, apathetic mien of the man in the boat, pushing his load of peats along the ditch, and of the people, men and women, who sat spinning gloomily in the picturesque cottages, I could not help feeling how many suffering persons must pay for my picturesque subject, and my happy walk. (Ruskin II, 492–493)

4.24 Unknown photographer. *S. Denis and angels (detail of sculpture), Rheims Cathedral*. Daguerreotype. The Ruskin Library, Lancaster University

4.25 John Ruskin. *Northern Porch, West Front, Amiens Cathedral, Before Restoration*, 1856. Photogravure from a drawing by Ruskin. From *The Bible of Amiens*. 33. facing 142. Photo by R. Martin Seddon

Ruskin's characteristic retort to the increasing wreck, from political revolution and 'restoration', of the architecture and its communities which he saw around him – 'there is not a street without fateful marks of restoration ... in twenty years it is plain that not a vestige of Abbeville, or indeed of any old French town, will be left' (8.xxix) – was to sketch significant architectural details everywhere he went and to commission and collect daguerreotypes and photographs of features from different northern French towns. The urge to record and salvage was fundamental to the composition of *The Seven Lamps*, published in the year that Eugène Viollet-le-Duc, the leading French Gothic architect, began his 'restorations' at Amiens which were underway during all Ruskin's future visits. Viollet-le-Duc was a reconstructor, who defined 'Restauration' in his exhaustive dictionary of French architecture: 'Restaurer un édifice ... c'est le rétablir dans un état complet qui peut n'avoir jamais existé à un moment donné' (Restoring a building ... is reinstating it in a complete condition which may never have existed at a given moment) (Viollet-le-Duc 1867: vol. 8, 14), and demonstrated his approach in his most celebrated recreation, the Château de Pierrefonds. Despite his respect for Viollet-le-Duc's writings (see Gamble, 1999: 192), Ruskin was deeply disturbed, as he had been by the architectural repairs in Venice which were partly inspired by the French

4.26 David Roberts. *The West Front, Amiens Cathedral, France*, 1830. Watercolour and bodycolour (heightened with white). The Whitworth Art Gallery, The University of Manchester

architect. There he had lamented the replacing of the mosaic over the central door of St Mark's in 1838, the refacing of the north and south sides in 1857 and 1865 respectively, and had actively, and successfully, campaigned against the 'restoration' of the west façade in 1876. His position was opposed to the destruction of all these exterior decorations, urging that the effects of the passage of time should not be effaced, and in 1856 he drew the Northern Porch of the West Front of Amiens Cathedral, before its imminent restoration. In 1870, he wrote:

> The colour of the front of Amiens, in 1856, was an exquisitely soft grey, touched with golden lichen; and the sheltered sculpture was fresh as when first executed, only the exposed parts broken or mouldering into forms which made them more beautiful than if perfect. All is now destroyed; and even the sharp, pure rose moulding (of which hardly a petal was injured) cut to pieces, and, for the most part, replaced by a modern design. (21.121)

More affirmatively, Ruskin embarked on his own last act of cultural restoration in his final architectural work, *The Bible of Amiens*. In it, he assumed and reinforced the well-established counter-revolutionary discourse of French antiquarianism which was mostly steeped in a reactionary Catholicism. In France, following the nationalisation of church property in 1789, a conflict resulted between those who wished to preserve the monuments for historical interest and those who wanted to erase them from sight and memory as a gesture of republican patriotism. A counter-discourse of imaginary medievalism, which had found influential expression in Victor Hugo's novel, *Notre Dame de Paris* (1831), and his subsequent cultural interventions, struggled to materialise under the Restoration of the Empire of 1852. Hugo went into exile, and though Ruskin was disgusted by Hugo's sensationalism and was ideologically alienated by his politics (see Hewison, 2009: 80–81), it was to be that tendency, broadened, re-sanctified, and opposed first to the modernising drive of Napoleon III and later to the anti-clericalism of the new Republic, which ultimately led to Ruskin's revisiting the Northern French Gothic of his youth in order to restore a vision of the good society in his final work of architectural criticism. That discourse had been disseminated in visual representations of the historical picturesque, proliferating societies, national grand projects and local guidebooks. The introduction of lithography at the end of the 18th century, then of engraving, which, with its capacity for precision in architectural details, found its fullest expression in the 20 volumes of *Voyages pittoresques et romantiques dans l'ancienne France* (1820–1878), directed by Baron Taylor, Charles Nodier and Alphonse de Cailleux, lent themselves to the same end. The last named project, which contrasted the lost chivalric paradise of the Middle Ages with the decline of modern times, initiated a vogue which led to a veritable industry after 1830, when the tendency for national preservation of monuments became concretised by the creation of the post of Inspector of Historical Monuments occupied first by the historian Ludovic Vitet and then the writer Prosper Mérimée. Part of the official programme was to create photographic records, which became available from 1839, offering more exactitude than drawings, and in 1851, the grand scheme ('mission héliographique') of photographing all major historical French monuments commenced (see Paccoud & Toubin, 2006). In the 1820s and 30s several antiquarian societies were founded in Normandy and Picardy, and from 1848 the church became a rising force in the nation, so that under the Restoration of 1852 religious medieval monuments were more actively conserved. But Ruskin's work was produced in the context of another movement towards secularism in the public policy of the Third Republic from the later 1870s. In relation to the local guidebooks which Ruskin followed, the abbé Roze's *Visite à la cathédrale d'Amiens* (1877), which is much relied upon, continued the interests and concerns of earlier works, including A.P.H. Gilbert's *Description historique de la Cathédrale d'Amiens* (1833), the abbés Edouard Jourdain and Charles Duval's *Stalles et les clôtures du choeur* (1867), and *Nouvelle description de la cathédrale d'Amiens* (1847) by Antoine Goze, associate inspector of Historical Monuments.

4.27 Charles Hugot. *Vue Général d'Amiens, Prise de la Citadelle, c.* 1847.
Photograph of lithograph. From Antoine Goze, *Description de la Cathédrale
d'Amiens*, 1847. Bibliothèque Louis Aragon, Bibliothèque d'Amiens Métropole,
Amiens

Ruskin contributed one small intervention. Kaltenbacher had produced a series of albumen photographs for the use of Viollet-le-Duc, but
Ruskin commissioned the reproduction of 'The quatrefoils on the foundation of the west front of Amiens cathedral ... [which] had never been
engraved or photographed in any form accessible to the public until last
year [1880]' (33.12–13) as an unparalleled 'exposition of the manner of central thirteenth-century sculpture' to illustrate his own book, and also separately for increased general perception, and memory. He then chose
four general views of the cathedral from Kaltenbacher's own stock,
making 25 photos in all, to 'form a complete body of illustrations for this
fourth number of the Bible: the lot costing a hundred francs in Amiens
and five pounds in London' (13).

What emerged as the *Bible of Amiens* was to have been part of a huge
project, up to 10 volumes, entitled, *Our Fathers Have Told Us*, evoking a
respectful and pious attention to the traditions of European Christianity:
its subtitle was 'Sketches of the History of Christendom for Boys and Girls
who have been held at its Fonts'. The central focus is the cathedral of
Notre-Dame d'Amiens, and its fourth chapter, 'Interpretations', is devoted
to it. The rest concerns the history of France and Christianity. Intended at
first for the Eton schoolboy, or thoughtful English girl, Ruskin's guide
came to be addressed to 'the Intelligent Traveller' in general. He had
already contemplated writing a *Stones of Abbeville*, and considered a further instalment, a *Bible of Rouen*. One of his last ideas was to write 'a little
guide to the cathedral [of Beauvais] like one of the *Mornings in Florence* – to
be called "the Choir of Choirs", or something of the sort' (37.606). But
in the West Front of Amiens Cathedral, he recognised the climactic, all-
embracing exposition of the whole medieval worldview: its avowal of the

4.28 Kaltenbacher, photographer. *General View of Amiens Cathedral, c.* 1880.
Albumen print. The Ruskin Library, Lancaster University. Photo by
R. Martin Seddon

4.29 Unknown photographer (probably Kaltenbacher). *The Three Western
Porches*. Photogravure from a photograph. From *The Bible of Amiens* (33.141).
Photo by R. Martin Seddon

history of the world since Creation, the dogmas of faith, the lives of the saints, the virtues and various branches of knowledge.

His underlying appeal is to the desire of the traveller to distinguish himself imaginatively from his fallen age:

> It is not easy for the citizen of the modern aggregate of bad building, and ill-living held in check by constables, which *we* call a town, – of which the widest streets are devoted by consent to the encouragement of vice, and the narrow ones to the concealment of misery, – not easy, I say, for the citizen of any such mean city to understand the feeling of a burgher of the Christian ages to his cathedral. (140)

He is in effect invoking a reversal of the 'counter-spirit' of his times:

> But the meaning of every act, as of every art, of the Christian ages, lost now for three hundred years, cannot but be in our own times read reversed, if at all, through the counter-spirit which we have now reached; glorifying Pride and Avarice as the virtues by which all things move and have their being .... (173)

Indeed, Ruskin even provided a prayer – from George Chapman, which he bids the Protestant English visitor recite there – thus engaging him in the avowal of and participation in Christian culture, tolerant of its Catholic continuities.

In order to produce a 'Separate Travellers' edition, Ruskin issued what would become Chapter Four, 'Interpretations', on its own in 75 pages, which in his Advice he describes as 'in a reduced size for the convenience of travellers, who may wish to possess this number only as a guide to the Cathedral, without bringing the whole work' (33.14). It was re-issued in 1909 as *Guide to the Cathedral*. In the guide, Ruskin offers to accompany his reader on the approach to the cathedral, making conversation and attempting to detach the tourist ironically from the usual attitudes and practices. He recommends that 'the really right thing to do is to walk down the main street of the old town, and across the river' and to walk to the top of the citadel, but he interweaves a mythic, biblical geography: 'then, returning, find your way to the Mount Zion of it by any narrow cross streets and chance bridges you can ...' (146). After all, that would take the tourist too long, and he makes apparent concessions – 'if you really must go to Paris this afternoon, and only mean to see all you can in an hour or two' – but only to lift his reader ashamedly above ordinary expectations as he provides redirections to enter the south transept through the Portail de St Honoré:

> ... you are still a nice sort of person, for whom it is of some consequence which way you come at a pretty thing, or begin to look at it – I think the best way is to walk from the Hôtel de France or the Place de Périgord, up the Street of the Three Pebbles, towards the railway station – stopping a little as you go, so as to get into a cheerful temper,

and buying some bonbons or tarts for the children in one of the patissiers' shops on the left. Just past them, ask for the theatre; and just past that, you will find, also on the left, three open arches, through which you can turn, passing the Palais de Justice, and go straight up to the south transept, which has really something to please everybody. (127–128)

Once there, he sees in the too pretty 'Madonna in decadence' in the porch, 'with her head a little aside', a sign of a fall beginning in the 14th century 'when the people first began to find Christianity too serious and devised a merrier faith for France' (148) and eventually leading to '"ça allait, ça ira," to the merriest days of the guillotine' (148). Yet, gazing more: 'But they could still carve in the 14th century, and the Madonna and her hawthorn-blossom lintel are worth your looking at, much more the field above, of sculpture as delicate and more calm, which tells St Honoré's own story, little talked of now in his Parisian faubourg' (148).

Having entered, he appreciates the fine structural immensity: 'this apse of Amiens is not only the best, but the very first thing done perfectly in its manner, by Northern Christendom' (151), but is really more concerned with significant decoration and its inner moral and social meanings as he guides the tourist to concentrate on the Choir, the labyrinth, some tombs, but especially on 'The Bible of Amiens', the West Front. His adaptation to the realities of the tourist's probable predicament suits his inclination to select the most memorable focus:

> Whatever you wish to see, or are forced to leave unseen, at Amiens, if the overwhelming responsibilities of your existence, and the inevitable necessities of precipitate locomotion in their fulfilment, have left you so much as a quarter of an hour, not out of breath – for the contemplation of the capital of Picardy, give it wholly to the cathedral choir ['flamboyant just past the fifteenth century']. (142)

What brings the whole building into immediate relation to the contemporary viewer is its realism: '. . . their own "Beau Christ d'Amiens" was as true a compatriot to them as if He had been born of a Picard maiden' (141). In this way, Ruskin attempts to impart a shared sense of reverence and an acuteness of response to the aesthetic experience: 'We talk foolishly and feebly of symbols and types: in old Christian architecture, every part is *literal*: the Cathedral is for its builders the House of God. . .' (141). The complete range of individual self-expression in the workman is the key to Ruskin's architectural hermeneutics:

> . . . and the glorious carvings of the exterior walls and interior wood of the choir, which an English rector would almost instinctively think of as done for the glorification of the canons, was indeed the Amienois carpenter's way of making his Master-carpenter comfortable, – nor

4.30 *The Golden Virgin, Amiens Cathedral.* Photo by K. Hanley

less of showing his own native and insuperable virtue of carpenter, before God and man. (142)

He employs his virtuoso prose style to convey the unfolding vitality of organic form:

> Sweet and young-grained wood it is: oak, *trained* and chosen for such work, sound now as four hundred years since. Under the carver's hand it seems to cut like clay, to fold like silk, to grow like living branches, to leap like living flame. Canopy crowning canopy, pinnacle piercing pinnacle – it shoots and wreathes itself into an enchanted glade, inextricable, imperishable, fuller of leafage than any forest, and fuller of story than any book. (143)

By now the tour is leading climactically to the West Front, the end of his Protestant pilgrimage – 'We will begin our examination of the Temple front . . .' (170) – to the *Bible of Amiens*. His interpretation, unfolded in all its richly detailed meanings as the summation of the Christian tradition in

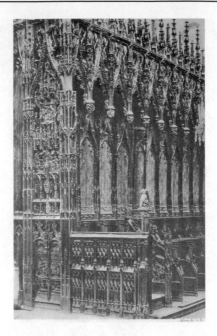

4.31 Unknown photographer. *The Choir Stalls, Amiens Cathedral*. Photogravure
from a photograph. 35. facing 125. Photo by R. Martin Seddon

life and art, depends on the book within the Book: 'What you have first to
think of, and read, is the scripture of the great central porch, and the façade
itself' (168). The underlying theme is the text in the New Testament in
which Christ compares himself to a gate through which the lambs came
into the fold. The route to the Lord (the 'Beau Dieu') is in their Biblical
order from right to left through the 12 Minor Prophets, urging the eye
towards the four great prophets at the centre: Isaiah and Jeremy on the
right, Daniel and Ezekiel on the left. They give way towards Christ, revealing the twelve apostles preaching about him. Entrance to the cathedral is
also aided by the first bishop and Our Lady: the right portal is devoted to
Mary; the left side portal to St Firmin, the first evangeliser of the Picard
region. The tympanum represents the Last Judgment: Christ proclaims
his judgement, and souls of the saved and damned are separated, while
angels hover all around. People rise from their graves, and St Michael
weighs the souls. The first man admitted to heaven is a friar from the
Order which had just settled in Amiens in 1244.

Ruskin certainly knows how precarious is his hold on the tourist's
attention to the minutiae which he lists for pages as he follows and comments on the extraordinary ramifications of the visual text: 'I give in clear
succession, the order of the statues of the whole front, with the subjects of
the quatrefoils beneath each of them ...' (177). Though for him they all
convey aspects of a richly comprehensive worldview, as he takes breath to

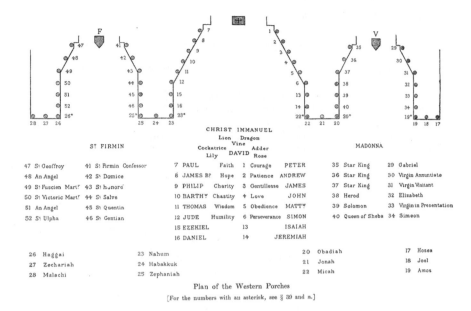

F   V

CHRIST IMMANUEL
Lion   Dragon
ST FIRMIN   Cockatrice Vine Adder   MADONNA
Lily   DAVID   Rose

47 St Geoffroy	41 St Firmin Confessor	7 PAUL	Faith	1 Courage	PETER	35 Star King	29 Gabriel
48 An Angel	42 St Domice	8 JAMES Bp	Hope	2 Patience	ANDREW	36 Star King	30 Virgin Annuntiate
49 St Fuscien Mart?	43 St honore	9 PHILIP	Charity	3 Gentillesse	JAMES	37 Star King	31 Virgin Visitant
50 St Victoric Mart?	44 St Salve	10 BARTH?	Chastity	4 Love	JOHN	38 Herod	32 Elizabeth
51 An Angel	45 St Quentin	11 THOMAS	Wisdom	5 Obedience	MATT?	39 Solomon	33 Virgin in Presentation
52 St Ulpha	46 St Gentian	12 JUDE	Humility	6 Perseverance	SIMON	40 Queen of Sheba	34 Simeon
		15 EZEKIEL		13	ISAIAH		
		16 DANIEL		14	JEREMIAH		

26 Haggai	23 Nahum	20 Obadiah	17 Hosea
27 Zechariah	24 Habakkuk	21 Jonah	18 Joel
28 Malachi	25 Zephaniah	22 Micah	19 Amos

Plan of the Western Porches
[For the numbers with an asterisk, see § 39 and n.]

4.32 John Ruskin. *Plan for the Western Porches, Amiens Cathedral*, 1880. 33.facing 144. Photo by R. Martin Seddon

continue with his exhaustive exposition he allows himself a final injection of ironic dialogue:

> ... having thus put the sequence of the statues and their quatrefoils briefly before the spectator – (in case the railway time passes, it may be a kindness to him to note that if he walks from the east end of the cathedral down the street to the south, Rue St Denis, it takes him by the shortest line to the station) – I will begin again with St Peter, and interpret the sculptures in the quatrefoils a little more fully. (182)

Ruskin will continue with his train of thought to the final exhortation to 'understand how thoroughly it was all believed' (173) and to enter into the profound imaginative appeal of Christian Hope. But all the time that other train is about to leave.

References

Bradley, A. (1987) *Ruskin and Italy*. Ann Arbor: UMI Research Press.
Buzard, J. (1993) *The Beaten Track: European Tourism, Literature, and the Ways to Culture 1800–1918*. Oxford: Clarendon Press.
Clegg, J. (1981) *Ruskin and Venice*. London: Junction Books.
Clegg, J. and Tucker, P. (1992) *Ruskin and Tuscany*. Sheffield and London: Ruskin Gallery, Collection of the Guild of St George, Sheffield, in association with Lund Humphries.
Coxe, W. (1789) *Travels in Switzerland: In a series of letters to William Melmoth, Esq., from William Coxe*. London: T. Cadell.

de Saussure, H.B. (1779–1796) *Voyages dans les Alpes*. Neuchâtel: Fauche, Fauche-Borel.
Gamble, C. (1999) John Ruskin Eugene Viollet-le-Duc and the Alps. In Douglas (ed.) *The Alpine Club Journal* 104: 185–96.
Gilbert, A.P.H. (1833) *Description historique de la Cathédrale d'Amiens*. Amiens: Alfred Carron.
Gotthelf, J. (1888) In J. Firth (trans.) and J. Ruskin (ed.) *Ulric the Farm Servant: A Study of the Bernese Lowlands*. Orpington, Kent: G. Allen.
Goze, A. (1847) *Nouvelle description de la cathédrale d'Amiens*. Amiens: Alfred Carron.
Green, V.H.H. (1961) *The Swiss Alps*. London: B.T. Batsford.
Hayman, J. (1990) *John Ruskin and Switzerland*. Canada: Wilfrid Laurier UP.
Hugo, V. (1831) *Notre Dame de Paris*. Paris: J. Hetzel.
Jourdain, E. and Charles, D. (1867) *Stalles et les clôtures du choeur*. Amiens: Alfred Carron.
Links, J.G. (1968) *The Ruskins in Normandy: A Tour in 1848 with Murray's Hand-book*. London: John Murray.
Norwich, J.J. (2003) *Paradise of Cities; Venice in the 19th Century*. New York: Doubleday.
Paccoud, S. and Toubin, A. (2006) *Pittoresques Monuments, De la Révolution du Patrimone Médiéval en Picardie 1789–1870*. Exhibition Catalogue. Abbeville: Musée Boucher-de-Perthes.
Parsons, N.T. (2007) *Worth the Detour: A History of the Guidebook*. Stroud: Sutton.
Proust, M. (1904) *La Bible d'Amiens*. Paris: Mercure de France.
Proust, M. (1987) In J. Autret, W. Burford and P.J. Wolfe (eds) *On Reading Ruskin: Prefaces to* La Bible d'Amiens *and* Sésame et les Lys *with Selections from the Notes to the Translated Texts*. New Haven, CT: Yale University Press.
Richardson, J. (1722) *An Account of Some of the Statues, bas-reliefs, Drawings and Pictures in Italy, Etc. with Remarks*. London: J. Knapton.
Rogers, S. (1830) *Italy*. London: T. Cadell and E. Moxon.
Roscoe, T. (1834) *The Tourist in France, Landscape Annual*. London: Jennings and Chaplin.
Rousseau (1761) *Julie, ou la nouvelle Héloïse*. Amsterdam: Rey.
Roze, abbé (1877) *Visite à la cathédrale d'Amiens*. Amiens: Alfred Carron.
Ruskin, J. (1972) In H. Schapiro (ed.) *Ruskin Family – Ruskin in Italy. Letters to his Parents*. Oxford: Clarendon Press.
Ruskin, J. (1955) In J.L. Bradley (ed.) *Ruskin's Letters from Venice, 1851–1852*. New Haven: Yale UP.
Ruskin, J. (1956–59) In J. Evans and J.H. Whitehouse (eds) *The Diaries of John Ruskin* (Vol. 2). Oxford: Clarendon Press.
Ruskin, J. (1973) In B. Van Aikin (ed.) *The Ruskin Family Letters*. (Vol. 2). Ithaca and London: Cornell UP.
Ruskin, J. (1982) In J. Hayman (ed.) *Letters from the Continent*. Toronto: Toronto UP.
Ruskin-Turner (2003) *Dessins et Voyages en Picardie Romantique*. Exhibition Catalogue. Amiens: Musée de Picardie.
Scott, Sir Walter (1829) *Anne of Geierstein; or The Maiden of the Mist*. Edinburgh: Cadell; London: Simpkin and Marshall.
Smedley, E. (1831–1832) *Sketches of Venetian History* (Vol. 2). London: John Murray.
Smollett, T. (1776) *Travels through France and Italy* (Vol. 2). London: R. Baldwin.
Taylor, B., Nodier, C. and Alphonse de C. (1820–1878) *Voyages pittoresques et romantiques dans l'ancienne France* (Vol. 20). Paris: P. Didot l'aîné.
Viollet-le-Duc, E. (1867) *Dictionnaire Raisonné de l' Architecture Française du XI au XVI Siècle* (Vol. 8). Paris: A Morel.
Wordsworth, W. (1959) In E. de Selincourt and H. Darbishire (eds) *The Poetical Works of William Wordsworth* (Vol. 5). Oxford: Clarendon Press.

Chapter 5
Ruskin and Tourist Destinations

Ruskin's most productive years as a writer coincided with an enormous expansion in tourist activity. The growth of the industrial, commercial and professional middle classes, in numbers and purchasing power, stimulated tourism markets among those with the requisite time, money and cultural capital, while the extension and articulation of transport, information and commercial hospitality systems made travel more accessible, comfortable and tempting in the new age of steam-powered transport and cheap print media. These developments have been caricatured as the first age of 'mass tourism', and summarised as 'from Grand Tour to Cook's Tour'; (Withey, 1997; Berghoff *et al.*, 2002) but they are actually much more complicated than the existing literature suggests. Tracing the influence of Ruskin on where British tourists went, what they saw and how they saw it, whether in the British Isles or on continental Europe, is a difficult but stimulating and necessary task. Ruskin's writings reinforced existing travel patterns inherited from the 18th and early 19th centuries, whether through the evolving agenda of the Grand Tour as it reached further down the social scale, (Chaney, 1998) or through the picturesque and romantic itineraries of tourists in England, Scotland and Wales. His own travels followed itineraries that were already laid down, and indeed conventional, by the 1830s, when his parents introduced him to the forms of cultural tourism that focused on the aesthetic and moral appreciation of architecture, townscape and scenery. As we saw in Chapter 2, and as Wolfgang Kemp points out, he was attracted to, and wrote about, less-frequented places within this framework, such as Abbeville and Lucca. But John Pemble argues that, 'Ruskin ... quite clearly owed as much to educated opinion as educated opinion owed to him, and his achievement was rather to formulate and mediate current ideas about Mediterranean history and art than to create them. He was influential only in a limited sense, because his large audience was wiling to be persuaded' (Pemble, 1987: 13). Alexander Bradley suggests that, 'Ruskin saw Europe through the eyes of his favourite artists', and many of his journeys were influenced by the painting itineraries of J.M.W. Turner, whose artistic relationship with

Ruskin was to be so important (Bradley, 1987: 7; Hanley, 2007; Hayman, 1990: 113). The influence of Romantic writers, especially Byron, also helped to direct Ruskin's footsteps: he recollected in *Praeterita* that, 'My Venice, like Turner's, had been chiefly created for us by Byron' (Bradley, 1987: 5). As Alice Meynell pointed out in 1900, 'John Ruskin's life was not only centred, but limited, by the places where he was born and taught, and by the things he loved. The London suburb and the English lakeside for his homes, Oxford for his place first of study then of teaching, usually one beaten round by France, Switzerland and Italy for his annual journeys – these closed the scene of his dwellings and travellings'. Here she edits out the full extent of his British travels, and his occasional visits to Germany, but the general point stands (Hayman, 1990: 2; Meynell, 1900: 1).

But Ruskin's work as artist, commentator and critic, and its influence on his growing body of readers (and on those who were aware of interpretations of what he had written), made a difference to the hierarchy of preferred journeys, halting points and objects of the tourist gaze. His journeys covered conventional ground, even as the pattern of directions and destinations changed over time, and what they omitted is of as much interest as what they contained and embraced; but his writings enjoined a different set of priorities within these conventions, a different ordering of 'what must be seen', from what had gone before. As the alpinist Douglas Freshfield put it, focusing on Ruskin and mountains: 'He saw and understood mountains, and taught our generation to understand them in a way no one – even of those who had been born under their shadow – had ever understood them before ... no writer has added so much to our appreciation of Alpine scenery' (Ring, 2000: 32). Anne Colley emphasizes the 'kinetic' relationship between Ruskin's vigorous climbing and scrambling, his ways of seeing at close quarters, and his ability to communicate the resulting understandings (Colley, 2009). On the other hand, Cardinal suggests that in spite of his intentions, Ruskin's 'articulate enthusiasm for the Alps helped to hasten their popularization and eventual kitschification', an unfortunate coinage and perhaps an over-simplified perception (Cardinal, 2007: 168). Ruskin's writings affected the directions, destinations and evaluations of Victorian tourists, whether directly or at one or two removes. In significant cases they changed the intensity, duration and appreciation of detail of the 'tourist gaze' when directed at objects that were singled out for special, serious, informed attention. They therefore helped to shape the nature and content of Victorian (and subsequent) cultural tourism, in terms of 'where to go and what to see', and above all of how to see it, in ways that had economic and environmental consequences for the development of tourist industries.

This chapter tries to assess the extent, nature and impact of those Ruskinian influences. It does so by examining tourist diaries, travel commentaries and commercial tourist itineraries (especially those of Thomas

Cook, because the survival and ready availability of extensive archives enables detailed analysis) to assess to what extent the places visited and the perceptions recorded map on to Ruskin's own itineraries and commentaries, and by building on earlier analyses of guidebook content and construction to examine commercially produced guidebooks (especially the most widely used), assessing the extent and nature of references to Ruskin and his representations of where to go, what to see and how to see it. We look especially at European journeys and destinations, focusing on Venice and the Alps. Analysis will proceed beyond the First World War, and embrace the post-war decline of Ruskin's reputation and influence as well as its rise and apogee. The methodological problems of trying to assess 'secondary' Ruskin influences, where there is no direct textual signposting, will be addressed in passing, and the conclusions will take account of them.

In the first place, we should emphasize that Ruskin's writings seldom, if ever, opened out new destinations: they did not feed into the 'discovery' phase of the imagined 'tourist area life cycle' (Butler, 2005). Ruskin was not himself a 'traveller', in the sense of blazing new trails, discovering new destinations, or interacting directly with societies that were unfamiliar, with curious strangers bearing alien expectations and speaking incomprehensible languages, although Ruskin himself had a good command of French and a less secure conversational grasp of Italian (Buzard, 1993; Hewison, 2004). This is an important issue, given the conventional assumptions about the higher status that came to be accorded to the 'traveller' as opposed to the mere 'tourist'. Ruskin was much closer to the latter category than the former, but the 'cultural tourism' that he practised and propagated demanded high levels of prior acculturation to 'where to go and what to see', and above all how to look at the object of the gaze, with fixity, concentration and the necessary attention to detail to develop an 'argument of the eye' (Hewison, 1976; Koshar, 2000; Urry, 1995). Ruskin was responsible for prompting tourists to see and respond to old sights in new ways, for adjusting the balance of the canon of culturally desirable or necessary experiences, for defining a hierarchy of what was to be seen within the established spectrum of recognised objects of the tourist gaze (though emphatically without, himself, reducing the process to grading on a scale of stars), and for extending or refining that spectrum by communicating the results of his own close observation and depiction. Within the context of established destinations, he brought about the positive revaluation of some sites and artefacts, and the downgrading of others, in the eyes of those who accepted his moral and aesthetic judgements and criteria.

It would be easy to load the dice in favour of interpreting Ruskin as 'traveller' rather than 'tourist' by emphasizing his antipathy to railways and other aspects of 'modernity', and some commentators take this to the point of caricature (Crook, 2003). To Michael Freeman, Ruskin's 'dislike of railways was legendary', and he did indeed deny that the traveller using them could know anything beyond the 'geological structure' of the country that was traversed, while suggesting that the railways reduced their users to mere 'human parcels (that) proceeded to their destination untouched by the space they traversed' (Freeman, 1999: 53, 79). But the railways themselves tended to follow 'the beaten track' that determined the directions and destinations of Ruskin's own journeys, thereby reinforcing the conventional. For their part, the railways did not reject him: the name 'John Ruskin' was given to a London and North Western Railway express locomotive, No. 5620, of the 'Prince of Wales' class, which entered traffic at around the height of Ruskin's pre-war popular visibility in 1913. This was quite a 'literary' group of locomotives, so too much should not be read into Ruskin's presence: other names in the series included not only Cowper, Thackeray, Macaulay, Southey and Sidney Smith, but also R.L. Stevenson, W.S. Gilbert, Mark Twain and Lewis Carroll. Thomas Carlyle had already been commemorated by the same railway company on a 'Precedent' class engine of 1894, so it might be thought that Ruskin's recognition was relatively belated. His absence would have been significant, however. Locomotive naming policies were significant indicators of 'official' attitudes, and we should not laugh this off (http://www.britishsteam. com, accessed 18 January 2009; Walton, 2005).

Ruskin certainly made damning or slighting comments on the impact of railways on landscapes, societies and architecture. He was an outspoken supporter of campaigns against their extension into the heart of the Lake District, especially when controversial schemes were proposed during his time at Brantwood in the 1870s and 1880s; he had been famously scathing (for example) about the building of the Derby-Manchester line through Monsal Dale in the Derbyshire Peak District; and he was dismissive of the whole concept of railway station architecture; but railways became a necessity and Ruskin made use of them for his own journeys as they became available, while tacitly accepting the presence of the Coniston branch line terminus as part of the view across the lake from Brantwood. It was one thing to object to, and campaign against, the extension of railways into what might be represented as pristine or innocent landscapes, with all that might entail in terms of mining and quarrying as well as tourist traffic, at a time when the planning regulations that later restrained urban sprawl and the intrusive smoke and scars of industry were still unthinkable. This lay behind Ruskin's support for organised opposition to railway extension in the heart of the Lake District from 1876 onwards, and his general dismay at the idea of mountain railways. His reaction to the impact of the railway on the experience of arriving in Venice was an urban variation on the theme: the terminus lay at the very edge of the city, but it was reached by a bridge across the lagoon that removed all idiosyncrasy and mystery from the arrival. But it was a different matter to abjure the speed, convenience and flexibility that were afforded by a form of transport whose existence was already a *fait accompli* from Ruskin's early youth, and a daily reality by the mid-19th century, at least in Britain; and he did not do so (Marshall & Walton, 1981: chap. 9; Pemble, 1995; Richards, 1995). He was even capable of actively enjoying a railway journey, as when he travelled by train to Turin in 1858 (Bradley, 1987: 36–37). Nor was he an instinctive or undiscriminating technophobe, as demonstrated by his eager embrace of the advantages of the daguerreotype (Colley, 2009: 56).

Ruskin's preference for older, slower, more leisurely and contemplative ways of travelling was compatible with the use of railways where necessary, especially to cover long distances to desired locations. His reservations were clear. Wolfgang Schivelbusch suggests that his dislike of railways 'created the most sensitive descriptions of the peculiar traits of pre-industrial travel', as he 'proposed an almost mathematical negative correlation between the number of objects that are perceived in a given period of time and the quality of that perception'. Ruskin asserted that, '...to any person who has all his senses about him, a quiet walk along not more than ten or twelve miles a day, is the most amusing of all travelling; and all travelling becomes dull in exact proportion to its rapidity'. For Schivelbusch, this reflected an inability to 'develop modes of perception appropriate to the new form of transportation' and enjoy the new ways of seeing that the railway provided; but such incapacity was not inevitable, as he points out, and there were exact contemporaries who were excited and stimulated by the aesthetic consequences of rapid motion framed by the carriage window in a succession of exciting, if ultimately tiring, images (Schivelbusch, 1986: 57–59). Lee's interpretation of Turner's famous railway painting *Rain, Steam and Speed* (1844) is interesting here: it is 'pioneering in the (a)esthetization of the steam engine', while Turner is interested in 'the essence of the steam locomotive – its motion, power and speed', expressing it through indistinctness and celebrating modernity and the 'industrial sublime'. This puts Turner on the opposite side of Schivelbusch's imagined divide from Ruskin: he had embraced the positive aesthetic consequences of the new mode of travel. As Lee remarks, Ruskin hardly mentions *Rain, Steam and Speed* in *Modern Painters*, and there is no chapter 'Of Turnerian Speed' (Lee, 1999: 13–15).

Ruskin was far from being unique in his rejection of the railway as an aesthetic experience; but the extent of that rejection was unusual. Schivelbusch cites similar reactions from Flaubert; and 'Arthur Sketchley', following the Cook's tourist track through Switzerland and Italy in 1870, commented that 'To those who remember the approach to Venice in other days, when one used to float from the mainland to the city in a gondola, the present mode of crossing the lagoon in the railway will appear very prosaic and commonplace'; but this was a special case, and the railway viaduct in itself was 'a very creditable piece of work', while elsewhere nostalgia for the days of the diligence were tempered by memories of its slow speed and discomfort, much was made of the railway as a vantage point for viewing landscape and society (such as the 'picturesque' peasant costumes on display in the fields between Rome and Naples), and the lamented lost views anticipated when the Mont Cénis tunnel was completed through the Alps were those obtainable from the current railway system ('Sketchley', 1870: 24, 33, 71, 98). This was a common mixture of nostalgia for a recent past with recognition of the value of innovations in long-distance transport, and provides a reminder of the many intermediate stages between embracing and rejecting the railways, whether on practical or aesthetic grounds.

Ruskin's preference for walking as an ideal (though not always practical) means of locomotion, associated with gaining a direct apprehension and understanding of landscape, terrain, geology, flora and fauna, was to exert a significant influence on 'alternative' modes of low-cost popular holidaymaking that prioritised energetic simplicity and proximity to Nature. This was to be a product of the growing visibility of his writings among a serious-minded lower middle-class and working-class public in the late 19th century, as we shall see in Chapter 6. But these preoccupations were to have more of an impact within Britain, and on this constituency and those middle- and upper-class radicals, reformers and preservationists who reached out to it, than on the tourists and sightseers to European destinations whose agenda was most strongly influenced by his mid-Victorian writings. It would, for example, be all too easy to exaggerate Ruskin's influence on the growing popularity of the Alps among British tourists in the 19th century.

The Alps were already well established on the Grand Tour and subsequent middle-class tourist itineraries long before the publication of *Modern Painters*, and the genesis of this project in 1842 at Chamonix itself reflected the conventional nature of the travel patterns of the Ruskin family (Heafford, 2006; Hilton, 2002: 69). Chamonix had become a staging post on a revised version of the Grand Tour from the late 18th century onwards, as mountains and glaciers became fashionable under the developing canon of the sublime; and by the year of Ruskin's birth it was already frequented by early climbers and mountain walkers, whose presence supported an infrastructure of accommodation and mountain guides. Ring may argue that *Modern Painters* was the single most important literary influence on the development of the Alps as a tourist destination and playground; but plenty of other early, and near-contemporary, influences were also at work, and the five volumes of *Modern Painters* took 17 years from 1843 to pass into print, while the key text for these purposes, Volume 4, *Of Mountain Beauty*, did not emerge until 1856. Laurent Tissot supplies a decade-by-decade profile of the number of editions of English language guidebooks to Switzerland published from the late 18th century onwards: there were three in the 1780s, two in the war-torn 1790s, three in the first decade of the new century, then seven in the 1810s, sixteen in the 1820s and fourteen in the 1830s. The real explosion came in the second half of the 19th century, as the number rose to 27 in the 1850s and 59 in the following decade before peaking at 85 in the 1890s. This was the period of Ruskin's maximum influence on this market; but the same applied (for example) to that of railways, Cook's tours and the rise of heliotherapy and winter sports (Barton, 2008; Hayman, 1990; Nicholson, 1959; Ring, 2000: 59; Tissot, 2001: 20). The key point is that there was plenty of Alpine tourist activity before Ruskin.

If we look specifically at the development of Chamonix as a tourist destination, and Mont Blanc as a goal for adventurous tourists as well as climbers (if these are indeed separate categories), we see the limitations of Ruskin's influence. Here, Ruskin was treading a beaten track. Wordsworth had visited 'the wondrous vale of Chamouni' in 1790, and undertaken a walking tour of the Alps. Shelley also visited Chamonix, and the first Englishman to reach the top of Mont Blanc, Col. Mark Beaufroy, did so in 1797. The so-called 'father of English mountaineering', James Forbes, made his first visit to Chamonix and the Mer de Glace in 1826, and by the 1830s the Alps in general had become fashionable among the expanding commercial and professional middle classes. As Dr Arnold put it in 1840, with an interesting imputation of the provincial nature of the Lake District's markets, 'Switzerland is to England, what Cumberland and Westmorland are to Lancashire and Yorkshire, the general summer touring place'. The first Murray's *Handbook* for Switzerland came out in 1838. So Ruskin's attachment to Chamonix brought him into contact with what was already becoming, as Murray described it, 'a large and important community which displays almost the bustle of an English watering-place in the most retired, heretofore, of the alpine valleys' (Ring, 2000: 20–28, 47–48). His Alpine climbs should not be underestimated, taking him to heights of over 10,000 ft and including ascents of several demanding peaks (Colley, 2009). But Chamonix, already popular, was rendered notorious by the activities of Albert Smith, a friend of the American showman P.T. Barnum, who turned his own ascent of Mont Blanc in 1851 into a burlesque commercial performance, celebrating the huge quantities of provisions that accompanied him up the mountain, shooting empty champagne bottles down the glacier, presenting the story to a crowded Egyptian Hall in London, and branding the performance with displays of edelweiss and a reproduction of a 'Swiss chalet'. Smith removed all sense of awe or aura from the mountain glories of Mont Blanc, turning the Alps into an adventure playground and offering an alternative, popular, commercial, frivolous vision of the mountain environment (Bevin, 2009; Cardinal, 2007: 159; Chamberlain, 2007; Hansen, 1995; and for the Egyptian Hall, Altick, 1978: chap. 18). Not that he was the first to represent Swiss mountain panoramas to the expansive commercial metropolitan market for such shows: as recently as 1849 'a view taken from the summit of Mount Righi' had been displayed at the Panorama, Leicester Square, and by that time there were several German precedents (Burford, 1849). Ruskin had endorsed the Leicester Square Panorama as an 'educational institution of the highest and purest value', but Smith was another matter: he alluded with irritation at the time to Smith's 'cockney ascent of Mont Blanc', and a few years later referred to Chamonix becoming 'a kind of Cremorne Gardens', a commercialised, artificial, metropolitan spectacle (Ring, 2000: 49, 61).

The state of the Chamonix tourist trade in the mid-1840s, together with the broader expectations and responses of the tourists themselves, can be illustrated by the travel journal of Marianne Wilkinson, a middle-class spinster travelling with her teenage niece in the summer of 1844. The road between Lausanne and Chamonix, traversed in a small carriage, was 'tremendous for a carriage of any sort' after Servoz, but saw plenty of traffic: 'the first evening we were at Chamouni 24 chars arrived, and the second 20'. The village was full of visitors on 20 August, and both beds and mountain guides were hard to find: 'Not only were the Hotels full, but every bed to be had in the village was occupied. There were 160 with us at the "(Hotel de l')Union"'. Miss Wilkinson was alert to the beauties of her surroundings, offering extended descriptions of views, mountains and cascades, together with the late summer flowers and berries; and she commented critically on her young companion's commonplace preference for the picturesque ahead of scenery of more complexity and magnificence. This was, of course, before Ruskin's writings could have affected the ladies' perceptions and vocabulary; but Miss Wilkinson did make full use of her Murray's *Handbook*, referring her readers at home to its pages for supporting detail that would be too tedious and lacking in originality to write down. A good deal of the text was taken up with family matters, questions of health, the discomforts and incidents of the journey, the behaviour and eccentricities of people encountered *en route*, and the content and quality of the sermons that were regularly sampled along the way (Heafford, 2008: iv, 72–74). But these conventional concerns stopped well short of the bovine behaviour of English tourists sailing along the Rhine, as satirised by Thackeray in 1850: 'Everybody looks at the ruins of Wigginstein – you are told in Murray to look at Wigginstein ... (the Rhine), who does not know it? How you see people asleep in the cabins at all the most picturesque parts, and angry to be awakened when they fire off those stupid guns for the echoes!' ('Titmarsh', 1850: 41–43).

For many (and probably most) Alpine tourists, Ruskin remained invisible or in the background even after the publication of Volume 4 of *Modern Painters* in 1856. Sightseers, and indeed walkers, sought sociable enjoyment as much as spiritual awakening as they shared the collective gaze at, and the expected experience of (for example) sunrise on the Rigi, as painted by Turner and praised by Ruskin, from the large inn that now occupied the summit. The Rev. Harry Jones, in his *The Regular Swiss Round*, published in book form in 1865, represented himself thus: 'I write merely as a common tourist, who brought no science to bear upon glaciers and lake dwellings, but walked the "Regular Swiss Round" for their recreation, unencumbered by any pressing desire to improve his own mind or that of his fellow creatures'. He regarded Albert Smith as the discoverer of Chamonix as a tourism venue, without endorsing either his enterprise or its consequences: 'Chamouni has been public property ever since poor Albert Smith established his entertainment. It has been described, re-described, and panorama'ed till every one has a tolerably familiar second-hand acquaintance with it ... to me there is something in the bustle and civilization of Chamouni itself, which takes off the edge of Alpine sensations. Instead of descending into a valley with its quiet inn and pleasant surroundings, you return after your day's work to a grand hotel, with its crowds of waiters and fine company, crinoline and kid gloves ... In fact the place itself is too much like Albert Smith's late exhibition ... much as I believe Albert Smith contributed to the fame of Chamouni, and the benefit of its innkeepers, one would have been glad if it had not smelt so strongly of the Egyptian Hall' (Jones, 1865: 28, 146–148). For all his denial of pretensions to the pursuit of intellectual stimulation or spiritual enlightenment among the mountains, Jones was dismayed by aspects of the level of commercialism and the predominance of fashion and luxury in Ruskin's old haunt; but he did not feel the need, or even imagine the relevance, of calling in a Ruskinian endorsement which would not have been appropriate to the overall tone and message of the book.

By this time Thomas Cook's tourists were already in evidence in the Alps, as railways, hotels and modern conveniences accelerated the spread of mainstream middle-class tourism, especially by the British. Cook, an enthusiast for and frequent defender of the railways which facilitated his operations and indeed made them possible (though it was astonishing how effectively he could marshal a fleet of horse-drawn *diligences* and *voitures* to bridge gaps in the system), was in no sense a Ruskinian, despite his interest in tourism as an influence for international brotherhood, the circulation of useful knowledge and the stimulation of spirituality (Brendon, 1991; Swinglehurst, 1974). His itineraries through the Alps, and elsewhere in Western Europe, generally matched Ruskin's preferred journeys, but perhaps only because these responded to the conventional inheritance of the Grand Tour. Cook was positive about the railways as a window on attractive landscapes (and feats of engineering), and enthusiastic (for example) about the opening of the Midland Railway route to Buxton through Monsal Dale, about which Ruskin's comments were famously damning. In the same issue of his *Excursionist* Cook advertised an exclusive special Swiss tour for 'Ministers' and Teachers' Vacations', a priority that encapsulated the earnest, 'improving' side of his activities. There was, of course, no inherent incompatibility here: there were many reputable and appropriate ways of pursuing knowledge, experience, understanding and excitement, and endorsing Ruskin's values and agenda was only one of the possibilities or alternatives (Thomas Cook Archives, *Cook's Excursionist*, 6 June 1863: 2, 4).

Cook's own account of his adventures with his first Alpine touring party in June 1863, under the heading 'Alpine Dreams and Realities', was datelined from '... famed Chamouny, immortalised by the histories and adventures of many an enthusiastic aspirant to the honour of having set foot on ... Mont Blanc! Is this the veritable and majestic mountain, so long pictorially and graphically set forth by the witty, the indefatigable, and the lamented Albert Smith? Is this that famous Chamouny where *Smith* met his friend *Brown* so often, and where *Jones* and *Robinson* have so frequently conspired against 'mother tongue' and murdered languages they could not articulate?' (Idem, 21 July 1863: 2). Chamonix and Mont Blanc featured prominently in all the early Cook's excursions, and on 28 August Cook returned to the idea of seeing in real life the Mont Blanc scenes presented by the 'lamented Albert Smith' and embodied in the paintings of 'Mr Beverley', the scene-painter and impresario William Roxby Beverley who had provided the backdrops for Smith's Egyptian Hall performance (Idem, 28 August 1863; Emanuel, 1921). Ruskin was not mentioned or indeed hinted at, and nor was Turner: the priority given to Beverley here is highly significant. Cook's points of reference were exclusively those of jocular, accessible popular culture as it related to Switzerland, including the erstwhile *Punch* artist Richard Doyle's much-reprinted *The Foreign Tour of Messrs Brown, Jones and Robinson*, a caricature catalogue of middle-class prejudice and misunderstanding which was first published in 1854 and by this time had become a point of household reference. Doyle also illustrated Ruskin's *The King of the Golden River* (Doyle, 1854; Engen, 1983). But Cook's main concern, understandably, was with practical questions of travel and accommodation.

In that same year of 1863, 'Miss Jemima's Swiss Journal', presented (as we saw in Chapter 2) as a record of the Cook's Alpine tour by a participant, reinforced the primacy of Albert Smith at Chamonix by drawing attention to a memorial stone in the 'little English church' to 'Chamonix's Egyptian Hall, advocate Albert Smith'. But this time Ruskin also came into the picture, alongside Wordsworth, with a long quotation on the view from the Col de Forchaz ('a pure and uninterrupted fullness of mountain characters of the highest order') and another on the view through the arches of the bishop's palace at Sion (Morrell, 1963: 27, 37–38, 41–42, 50, 58). Ruskin appeared occasionally in subsequent Cook publications: in the *Tourist Handbook* for 1874, for example, the description of the falls of Schaffhausen by 'the great word-painter, John Ruskin' follows a similar long extract from Professor Forbes; but this is one of an eclectic collection of quotations from authors as diverse as Longfellow and Rev. Harry Jones, and Ruskin does not reappear. 'Ruskin's Works' are listed among the 'works consulted and quoted', but among many others (*Cook's Tourist Handbook*, 1874: 174, 199).

Ruskin was never a prominent point of reference in the developing Thomas Cook Swiss tourism universe, despite the prominence given to favourite Ruskin haunts like Chamonix and the Falls of Giessbach on Cook's itineraries. Nor did he feature strongly in Murray's guides to Switzerland. In Swiss urban settings, Hayman uses Murray's *Handbooks* as a kind of counterpoint to Ruskin's evolving preoccupation about the damaging impact of demolition and redevelopment; and the contrast between their representations of 'progress' and 'improvement', and his laments over the loss of the distinctive character of towns like Geneva and Rheinfelden to demolition and redevelopment, is particularly striking (Hayman, 1990: 78, 119). But in other literatures of Alpine tourism Ruskin was much more in evidence by the late 19th century. Among the mountaineers, the philosopher and climber Leslie Stephen shared many of Ruskin's dislikes, referring to 'the common tourist' as an 'offensive variety of the species of primates', who did everything possible to 'cocknify ... the scenery', a development which he associated with 'Mr Cook and his tourists'. He complained particularly about a 'cockney' at St Moritz who ignored the dying beauties of a roseate sunset to discourse knowingly on the quality of the brandy, interspersing a few commonplaces on the landscape which Stephen assumed to be lifted from Murray or Baedeker. 'There are persons, I fancy, who "do" the Alps; who look upon the Lake of Lucerne as one more task ticked off from their memorandum book...'. But much more important were positive perceptions that were shared with Ruskin, as Stephen insisted on 'the imperishable majesty' of the mountains, like 'the Pyramids or a Gothic cathedral'. His book on the Alps, scenery and mountaineering, significantly entitled *The Playground of Europe*, made only occasional direct reference to Ruskin, but with respect. He was self-conscious, but unrepentant, about his own purple passages, and remarked that 'most humble writers will feel that if they try to imitate Mr Ruskin's eloquence they will pay the price ... of becoming ridiculous. It is not everyone who can with impunity compare Alps to archangels' (Stephen, 1894: 49, 102–103, 219–220, 349, 353, 366–367). This occasional passing homage, conveying an assumption that the reader is aware of Ruskin's writings and reputation, is characteristic, and illustrates the increasing difficulty of tracing the direct threads of Ruskin's influence with the passage of time. It was also Stephen who wrote that, 'The fourth volume of *Modern Painters* infected me and other early members of the Alpine Club (founded in 1857) with an enthusiasm for which we are, I hope, still grateful' (Ring, 2000: 60).

Edward Whymper, 'conqueror' of the Matterhorn and Stephen's Alpine Club colleague, subsequently provided a vehicle for bringing Ruskin closer to centre stage. He published a set of Alpine sketches with an accompanying text by Rev. S. Manning, who made a fulsome acknowledgement to Ruskin's publishers for 'permission to enrich his pages by several subsequent passages' from his works, mainly describing Swiss mountain scenes. In fact, the text was a tapestry drawn from several writers, with Dr Cheever challenging Ruskin for pre-eminence, Coleridge and Longfellow being quoted on the view of Mont Blanc from Chamonix, and Wordsworth and Byron putting in appearances (Whymper, 1891: 6, 22, 70–75, 93, 107–108). It was at these more elevated and intellectual levels, where writers sought to distance themselves from the swelling invasion of 'cockneys' and of 'common' or 'Cook's' tourists, that Ruskin's influence was most directly and sympathetically signalled; but always among a host of others. But to follow Cardinal in blaming him for the 'kitschification' of the Alps seems a step too far, given the timing of developments, the variety of influences and the ease experienced by enterprising travellers and climbers like Stephen in getting away from the beaten tourist track and the handful of honey-pots. What mattered was the transformative impact of Ruskin's perceptions of mountains on the attitude of early mountaineers; but this did not extend to any broader influence on the mainstream middle-class traffic flows that dominated the mid-Victorian development of the Swiss tourist trade, where the dominant values, in spite of social snobbery, were those exemplified by Thomas Cook.

What of Ruskin's influence on artistic and architectural tourism? Here it will again be helpful to focus primarily on a particular location with which he is strongly associated; and we move on now to examine the relationship between Ruskin and urban cultural tourism, especially through the well-documented example of Venice (Cosgrove, 1982; Norwich, 2003). It will become clear that, here and in other European (and especially North Italian) cities, Ruskin made a bigger difference to the agenda of what might be called architectural and artistic tourism than he did to the growth of Alpine tourism. In northern Italy as in the Alps, however, his writings made more difference to patterns of sightseeing within urban destinations, to what was seen and how it was perceived, and to the activities of a minority of literary and aesthetic tourists, than to the older patterns of journeys and destinations that were inherited from the Grand Tour and reinforced by the railways. But in the case of Venice he also enhanced the visibility, and attractiveness as a tourist destination, of a city which had remained on the fringes of the main Grand Tour circuit. Not that Venice had been completely unfrequented before Ruskin brought it to the forefront in the mid-19th century by publishing *The Stones of Venice*. Indeed, as Tony Tanner reminds us, 'Between Byron's time and Ruskin's, Venice had become a tourist city – as opposed to a possible stopping-off point on the

Grand Tour... The change may be most conveniently marked by the publication of the first tourist guide to Venice – Murray's *Handbook of Northern Italy*, published in 1842...' (Tanner, 1992: 75).

Miss Wilkinson, supervising a version of the Grand Tour for her niece in 1844, reached Venice shortly before her travels were curtailed by a death in the family, to find the town almost full 'for the approaching regatta'. She was enchanted by the 'indescribably pretty' maritime approach, a 'charming succession' of pictures which she 'knew before through Canaletti; he is inferior only to the reality'. She was surprised by the excellence of Venetian painters, but had more to say about the prisons and the experience of travelling by gondola (Heafford, 2008: 189–191). Miss Wilkinson describes, as do others, a city geared up to the reception of tourists, but attractive for its pretty quaintness and curiosity rather than for its artistic or architectural treasures or the lessons of its history. This was how travelling Britons saw Venice, before the impact of Ruskin's writings; and John Pemble describes a further transition after mid-century, into what might be called the 'age of Ruskin': 'Before the middle of the nineteenth century the British ... admired and described the city's canals, bridges and palaces ... (but) they did not regard its architecture as the best ... It was not until the second half of the nineteenth century that evangelical prejudice was overcome and the mental map redrawn. Venice was shifted from the frontier between civilization and barbarism to the eminence where civilization and culture intersected' (Pemble, 1995: 9–10).

This is a bold claim, and Ruskin is central to any attempt at substantiating it, not least because the overcoming of his own evangelical prejudice was part of the process. *Modern Painters* and *The Stones of Venice*, together with later works like *Mornings in Florence*, set out new, specifically artistic and architectural criteria for 'what should be seen' in the towns of northern Italy, offered new evaluations of artists, infused their interpretation with moral judgements about the nature of work and the meaning of historical change, and in the process accorded a new importance to medieval and post-medieval Venice. We shall see that many of Ruskin's texts, appraisals and judgements found their way into guide-books and tourist diaries, and helped to direct and give meaning to the 'tourist gaze'. But we need to remember that Ruskin's perceptions entered an existing literature alongside a multiplicity of alternative or supplementary viewpoints, and that the texts that reproduced or alluded to them as they informed and influenced their readers were sometimes critical, while their reception entailed a spectrum of modes of engagement, from full endorsement and acceptance of their values to passive 'reading over' and outright hostility. The balance would change with the generations and within the lifetimes of individuals (Pemble, 1987: chapter 17). The first volume of *Modern Painters* almost coincided with the publication of Charles Dickens's *Pictures from Italy*, which focused on colourful depictions of exotic social circumstances, represented Venice as if through a hazily-remembered dream of prisons, torture, gondolas, wharves and eclectic architecture, and offered lively and undemanding entertainment to the armchair tourist (Dickens, 1846: chap. 7). Ruskin was himself able to make a difference to the second edition of Murray's *Handbook for Travellers in North Italy*, when his objections to the treatment of Italian Renaissance painting in the 1842 edition led to his being invited to make extended contributions to that of 1847 (Bradley, 1987: 20). But he thus became incorporated into the tourist practice that James Bryce referred to as 'verifying their Murray', earnestly passing from one prescribed site to another, Murray in hand, inspecting what was there in the prescribed manner, and moving on to the next item (Pemble, 1987: 72). By the time of *Mornings in Florence* (beginning in 1875) Ruskin was making teasing references to Murray's tendency to refer to 'judicious restoration' where he himself saw damage and destruction, and to state the obvious when describing buildings; but he was nevertheless part of the system himself. Indeed, as we saw in Chapter 3, he brought himself into it explicitly from the mid-1870s onwards, and his little, targeted pamphlet guides to treasured places out-sold Murray by a long distance, extending the sway of Ruskin's ways of seeing in the process. Nevertheless, Ruskin's own books came to be used in a similar manner to Murray, as part of the repertoire of performative practices that came to be associated with British tourists in post-Grand Tour Europe. He was well aware of this tourist appropriation of *The Stones of Venice*, alluding to the way in which tourists carried the book around while relieving the tedium with ices, music by moonlight, paper lanterns and English newspapers (Garrett, 2001: 200; Steward, 2004).

By the 1860s and 1870s Ruskin's artistic and architectural dicta had come to be incorporated into tourist guide-books and diaries, at a more conventional and mainstream level than were his writings about the Alps. They were used selectively: in Thomas Cook's 1875 *Handbook*, for example, the dominant acknowledged influences on the text for much of northern Italy came from Dickens and his fellow novelist William Dean Howells, who had been the United States consul in Venice in 1860, and Ruskin only came to the fore in the long section on what to do and see in Venice itself. After Venice, the main source of quotations reverted to Dickens (Thomas Cook Archives, *Handbook*, 1875). Howells himself, in his *Venetian Life*, reinforced Ruskin's exposure of the adventitious nature of 'that Venice of modern fiction and drama', of the Bridge of Sighs and the Rialto, quoting *The Stones of Venice* for that purpose; but he was also well aware of Ruskin's defects. He was 'undoubtedly the best guide you can have in your study of the Venetian painters'; but the reader was left in 'confusion and ignominy' by the contradictory lack of clarity of his 'theories and egotisms'. Howells also leaves the reader in no doubt that no-one who associated with the Austrians in the Venice of the last years of imperial rule could be acceptable in local society, thereby implicitly undermining any credibility Ruskin might have sought as a commentator on the current state and conventions of Venetian society; but this was, after all, not his goal (Howells, 1867: 13, 155). In this Thomas Cook publication Ruskin also shared his billing as historian of Venice with Edmund Flagg (another former United States consul in the city), although the latter's chosen remit covered only the period from 1797 to 1849 (Flagg, 1853).

Even so, Ruskin dominated Thomas Cook's representation of Venice in the mid-1870s, and indeed afterwards. *The Stones of Venice* was the key text, quoted extensively (though not always acknowledged) on Venetian history, on the Hall of the Grand Council and Tintoretto's 'Glory of Paradise', the Hall of the Senate, the interior of San Marco, and the Scuola di San Rocco, among others. But his verdicts were not always unchallenged, directly or implicitly: 'Ruskin speaks of this (Tintoretto's 'The Glory of Paradise') as ... "the most precious thing that Venice possesses", but tastes differ materially on this point...'; 'Ruskin rather exhausts himself in calling it "intolerable in affectation, ridiculous in conception", and so on'; 'Mr Ruskin objects to this monument on various grounds, too lengthy to quote'; 'The art student will inspect them all (the Tintoretto paintings in the Scuola di San Rocco) with diligence (and some amount of disappointment) and will then read with intense interest the glowing description given in *The Stones of Venice*...' (Thomas Cook Archives, *Handbook*, 1875: 118, 127–128, 132, 146, 150, 174). A quarter of a century later the equivalent publication for 1899 had amplified some references to frescoes and the Spanish Chapel in Florence, in recognition of Ruskin's *Mornings in Florence*, while the numerous Ruskin references in the Venice section remained intact (Thomas Cook Archives, *Handbook*, 1899: 314, 330).

Some of the holiday journals which are lodged in the Thomas Cook archives make reference to Ruskin in revealing ways. George Couch Heard, narrating his three weeks in Switzerland and North Italy in September 1865, pays extended attention to Venice, and alludes to the difficulty of summarising his reading of *The Stones of Venice*, which is reserved for an attenuated appendix. He remarks that, 'Everybody is supposed to know about the "Rise and Fall" of Venice, whereas scarcely any one knows anything at all about it', reinforcing ideas about the limited extent to which Ruskin might be *read* as opposed to being used as a *vade mecum*; and his own comments on what he sees do not pass far beyond lists, together with complaints about the tiring superficiality of high-pressure sightseeing (Thomas Cook Archive, *Journal of George Couch Heard*, 1865: 86–87, 183–186). Twelve years later Miss J. Furby, daughter of a Bridlington bookseller and stationer, quoted *The Stones of Venice* alongside works by (for example) Dickens, Shelley and Byron in a lengthy sightseeing diary of a 'trip to Switzerland and Italy' under Cook's auspices, but without using Ruskin as more than a supplier of occasional bursts of second-hand eloquence, a role he must often have played (Thomas Cook Archive, Diary of Miss J. Furby, 1877: 12, 23).

Recognition of Ruskin as a necessary authority on the historic buildings and art treasures of northern Italy, as someone who should be quoted and who was worthy of directing the gaze, was thus evident among Thomas Cook's customers, and presumably among a broader middle-class constituency, from the 1860s onwards. Some publications, like the American artist Joseph Pennell's *Venice: City of the Sea*, went further, emphasizing in this case that the text that accompanied the illustrations was drawn from Ruskin's writings, along with others (Pennell, *c*. 1903). Others, like Murray's *Knapsack Guide* to Italy, made no mention of Ruskin, confining themselves to topographical description without any overt aesthetic or historical judgements (*Knapsack Guide*, 1864). If the frequency of new printings of *The Stones of Venice* is indicative, his influence on the reading public was at its peak between 1885 and 1907, when the longest gap in the British Library record covers the three years 1895–1897, and only three other years are missing. Two more printings are visible in 1911 and 1912, after which there are isolated reprints in 1921 and 1925, and this record then falls silent for several decades. The availability of small format, cheaper editions, and of 'selections', contributed to this process, including the significant combination (in 1879) of introductory chapters and local indices for the use of 'travellers' in Venice which was part of his programme of outreach to the mainstream guidebook-using travelling public, as discussed in Chapter 3. But the extent to which this late Victorian and Edwardian proliferation of new editions and printings was used by tourists, as opposed to domestic readers in pursuit of cultural enhancement and moral enlightenment, must remain unclear.

Ruskin's influence on 'mainstream' middle-class continental tourism peaked earlier than the acknowledged contributions to 'alternative' popular tourism which are discussed in the next chapter. By the Edwardian years he was already disappearing from new guidebooks to Italy's landscapes, towns, architecture, and art treasures, as new generations of writers occupied his territory. The established popular travel writer Douglas Sladen made no mention of his work or influence in *How to See Italy* (1912). Its immediate precursor in the same series, Paul Konody's *Through the Alps to the Apennines*, was a hymn of praise to the joys of road travel (in this case by steam-powered car) and the new vistas and neglected architectural gems it opened out, despite the hazards of punctures and interested spectators. Konody acknowledged the continuing dominance of the 'commands of Baedeker and Murray' in Siena (while using Baedeker himself to smooth his path through Florence), and commented that Assisi was 'simply swarming with lady artists'; but his architectural and artistic agenda was at variance with Ruskin's, and the nearest he came to a display of fellow-feeling was an attack on a party of fellow British motorists for rushing from Florence to Rome in a day, through lovely country and countless places of historic and artistic interest, 'at a speed which debars you from using your eyes'. But this was a far cry from preferring the closer 'feel' of landscape and countryside that went with the slower pace of horse-drawn or pedestrian travel; and Konody, like Sladen, makes no allusion at all to Ruskin or his work (Konody, 1911: 156, 195, 276; Sladen, 1912).

This was a generational change, which gathered momentum after the First World War. Pemble suggests that in the 1920s, 'Ruskin was still read by the Anglo-Saxon travelling public, and was even revered among the elderly; but he lost his influence and prestige among those of the younger generation who took themselves seriously as intellectuals' (Pemble, 1995: 189). Pre-war publications like those of Konody and Sladen suggest that this process began earlier, and was not confined to *soi-disant* intellectuals: it was a more general trend among those strata of mainstream conventional tourists for whom Ruskin had perhaps always been a voice to be conciliated by lip service or passing acknowledgement rather than to be recognised as a mentor at deeper levels of commitment. The drying up of new editions and printings of Ruskin's work during and after the First World War is indicative of more than just the saturation of the market. But, in this expansive sector of Victorian and Edwardian tourism, its influence had been pervasive (though often superficial) for half a century.

Ruskin also played his part in the revaluation of old buildings more generally, with additional implications for the varieties of 'tourist gaze'. He had to address the twin threats of decay and decomposition through the continued neglect of fabrics and frescoes, and of the kind of modernising 'restoration' that scraped the textures of time from stonework and, at its worst, re-created buildings in an idealised, but inauthentic, historic image. His interventions in Venice, as he enlisted sympathetic local help to modify the restoration of San Marco as part of more general campaigns against unsympathetic modernisation in all its forms, were making a difference by the late 1870s. The distinctive aesthetic that embraced the visible workings of time, age and even neglect was not of course Ruskinian in itself, growing as it did out of the Romantic movement to which Ruskin became harnessed; but he made his own contributions to this rhetoric and sensibility (Pemble, 1995: 134–135, 174–175). Dismay or at least disquiet at the loss of quaint, historic urban areas to 19th-century 'improvement' was far from being peculiar to Ruskin, of course: as prosaic an observer as 'Arthur Sketchley' in 1870 might show awareness of the problems associated with 'progress' in Dieppe and Rouen, where 'one of the most picturesque places in France' was 'fast assuming the style and tone of a thriving manufacturing town, which ... will not enhance its value as a place of sojourn to the antiquarian or the ecclesiologist who sigh at the recollection of its quaint gables and narrow streets, now passed away and gone' ('Sketchley', 1870: 22, 24).

Similar sentiments were being expressed in late Victorian England, of course, as applied to urban vernacular as well as ecclesiastical and 'polite' architecture; but it is impossible to tease out (for example) a distinctive Ruskinian contribution to the growing attachment to old fishing ports and harbours that developed in conjunction with artistic colonies, and generated a new kind of middle-class tourist demand, from Staithes in North Yorkshire to St Ives in Cornwall and beyond. His contribution to *The Harbours of England* in 1856 makes it tempting to try, not least because this textual commentary on etchings taken from Turner was also reissued so often in the late Victorian and Edwardian years; but this was more than just a British development, and here Ruskin's sentiments were part of a much broader flow (Crouch & Lubbren, 2003: chapters 5–7; Ousby, 1990; Ruskin, 1856; Walton, 2008).

Even in the particularly tempting case of the English Lake District, it is hard to make the case for Ruskin as a definer of destinations or a regenerator of the tourist gaze. Here, far more so than in Venice or the Alps, he was the heir to pre-emptive traditions: Wordsworth, in particular, had already conducted most of the creative work in rendering sacred this particular literary landscape. Ruskin's contributions to campaigns against the extension of railways, in association with mining and the sort of tourists who would not appreciate what they ought to be seeing and experiencing, were forceful and histrionic, and he provided ammunition and moral support for the landscape protection organisations of the 1880s onwards in which his disciple Canon Rawnsley played a formative, if ill-disciplined, role; but even in the days of the National Trust he was never to define 'what was to be seen' or even how to see it (Marshall & Walton, 1981: chapters 8–9; Walton, 1998; Walton & O'Neill, 2004). This point is driven home when we look at the role of Brantwood as a tourist destination in Chapter 7. The analysis in the present chapter suggests that Ruskin's greatest contribution to 'mainstream' middle-class tourism lay at the international level, and more obviously in northern Italy (especially Venice) than in the Alps. But this was far from being the whole story; and in the next chapter we investigate the extent and nature of Ruskinian influences on 'popular' tourism, especially in the late 19th and early 20th century.

References

Altick, R. (1978) *The Shows of London*. Harvard: Belknap Press.
Barton, S. (2008) *Healthy Living in the Alps: The Origins of Winter Tourism in Switzerland, 1860–1914*. Manchester: Manchester University Press.
Berghoff, H., Korte, B., Schneider, R. and Harvie, C. (eds) (2002) *The Making of Modern Tourism: The Cultural History of the British Experience, 1600–2000*. Basingstoke: Palgrave.
Bevin, D. (2009) The struggle for ascendancy: John Ruskin, Albert Smith and the Alpine aesthetic. PhD thesis, University of Exeter.

Black, J. (2003) *The British Abroad: The Grand Tour in the Eighteenth Century*. Stroud: Sutton.

Bradley, A. (1987) *Ruskin and Italy*. Ann Arbor: UMI Research Press.

Brendon, P. (1991) *Thomas Cook: 150 Years of Popular Tourism*. London: Secker and Warburg.

Burford, R. (1849) *Description of a View Taken from the Summit of Mount Righi*. London: T. Brettell, painter.

Butler, R.W. (ed.) (2005) *The Tourist Area Life Cycle: Applications and Modifications* (Vol. 1). Clevedon: Channel View.

Buzard, J. (1993) *The Beaten Track*. Oxford: Clarendon.

Cardinal, R. (2007) Ruskin and the Alpine ideal. In C. Casaliggi and P. March-Russell (eds) *Ruskin in Perspective* (pp. 157–176). Newcastle: Cambridge Scholars Press.

Chamberlain, C. (2007) 'Mont Blanc montage', *Cabinet* 27, Fall. On WWW at http://www.cabinetmagazine.org/issue/27chamberlain.php. Accessed 20.04.09.

Chaney, E. (1998) *The Evolution of the Grand Tour*. London: Frank Cass.

Colley, A.C. (2009) John Ruskin: Climbing and the vulnerable eye. *Victorian Literature and Culture* 37, 43–66.

Cook's Tourist Handbook to Switzerland, via Paris (1874) London: Thos. Cook and Son & Hodder and Stoughton.

Cosgrove, D. (1982) The myth and the stones of Venice. *Journal of Historical Geography* 8, 145–169.

Crook, J.M. (2003) Ruskin and the railway. In J. Simmons, A.K.B. Evans and J. Gough (eds) *The Impact of the Railway in Britain* (pp. 129–134). Aldershot: Ashgate.

Crouch, D. and Lubbren, N. (2003) *Visual Culture and Tourism*. Oxford: Berg.

Dickens, C. (1846) *Pictures from Italy*. London: Bradbury and Evans (also published in Paris and Leipzig in the same year).

Doyle, R. (1854) *The Foreign Tour of Messrs Jones*. London: Brown and Robinson.

Emanuel, F.L. (1921) *William Roxby Beverley*. London: Walker's Quarterly.

Engen, R.K. (1983) *Richard Doyle*. Stroud: Catalpa Press.

Flagg, E. (1853) *Venice: The City of the Sea*. New York: Charles Scribner.

Freeman, M. (1999) *Railways and the Victorian Imagination*. New Haven, CT: Yale University Press.

Garrett, M. (2001) *Venice*. Oxford: Signal.

Hand-Book for Travellers in Switzerland (1852) London: John Murray.

Hanley, K. (2007) *John Ruskin's Northern Tours, 1837–1838*. Lampeter: Edwin Mellen Press.

Hansen, P.H. (1995) Albert Smith, the Alpine Club, and the invention of mountaineering in mid-Victorian Britain. *Journal of British Studies* 34, 300–324.

Hayman, J. (1990) *John Ruskin and Switzerland*. Waterloo, Ontario: Wilfrid Laurier University Press.

Heafford, M. (2006) Between grand tour and age of tourism: British travellers to Switzerland in an age of transition, 1814–1860. *Journal of Transport History* 27, 25–47.

Heafford, M. (2008) *Two Victorian Ladies on the Continent*. Cambridge: Postillion Books.

Hewison, R. (1976) *John Ruskin: The Argument of the Eye*. London: Thames and Hudson.

Hewison, R. (2004) 'Ruskin, John (1819–1900)', *Oxford Dictionary of National Biography*. Oxford: Oxford University Press.

Hilton, T. (2002) *John Ruskin*. New Haven, CT: Yale University Press.

Howells, W.D. (1867) *Venetian Life* (2nd edn). New York: Hurd and Houghton.

Jones, Rev. H. (1865) *The Regular Swiss Round*. London: Alexander Strachan.

Knapsack Guide for Travellers to Italy (1864) London: John Murray.

Konody, P.G. (1911) *Through the Alps to the Apennines*. London: Kegan Paul.

Koshar, R. (2000) *German Travel Cultures*. Oxford: Berg.

Lee, S-S. (1999) "Indistinctness" in J.M.W. Turner's paintings of steam power. *Intergrams: Studies in Languages and Literature* 1. On WWW at http://benz.nchu. edu. Accessed 18.04.09.

Marshall, J.D. and Walton, J.K. (1981) *The Lake Counties from 1830 to the Mid-Twentieth Century*. Manchester: Manchester University Press.

Meynell, A. (1900) *John Ruskin*. Edinburgh: Blackwood.

Morrell, J. (1963) *Miss Jemima's Swiss Journal*. London: Putnam and Co. for Thomas Cook and Son.

Murray, J. (1904) *A Handbook for Travellers in Switzerland* (19th edn). London: Edward Stanford.

Nicolson, M.H. (1959) *Mountain Gloom and Mountain Glory*. Ithaca: Cornell University Press.

Norwich, J.J. (2003) *Paradise of Cities: Venice in the Nineteenth Century*. New York: Doubleday.

Ousby, I. (1990) *The Englishman's England: Taste, Travel and the Rise of Tourism*. Cambridge: Cambridge University Press.

Pemble, J. (1987) *The Mediterranean Passion*. Oxford: Clarendon Press.

Pemble, J. (1995) *Venice Rediscovered*. Oxford: Clarendon Press.

Pennell, J. (n.d., c. 1903) *Venice: The City of the Sea*. London: T.N. Fouls.

Ring, J. (2000) *How the English made the Alps*. London: John Murray.

Ruskin, J. (1856) *The Harbours of England*. London: Gambat and Co.

Schivelbusch, W. (1986) *The Railway Journey* (2nd edn). Leamington Spa: Berg.

'Sketchley, A.' (pseudonym of G. Rose) (1870) *Out for a Holiday with Cook's Excursion through Switzerland and Italy*. London: George Routledge.

Sladen, D. (1912) *How to See Italy by Rail*. London: Kegan Paul.

Stephen, L. (1894, first published in 1871) *The Playground of Europe*. London: Longman, Green and Co.

Steward, J. (2004) Performing abroad: British tourists in Italy and their practices, 1840–1914. In D. Medina Lasansky and B. McLaren (eds) *Architecture, Performance and Space* (pp. 73–93). Oxford: Berg.

Swinglehurst, E. (1974) *The Romantic Journey: The Story of Thomas Cook and Victorian Travel*. London: Pica Editions.

Tanner, T. (1992) *Venice Desired*. Oxford: Blackwell.

Thomas Cook Archive (1863) *Cook's Excursionist and International Tourist Advertiser*, Peterborough.

Thomas Cook Archive (1865) *Typescript Journal of George Couch Heard*. Peterborough.

Thomas Cook Archive (1875 and 1899) *Cook's Tourist Handbook for Northern Italy*. Peterborough.

Thomas Cook Archive (1877) *Diary of Miss J. Furby*. Peterborough.

Tissot, L. (2001) *Naissance d'une Industrie Touristique: Les Anglais et la Suisse au XIX Siecle*. Lausanne: Payot.

Titmarsh, M.A. (pseudonym of W.M. Thackeray) (1850) *The Kickleburys on the Rhine*. London: Smith, Elder.

Urry, J. (1995) *Consuming Places*. London: Sage.

Walton, J.K. (1998) Canon Rawnsley and the English lake district. *Armitt Library Journal* 1, 1–17.

Walton, J.K. (2005) Power, speed and glamour: The naming of express steam loco-motives in inter-war Britain. *Journal of Transport History*, third series 26, 1–19.

Walton, J.K. (2008) Whitby: Une station balnéaire, du XVIIIe au XXe siecle. In Y. Perret-Gentil, A. Lottin and J-P. Poussu (eds) *Les villes balnéaires d'Europe occidentale du XVIIIe siecle a nos jours* (pp. 233–259). Paris: Presses de l'Université Paris-Sorbonne.

Walton, J.K. and O'Neill, C. (2004) Tourism and the lake district: Social and cul-tural histories. In D.W.G. Hind and J.P. Mitchell (eds) *Sustainable Tourism in the English Lake District* (pp. 19–47). Sunderland: Business Education Publishers.

Whymper, E. (1891) *Swiss Pictures drawn with Pen and Pencil*. London: The Religious Tract Society.

Withey, L. (1997) *Grand Tours and Cook's Tours*. New York: Morrow.

Chapter 6
Ruskin and Popular Tourism

As Ruskin's writings extended their reach to wider reading publics among the lower middle and working classes, whether directly (especially through cheap editions) or through various mediations, between the 1870s and the First World War (Cockram, 2007: Chaps 4 and 7; Goldman, 1999; Waller, 2006: 218–219), they exerted both positive and negative influences on the concurrent rapid development of 'popular' and working-class tourism markets. On the one hand, Ruskin's demanding assumptions about the necessary degree of leisure, time and appropriate knowledge and understanding for the satisfactory carrying out of the role of cultural tourist could easily be adapted for snobbish, exclusive purposes, and directed scornfully against the 'Cook's tourists' who rushed industriously to take in every possible site, guidebook in hand. (Brendon, 1991; Fraser Rae, 1891) Ruskin's ambiguous attitudes to culture, democracy and popular tourism set standards that were very difficult to meet. His views on the idea of the public museum, as an 'example of perfect order and perfect elegance to the disorderly and rude populace', are symptomatic of his expectations of popular tourism (Lowenthal, 2009: 21). On the other hand, just as the geographical distribution of suitable tourist destinations within the Ruskin canon was limited even in European or Mediterranean terms, so the development of large popular resorts specialising in 'mass entertainment' was and remained beyond the pale (Berghoff *et al.*, 2002; Cross & Walton, 2005; Gray, 2006; Toulmin, 2006; Walton, 1983).

These rapidly developing phenomena of the later 19th century, especially in England, constituted the 'wrong' kind of democracy of taste; and Ruskin's articulate followers, transmitting his doctrines to wider publics as part of a more extensive mix of proposals for cultural and moral improvement through landscape, architecture, art and high moral purpose, were forceful in their condemnation of high-pressure commercial resorts such as Blackpool and Brighton, and in their advocacy of the alternative virtues of the upland walking tour or the tranquil, picturesque fishing village. They were not alone in this, however, and we shall see that opposition to the development of the popular commercial seaside holiday system, the orthodoxies of pier and promenade, boarding-house and bathing-machine, pierrots and variety programmes, came from a variety of sources. In some cases these were close to Ruskin's values, and direct genealogies of influence can be traced; in others the dominant attitudes were more strongly influenced by radical protestant Nonconformity, by various tendencies within late Victorian and Edwardian socialism (in which Ruskin's ideas were sometimes mediated through the influence of William Morris or Edward Carpenter), and by an emergent 'outdoor movement' which campaigned for access to uplands, brought together both these strands, and sometimes (as in the case of the Manchester and Sheffield ramblers' organisations and the 'Dark Peak' of Derbyshire) transcended them by espousing an alternative aesthetic of moorland wilderness that prioritised physical interaction with as well as contemplation of bleak expanses of heather, bog and rocky outcrop (Darby, 2000; Hollett, 2002; Readman, 2001; Taylor, 1997; Tebbutt, 2006).

This chapter teases out the influence of Ruskin, as always among other related influences, on the late Victorian and Edwardian (and subsequent) development of those strands of popular tourism that rejected or reacted uneasily towards the development of the conventional commercial holiday industry of Victorian and Edwardian Britain, especially the popular seaside resort. The 'outdoor movement' of this period, heavily influenced at organisational level by a reformist mix of ethical socialism, romantic Nonconformity and advocacy of closeness to Nature and the virtues of the simple life, constituted an articulate body of opinion which sought to 'reform' the holiday habits of the 'toiling masses' away from commercial consumerism and packaged entertainment (Taylor, 1997; Waters, 1990). Some of its members, like the Lancashire romantic socialist writers Allen Clarke and Arthur Laycock, eventually moved across into celebrating the democratic participatory vigour of the popular seaside holiday (Walton, 2007) but this was a minority perception, and its votaries had never been among Ruskin's overt followers. In practice, most holiday guides and diaries found room for a mixture of perspectives and enjoyments, and the 'outdoor movement' always found room for a mixture of the athletic and the aesthetic in which 'hearty' aspects of the former often predominated, sometimes to the dismay of the more serious-minded of the organisers and participants. The bicycle was an ambiguous piece of accessible technology from the late 19th century onwards, allowing both individual self-expression (together with new freedoms from surveillance for women) and collective camaraderie, and letting some find new locations for tranquil contemplation while enabling others to use rural roads as adventure playgrounds for trials of strength, speed and endurance through competitive 'scorching' (McGurn, 1987; Pye, 1995; Rubinstein, 1977). We shall use a detailed analysis of the archives, publications and activities of organisations at the core of the 'outdoor movement', especially the Co-operative

Holidays Association, to gauge the extent of overt and indirect Ruskinian influences on the values that were propagated, alongside an investigation of Ruskin's role in the development of campaigns for the safeguarding of the 'natural beauty' of the Lake District, and his influence on the foundation and early work of the National Trust. An examination of the sharp and sudden decline of direct Ruskinian allusion in this culture at the end of the First World War, and the changing nature of the 'outdoor movement' during the 1920s and 1930s, will conclude the chapter.

Ruskin was one of the influences on the development of a popular late Victorian and Edwardian 'outdoor movement'; but even where his fingerprints can be identified on the ideas, perceptions and activities of some of the relevant organisations and participating individuals, they always operated in combination or conjunction with other philosophies, and in some of the liveliest strands his direct input is invisible. The secular strands of romantic socialism, with their recreational offshoots into self-organized and relatively uncommodified rural tourism, were at one remove from Ruskin's influence, although that of Morris's *News from Nowhere* would bear detailed inspection. An initial investigation of the Clarion rambling and cycling clubs, which operated (initially, at least) under the umbrella of the newspaper of that name and the tutelage of the charismatic journalist Robert Blatchford, finds little or no direct input from Ruskin's writings. The Clarion Cycling Clubs, in particular, founded in Birmingham in late 1894 and soon extending across England, aimed at spreading socialist ideas in rural areas while developing, expanding and entertaining a committed membership drawn from the urban working (and, in practice, lower middle) class. This was popular tourism with a strongly political, sociable and communtarian bent, organised around the voluntary distribution of the *Clarion*, which was founded by Blatchford in December 1891 after he was dismissed by the Manchester newspaper proprietor Edward Hulton for writing socialist propaganda in his *Sunday Chronicle*, and soon became firmly based in the city. By 1908 the *Clarion* had achieved a circulation of 80,000, and the cycling and rambling clubs had been augmented by a well-supported choral section. Blatchford's socialism was humanitarian and ethical, secular in tone, and influenced by Ruskin's disciple (in some senses) William Morris as well as by the Marxist-oriented H.M. Hyndman, but it by-passed Ruskin's aesthetic and conservationist concerns, and its educational interests were not his. Blatchford's message included a strong strain of English patriotism, of which the celebration of the beauties of the English countryside formed part; but this was always inflected through his military background. It increasingly shaded over in the early 20th century into jingoism and eventually into assertive support for British involvement in the First World War, a stance that divided the movement and weakened it fatally in the long run (Prynn, 1976; Pye, 1995). Where the broader Clarion movement did link up directly with Ruskin was through the Clarion Field Club, which looked outwards to other socialist and Co-operative organisations, encouraged the detailed study of geology and natural history, and promoted the virtues of fresh air and the moral superiority of the countryside over the town. Its founder, Bellerby (Harry) Lowerison, has been described as 'son of a Durham miner and disciple of Ruskin and Morris' (Taylor, 1997: 107). He was an early member of the Fabian Society, serving on the national executive during 1891–1892, a friend of H.M. Hyndman, and the proprietor of the Ruskin School at Hunstanton and Heacham in Norfolk from the start of the 20th century; and he also contributed an article on Whitby to *Comradeship* in 1911 (*Comradeship*, April 1911: 80; Manton, 1997). Despite such occasional links, however, the Clarion movement drew people together in a common attachment to fresh air, exercise and countryside, but in a comradely, informal, physical, gregarious, jocular, buttonholing idiom that was alien to Ruskin's mode of presentation. As Taylor points out, 'A drink and a smoke were part of the convivial atmosphere of the Clarion fellowship'. So was communal singing late at night (Taylor, 1997: 228).

The limited extent of Ruskin's influence on this powerful ethical socialist movement, with its strong elements of participatory popular rural tourism, is underlined by the lack of references to his work or ideas during the *Clarion*'s first year of publication. An early discussion of 'Venice in London', featuring an author's sounding-board character called Tintoretto, focuses solely on the spectacular exhibition of that name at Olympia, with its gondolas, masquerade, mock naval battle and catering by Lyons. Theatre coverage, pantomime reviews, a 'Parisiana' section (edited by 'Flaneur') and commentary on northern rugby football added up to a determined attempt to capture an audience by providing entertainment alongside (for example) support for the guards of the Manchester, Sheffield and Lincolnshire Railway in their pursuit of shorter working hours, a concern that might well have appealed to Ruskin without ever being peculiarly his own (*Clarion*, 19 December 1891, 2 and 9 January 1892). Summer commentary on popular holidays and excursions included an idiosyncratic and broadly celebratory account of a trip by sailing vessel down the River Weaver, past salt and chemical works, to join the Manchester Ship Canal and reach the commercial entertainments of Eastham on the Cheshire side of the Mersey, alongside a denunciation of the crowded, regimented experience of railway excursions to the seaside at August Bank Holiday (*Clarion*, 23 April 1892, 6 August 1892). The only extended reference to Ruskin himself was taken from an interview with Tolstoy in the *Cornhill Magazine*, in which the Count 'expressed his surprise that English public opinion did not accord Ruskin his proper place as one of the greatest men of the age in any country ... a much greater man than Gladstone...' (*Clarion*, 28 May 1892). But there was no follow-up to this, and no discussion of any possible relationship, positive or negative, between Ruskin's ideas and the preferred excursion and holiday practices of the paper's contributors. Blatchford himself, under his pseudonym 'Nunquam', had more to say in praise of Walt Whitman and Edward Carpenter, with favourable commentary on the latter's *Towards Democracy* but an erroneous reference to Whitman's *Blades of Grass* which hinted at a lack of genuine familiarity with the work of the American poet. Ruskin was, of course, an influence on Carpenter; but one of many (*Clarion*, 16 April 1892). Blatchford did eventually acknowledge Ruskin's importance in an obituary in the *Clarion*: 'Ruskin's genius has become part of the national thought, his high ethical ideals have entered into and coloured the national conscience... The nation has learned his lesson, has assimilated his gospel, although we do not always repeat his words between quotation marks' (Cockram, 2007: 194). Blatchford here drew attention to a key general problem in tracing Ruskin's influence, especially with the passage of time; but his praise, though fulsome, did not connect at all specifically with the *Clarion*'s main agenda.

These were, indeed, more powerful influences on those areas where romantic, ethical socialism met the ramblers, cyclists and celebrants of rural landscape and countryside of the emergent 'outdoor movement'. The Bolton socialists, ramblers, cyclists and campaigners for access to moorland, who are examined in Paul Salveson's writings on this distinctive and enduring group, were much more interested in Whitman and Carpenter than in Ruskin, and in local landscapes and nature rather than the 'high culture' landscapes, validated by art and literature, of the Lake District or parts of the Yorkshire Dales, which were out of reach for everyday purposes. Some of them were, perhaps, the heirs of the self-taught working-class naturalists, geologists, herb-gatherers and 'weaver botanists' who had enjoyed and used the rural environs of the 'cotton towns' since the early Industrial Revolution (Percy, 1991; Taylor, 1995). The early Bolton socialist and dialect writer Allen Clarke ('Teddy Ashton'), who was also an early *Clarion* contributor (and originally a fierce critic of the high-pressure, ultra-commercial Blackpool model of holidaymaking), seems to have derived his celebratory attachment to the moorlands and informal countryside of Rivington Pike and the Lancashire Fylde from these sources; and his celebration of 'the fair places of steam-engine land', and of 'rambles in a rural, old-fashioned country, with chat about its history and romance', emphasized a focus on popular histories and traditions, and on homely, accessible places (Clarke, 1916, 1920; Salveson, 2009). These are not really Ruskinian landscapes, except in the restrictive sense that he preferred most working-class people to enjoy the countryside on their doorstep, as suggested by Dorothy Wordsworth's comment that all they needed was a 'green field with buttercups', rather than to invade the sacred precincts of the Lake District by excursion train (Taylor, 1995: 25). They are either too commonplace or, where moorland is at issue, too lacking in the conventional 'sublime', the picturesque or the associations with Turner's painting or Wordsworth's writing that hallowed other settings. The same applied to the Dark Peak, that haunt of 'Manchester ramblers' and their Sheffield counterparts, which became the site of better-known conflicts over access to uplands than the late Victorian ones that focused on the uplands at the back of the Lancashire 'cotton towns' (Salveson, 1996, 2008; Stephenson, 1989; Taylor, 1997; Tebbutt, 2006). The appeal to the 'old-fashioned' and unpretentious, with its concern for legend rather than history, the local rather than the national, and the enjoyment of superstitions and stories (ghosts and boggarts, dialect stories and the celebration of 'characters') fits in with a more generalised desire to hark back to 'the good old times', as discussed by Bann and Mandler, than can be distilled from Ruskin. Patrick Joyce, who offers useful commentary on such themes in late Victorian and Edwardian Lancashire, significantly makes only the most limited and indirect connections between this culture and the ideas of Ruskin (Joyce, 1991: chapters 6–7 and 40, 77). Strong elements of these values can certainly be found in Ruskin's writings, but on a wider canvas: the widely felt attachment to the romantic appeal to the palimpsest and patina of the past as expressed through mossy stones and weathered walls has particularly powerful Ruskinian resonances, especially when we take into account the formative influences of Sir Walter Scott's romantic historical novels on Ruskin himself (Chandler, 1970; Durie, 2003, 2006) In this case they seem to be mediated through William Morris, and a range of less 'political' and more independent influences, including the historical novelist Harrison Ainsworth and a long tradition of Lancashire dialect and antiquarian writing (Bann, 1990; Carver, 2003; Deacon, 2001; Mandler, 1999).

Ruskin's direct influence was, then, often hard to tease out even among the working-class apostles of alternative, healthy, improving holidaymaking as an alternative to the crowded, brash, commercial popular seaside resorts which were consolidating their hold on working-class imagination and aspiration towards the end of the 19th century. The suffrage campaigner and trade union organiser Ada Nield Chew, writing her personal experience as thinly disguised fiction in 1913, cannot have been alone in enjoying Devonshire coastal scenery as 'something the exact opposite of an industrial town', with an 'ever-changing panorama of sea, sky, rocks and tree-clad hills'; and she imputed 'a keen sense of beauty' to her working-class Lancashire protagonists, who had made the long journey from industrial Lancashire at the Wakes holidays in search of novelty and beauty, without necessarily rejecting the Blackpool alternative ('We can have a weekend in Blackpool any time'). But all this was presented as a matter of 'common sense', without entanglement with the ideas of any 'great thinkers'; and this must have been how many people saw it. Chew read widely, but her preferred authors were Arnold Bennett and George

Bernard Shaw (Chew, 1982: 188–189, 213). But there were important elements of the working class, in Lancashire and elsewhere, among whom the influence of overtly Ruskinian values on lifestyle choices, including holiday travel and arrangements, was already gaining ground by the 1890s. Where such developments took organised form, they tended to be associated more with advanced or 'new' Liberalism than with socialism or the labour movement as such, and to be more identified with politically reformist wings of Nonconformity or, sometimes, the Church of England than with organisations of a more secular bent like the Social Democratic Federation or, as we have seen, the *Clarion* movement (Taylor, 1997). They had more affinities with the Independent Labour Party, which might harbour its own cycling or rambling groups, although we should remember that there was always common ground at grassroots level between all of these organisations (Eagles, 2007: 95; Howell, 1983).

The Co-operative Holidays Association (CHA), in its origins an off-shoot of the National Home Reading Union (NHRU), provides a particularly clear example, which has not attracted the attention it deserves from scholars working in this field. It does not feature, for example, in Jonathan Rose's generally impressive *The Intellectual Life of the British Working Classes*, which misses out on the theme of holidays and tourism while giving Ruskin his due as an influence on the culture of the serious-minded working classes more generally (Rose, 2001). Patrick Joyce also ignores it, and Susan Barton, in her (also impressive) survey of working-class organisations and popular tourism, picks up on it as a noteworthy dimension of 'alternative' holidaymaking while missing out on the Ruskin connection and indeed the general ideological orientation of the CHA (Barton, 2005: 144–145; Joyce, 1991). The NHRU and CHA have their historians, but these aspects of the organisations' work and identity need (and deserve) to be more widely known (Leonard, 1934; Snape, 2002, 2004; Speake, 1993; Taylor, 1997). Harvey Taylor's chapter on 'Rational Holidays', in his excellent *A Claim on the Countryside*, provides the best introduction to the genesis, context and development of the CHA, despite the potentially misleading and reductive connotations of his chapter title (Taylor, 1997: chapter 6). The CHA remained a minority organisation, especially when compared with the four million visitors per year (on one calculation) who were visiting Blackpool on the eve of the First World War. It soon counted its holidaymakers in thousands, but its actual membership grew only from 268 in 1893 to 13,719 in 1911, with (according to Snape) a sudden leap to over 30,000 by 1914 (Snape, 2004; Taylor, 1997: 207; Walton, 1974: 263, Table 5.2). Its patrons, promoters and activists always lamented that it failed to reach the core working-class constituency to which its founders aspired; but as the most Ruskinian of organised holiday providers, with connections across a spectrum of related currents of thought, its significance transcends mere numbers, offering as it does a window on the intersection between leisure, holidays, unconventional religion and politics, health and the 'simple life' at the turn of the 19th and 20th centuries, and for some time afterwards.

From its foundation in 1887–88 the NHRU, with its aspirations to making stimulating reading and serious discussion available to working-class people for whom more formal further education was out of reach, was interested in encouraging the displacement of the popular seaside holiday by less expensive and more 'improving' uses of free time involving the communal sharing of fresh air, exercise, the simple pleasures of landscape and countryside, and the appreciation of history 'on the ground'. The choice of Blackpool for its summer assembly in 1889 (the first had been in Oxford) expressed a determination to engage the enemy, as defined by the seaside holiday based on fashion, flirtation, fairgrounds, dancing, shows, piers, promenades and pierrots, on its perceived home territory. Blackpool was, by this time, the epitome of the commercial, frivolous, artificial seaside holiday, which was adapting itself to working-class tastes and in turn helping to form consensual expectations about what a holiday should be. As regards its target, though not its initial chosen battleground (although the Independent Labour Party also held proselytising meetings at Blackpool), the NHRU was at one with a spectrum of organisations, generally blending popular education, ethical socialism and Nonconformity in various proportions, that was emerging at about the same time across Britain (Snape, 2002; Taylor, 1997: 194–195; Waters, 1990; Yeo, 1977). But the enemy was already well entrenched. By 1911 there were over 50 substantial seaside resorts with resident populations of over 8000 scattered along the coasts of England and Wales, clustering wherever there was easy access from London and the industrial population centres; and the eight largest destinations were major towns with over 50,000 off-season inhabitants each (Walton, 1983: 65). By the turn of the century the seaside resort, with its pier, promenade, band, amusements, entertainments and cheap consumerism through holiday clothes and souvenirs, was already established as the dominant mode of popular holidaymaking, while even the Lake District was developing similar kinds of pleasure towns (Gray, 2006). Such urban holiday experiences were easy to access by cheap trains, at once attainably fashionable and reassuringly conventional, and already the stuff of habit and routine. There were many smaller, quieter, more 'natural', less intensively commercial resorts, on the edge of or beyond the full-blown railway system of Edwardian Britain; but to reach them required demanding resources in finance, information and ability to make longer and more complex journeys. They tended to be the preserves of the professional middle classes, who often reacted to working-class visitors of any kind with snobbery and disdain (Chew, 1982: 190–194; Walton, 1983). The same applied to early versions of the 'plotland' settlements, with their bohemian ethos and cheap self-built accommodation that recycled old tramcar bodies and railway carriages (Ward & Hardy, 1984). The dominant commercial modes of popular holidaymaking were to prove difficult to challenge.

In 1891 the Congregationalist minister T.A. Leonard decided, with NHRU prompting and encouragement (as prefigured in its monthly journal in April 1890, which set out in outline what became the CHA's programme), to take a party of young men from his congregation in the weaving town of Colne, in the Lancashire Pennines, on a Spartan, energetic walking holiday (a long week-end, from Saturday to Tuesday) based on Ambleside in the Lake District (Taylor, 1997: 196). This began an enduring tradition that produced two new organisations, the CHA and later the Holiday Fellowship (HF), and helped to lay the groundwork in the interwar years for the Youth Hostels Association (YHA). All can trace connections back to Ruskin's writings and personal influence; but these are at their most obvious and direct in the CHA, especially during its early years. The early records of the CHA and its periodical publication _Comradeship_ (from 1907) are suffused with Ruskinian associations, especially before the secession of Leonard to form the HF in 1913, which he saw as an attempt to recover the early purity and simplicity of the CHA's ideals and practices. Leonard started from the premise that 'the devil wields no small influence over holiday times' in Colne, at the core of Blackpool's resort hinterland, and he sought to promote an alternative model that encouraged physical and moral renewal through strenuous walking in rugged scenic surroundings, proximity to nature and therefore Nature's God, and serious reading and discussion in the evenings. He repeated the 1891 experiment in North Wales in the following year, and in 1893 he opened out his 'simple', 'strenuous' and 'democratic' holiday system to other Adult Classes and Pleasant Sunday Afternoon groups, with music and 'lecturettes' in the evenings, a University 'companion guide' and centres at Ambleside and Keswick, all under the auspices of the NHRU and advertised nationally in the _Review of Reviews_. The two parties exchanged places on the summit of Helvellyn, half way through the holiday. This marked the origin of the CHA as an enduring organisation. As the operation began to grow Leonard resigned his ministry in 1894, and devoted himself to it full-time. Annual conferences began in that same year, and the CHA as such, with name and constitution, was formally established in 1897 (Leonard, 1934; Snape, 2004; Speake, 1993: 36).

The CHA was, in its origins, grounded in Congregationalism. It was Leonard's mentor, John Brown Paton, principal of the Congregational Institute in Nottingham where Leonard had trained for the ministry, who fostered the link between the holidays and the NHRU, which he had established following the principles of the Chautauqua movement in the United States, a product of the 1870s which expanded rapidly in the late 19th century and also combined rural and coastal holidays with serious reading and discussion, with connections to Ruskin, Morris and the Arts and Crafts movement. It was Paton who made the resources available in 1893 and encouraged Leonard to expand the operation (Aron, 1999; Snape, 2002: 88–90). Paton's son John Lewis Paton, who became High Master of Manchester Grammar School between 1903 and 1924 after an earlier stint as master of the Sixth Form at Rugby School, was an active stalwart of the CHA from the very beginning (Carew, 1968; Snape, 2004; Speake, 1993: 38) But there was nothing sectarian about the CHA, as in the early 20th century it moved away from initial NHRU domination to carve out an identity of its own. The NHRU itself had never been a purely Congregationalist body: its founders had included the Bishop of London and 'several officials of the Co-operative movement' (Taylor, 1997: 198). Leonard himself took an ecumenical approach to his task, and his ideas were strongly and directly influenced by Ruskin, as indeed were those of John Brown Paton, who remarked, in words that closely follow the core argument of *Unto this Last*, 'The wealth of a country does not consist in the number or exchangeable value of its agricultural or manufactured or artistic products, so much as in the strength and intelligence and virtue of the men and women whom it rears' (Speake, 1993: 35; Taylor, 1997: 199). Robert Snape describes Leonard as 'a Christian Socialist and a disciple of Matthew Arnold and John Ruskin, both of whom he quoted in sermons'; and he argues that the CHA was '...largely inspired by Ruskin. Indeed, the CHA's ideological outlook clearly reflected Ruskin's contrast of the materialistic nature of urban leisure and the potential of the countryside as an alternative leisure space'. He supports this contention with an extended quotation from *Modern Painters*, 'The Moral of Landscape' (Snape, 2004: 152). Ruskin's own statement of belief in 'The Code of the Guild of St George', with its ecumenical embrace of broad Christian principles, helps to explain the readiness with which the CHA endorsed and propagated his ideas (Cockram, 2007: 168).

The most obvious personal link between the CHA and Ruskin was also an ecumenical one. Canon Rawnsley himself was directly associated with the CHA from the beginning, addressing Leonard's first parties of Lake District visitors and introducing the ideas of Ruskin and Wordsworth in that setting. Leonard acknowledged Rawnsley as 'a fine spirit who helped us to the last days of his life'. Rawnsley was also associated with the CHA's headquarters at Abbey House, Whitby, and the CHA provided a donation of £5 in 1898 in support of the Caedmon Memorial Fund for a commemorative statue at the top of the 199 steps leading to Whitby Abbey, as the minutes record, 'not only as a tribute to the memory of the Saxon poet, but more as an Expression of the Gratitude of the Association for all the kindly help it has received from Canon Rawnsley'. He served as a Vice-President of the CHA, welcomed its members to his parish church at Crosthwaite near Keswick, and entertained a group at Brandle How Woods (GMCRO B/CHA/ADM/1/1, 8 October 1898; Snape, 2004: 154; Speake, 1993: 39).

Rawnsley in turn brought the CHA into contact with Lake District and other landscape and heritage protection societies, including the National Trust, and it supported his campaigns against (for example) footpath closures in the Lake District and insensitive tree felling at Launchy Ghyll, while contributing to the National Trust appeal for the acquisition of Gowbarrow. We shall see that it fitted into a network of similar organisations and movements (Taylor, 1997: 211; Walton, 1998).

But the CHA was also hospitable to socialists, even those with a predominantly secular cast of mind; and Leonard had friendly contacts with H.M. Hyndman and Keir Hardie. In 1895 he encouraged *Clarion* readers, cyclists included, to join the Co-operative Holidays movement as a healthy alternative to 'the whirligig holidays spent by the average north-country toiler at Blackpool or Douglas'. John Trevor of the Labour Church movement joined an early CHA group at Barmouth in 1894, and recommended 'the happiest and healthiest of holidays' to readers of the *Labour Prophet*. The five principles of the Labour Churches have been described as 'a clear expression of Ruskinian thinking' in their embrace of non-sectarian religion and obedience to God's moral and economic laws (Cockburn, 2007: 180; Taylor, 1997: 201–202, 205–206). Selina Cooper, the socialist cotton winder from Brierfield in north-east Lancashire who became a prominent women's suffrage campaigner in the early 20th century, was an early recruit to Leonard's cause. Her first child was named John Ruskin Cooper. Leonard conducted her marriage ceremony in 1896, and when the CHA became formally established he was quick to recruit Selina and her husband Robert to run a new centre at Keld, in Swaledale, which opened in 1899. This provided basic accommodation in a remote place, reached by an eight-mile walk over Buttertubs Pass from the nearest railway station at Hawes. The Coopers looked after their guests, with Robert's local knowledge as a Swaledale native proving important for constructing the programme of daily rambles; but Leonard's philosophy enjoined that they be treated as equals. This involved Selina in demanding defences of her socialist principles, in debate with guests whose political beliefs were altogether more conventional. Most were middle-class, including John Lewis Paton himself; and the 'Golden Maxims' that Selina collected from them in her autograph book featured Ruskin in religious vein alongside Wordsworth and Tennyson. Here is a good illustration both of the diversity of points of view that the CHA accommodated, and of the importance of Ruskin's influence across the spectrum (Liddington, 1984: 67–68, 83–87).

As the CHA gathered strength and momentum from the late 1890s onwards, its holiday centres included several locations with Ruskin associations. Barmouth stands out particularly strongly. As represented in a guide to the 'seaside watering places' of England and Wales in 1885, it might appear a conventional small resort, albeit in a picturesque setting: 'one of the most favoured watering places in North Wales ... improving every year'. The arrival of the railway in 1867 had stimulated its growth, and new accommodation was provided in Marine Terrace and the Marine Hotel. There was a concert room and a circulating library, and an ample supply of shops and 'bathing coaches'. So far, so conventional; and this was the guidebook doing its job. But there is also unusual emphasis on the beauties of the surrounding scenery, on the variety of upland walks available to the serious pedestrian, and on the diversity of local ferns and flowers. Moreover, 'The town consists principally of one long irregular street, with a few terraces and picturesque old cottages built on the sides of the hills and rocks, somewhat resembling the old part of Clovelly, in Devonshire'. This combination of the scenic, the natural and the informally historic was obvious territory for the CHA (*Seaside Watering Places*, 1885: 230–232). There were also strong associations with Ruskin, especially through his Guild of St George, dedicated to reconstituting an older paternalistic mode of living, close to nature and in tune with its rhythms. Mrs Fanny Talbot, a correspondent and friend of Ruskin and Canon Rawnsley, had made over 13 cottages in the quaintest part of the little town to Ruskin's Guild in 1874 (Scott, 1931; Spence, 1957–1958; Spence, 1959–1960). She was also the first person to give land to the National Trust, as early as 1895, when she donated four and a half acres of hillside at Dinas Oleu, explaining that she wished 'to put it into the custody of some society that will never vulgarize it or prevent wild nature having its way' (Murphy, 1987). The original Barmouth centre of what became the CHA opened in 1894, and in 1898 the officers of the Association were urged, by Miss Atkinson of Barmouth, to sign a protest against a proposed light railway to nearby Beddgelert (GMCRO B/CHA/ADM/1/1, Executive Committee, 19 Feb. 1898). Ruskin and Rawnsley had been staunch campaigners against railway extension into the heart of the Lake District since the mid-1870s, and the CHA's involvement in this campaign brought it into battle alongside the National Trust, which marshalled its big legal and parliamentary guns on behalf of the opposition. The main thrust of the campaign was to prevent a proposed narrow-gauge electric railway from damaging the scenery of the Abergynolwyn Pass, and extracting water for hydro-electricity from nearby Llyn Llydaw; and the struggle continued, on shifting terrain, into the new century (Marshall & Walton, 1981: chapter 9; National Archives, MT6/1721; Walton, 1996). But the key point here is the close relationship between the infant CHA, the emergent National Trust and the preservationist concerns of Ruskin, Rawnsley and their allies, expressed in the context of a shared attachment to Barmouth which can be no coincidence. Admittedly, it disappeared from the CHA's list of centres between 1899 and 1910, but only to reappear in 1911 and retain its place for over seventy years (Speake, 1993: 12–13). Everything about its character, personal associations included, made Barmouth an obvious location for the kind of Ruskinian tourism the CHA favoured.

Other early CHA venues shared similar characteristics. Its first twin centres in Ambleside and Keswick began an enduring association with the Lake District, including at different (and overlapping) times Bassenthwaite, Borrowdale, Grasmere, Newlands and Stanley Ghyll in Eskdale. This was an obviously attractive area for reasons not necessarily connected with Ruskin (the literary landscapes of the Lake Poets, and relative accessibility from the industrial districts of Lancashire and the West Riding of Yorkshire where the CHA became particularly strong, were attractions enough in themselves); but this was, nevertheless, Ruskin territory, and recognised as such. Conwy, in North Wales, had Ruskin connections, and the first Peak District centre at Buxton had well-known associations with Ruskin's anger at the destruction of a local valley to build the railway between that town and Bakewell: these were both early, but short-lived, centres. Nearby Matlock, where Ruskin convalesced in 1871, was a CHA venue between 1911 and 1916. The CHA centre at Keld survived for only three seasons, but Richmond, which had been part of a youthful Ruskin itinerary, featured briefly on the list, while further south in the Yorkshire Dales a more accessible centre in a purpose-built 'bungalow' at Hebden, near Bolton Abbey in Wharfedale, was to be popular for nearly half a century, in an area frequented both by Turner and Ruskin, who was particularly fond of Malham and Gordale Scar. It was not until 1929 that the CHA acquired a base in Kirkby Lonsdale, the site of 'Ruskin's View' of the River Lune from the edge of the churchyard (which had already been celebrated by Wordsworth and painted by Turner before it acquired Ruskin's endorsement); and Kirkby, a small market town several miles from the nearest railway station, never acquired a tourist industry to match those of more accessible locations in the Lake District and Yorkshire Dales. This should remind us that Ruskin was always part of a much broader picture; and CHA centres from the earliest days included locations in the northern Peak District (especially Hayfield and later Hope, already favourite haunts of working-class ramblers from Manchester by the turn of the century), Devon and Cornwall, Scotland, Ireland, the Isles of Wight and Man, rural Surrey, and even Eastbourne, in places where any Ruskin connections were altogether more distant or fanciful, although (for example) Ruskin mentioned Boscastle in *St Marks' Rest* and acknowledged hazy memories of Whitby in his commentary on *Harbours of England*. But we should not make too much of the apparent Ruskinian connections of the CHA holiday centres, especially as they are easier to identify in retrospect than to associate with the immediate, and practical, priorities of the CHA in looking for suitable accommodation at the time (Hanley, 1992; Speake, 1993: 12–13, 26–27, 57).

From 1902 onwards the CHA extended its operations across the Channel, in the furtherance of ideals of peace and international brotherhood. It began with St Luc in Switzerland in 1902 and soon extended operations in Brittany, where rustic surroundings, quaint old villages and religious customs had long attracted British visitors, and in the upland Eifel and Taunus districts of Germany (Speake, 1993: 30–33). In 1909 Finhaut in Switzerland, not far from Ruskin's beloved Chamonix, was added to the list. Herbert Wroot, a writer on Yorkshire geology and pillar of the Bronte Society, introducing Finhaut to readers of the CHA journal *Comradeship* under the Ruskinian title 'Mountain Glories', wrote lyrically about colour, flora, fauna and geology, and made cross-references to the Craven district, adopting thoroughly Ruskinian idioms and ways of seeing without actually mentioning the author's name (GMCRO B/CHA/PUB/1/1, cited hereafter as *Comradeship*, April 1909: 60–62). But generally these destinations, although entirely in keeping with Ruskinian values, lacked specific, direct connections with his writings, sketches or itineraries; and plenty of other cultural links and established travel flows were pulling in similar directions.

The most direct evidence of strong Ruskinian influences on the values of the CHA comes from the pages of *Comradeship*, which began publication in October 1907. The first five issues featured, under the heading 'Citizenship', a supportive exposition and critical analysis of Ruskin's *Unto This Last*, probably his most influential piece of writing for a working-class readership, by no less a figure than J.A. Hobson. The first edition of Hobson's influential *John Ruskin: Social Reformer* had been published in 1898, and the publication of his introduction to a new edition of *Unto This Last* practically coincided with the series in *Comradeship* (Hobson, 1898; Ruskin, 1907). This was followed immediately by John Ernest Phythian's discussion of Marshall Mather's popular digest of Ruskin's ideas, with a series of questions appended for discussion, and an addendum that, 'A portfolio of prints illustrating Ruskin's life may be borrowed from the Editor'. Phythian, a former Manchester city councillor and secretary of the Manchester Ruskin Society, had met Ruskin at Walkley in 1880. Subsequently he acted as chair of Manchester's municipal Art Gallery Committee, and published books on G.E. Watts, Turner and Millais. Here, he argued that readers of Mather will need 'to take into serious consideration the possibility – rather the necessity and the certainty – of such a communistic society as Ruskin advocates'. He concluded with a question expecting an affirmative answer: 'Reader, do you and I want to be followers of Ruskin?' (*Comradeship*, October 1908; Eagles, 2007: 94; Walton, 1995). In the very next issue we find John W. Graham, whose book on smoke pollution had come out in 1907 and whose *The Harvest of Ruskin* was to appear in 1920, reviewing Hobson's *John Ruskin: Social Reformer*, not as a new book but as an important interpretation. To complete the initial barrage of informed, sympathetic commentary on Ruskin's thought we find John Howard Whitehouse, later to become the founder of Bembridge School and the purchaser of Brantwood, examining 'The Two Paths' (*Comradeship*, December 1908, February 1909; Graham, 1907, 1920).

This overwhelming focus on Ruskin owed much to the agenda of the NHRU, but it also helped to define a dominant ethos for the core membership of the CHA, whose journal *Comradeship* was. Apart from the set-piece articles on Ruskin's philosophy, his citation index in the early issues would look very impressive. He is quoted at the end of the second issue in opposition to mountain railways and the disfigurement of mountain streams by electrical works (*Comradeship*, December 1907). In the following spring, alongside a paean of praise to the scenic beauties of the railway through the Western Highlands to Kyle of Lochalsh, we find a quotation from Ruskin, identifying Yorkshire as the source of Turner's 'first conception of mountain scenery', in an article by Leonard himself on 'Celtic Grassington', in Wharfedale (*Comradeship*, April 1908: 51–52). In early 1909 the Co-operator (and commentator on Tolstoy) Percy Redfern's 'Wintertime in Whitby' did not mention Ruskin specifically, but his description of the Monk's Walk near Abbey House concluded that, 'It is not pleasant to think that the fine or beautiful or pretty things, the abbeys and cathedrals, the villages, old inns, wild-flower lanes, nooks and squares of historic cities, and the rest, are mere legacies, really crumbling, decaying, passing away' (*Comradeship*, February 1909: 35–38; Redfern, 1907). This pulls together a lot of the Ruskinian values that were central to the CHA's 'official' agenda. It is also significant that the review *Public Opinion* advertised itself in the April 1909 issue as 'Ruskin's ideal paper'. In May we find Mildred Spencer recommending *Modern Painters* in a feature on 'Books about Switzerland', while in the same issue Canon Rawnsley, author of *Ruskin and the English Lakes*, contributed on 'Ambleside and Rydal' (*Comradeship*, May 1909: 71–73, 75–76; Rawnsley, 1902). Ruskin is cited in the supporting reading-list for R. Balmforth's *Social and Political Pioneers* in the September issue, and in an article on 'Our Wharfedale Centre' in December, celebrating the attachment of Ruskin and Turner to Bolton Abbey, a theme that reappears in Leonard's own article on 'Wharfedale' in April 1910 (*Comradeship*, September 1909: 16; December 1909: 35–36; April 1910: 75). A year later we find *Sesame and Lilies* appearing on a list of presentation volumes offered by a publisher, while no less a figure than Patrick Abercrombie, contributing an article on town planning, quotes *The Seven Lamps of Architecture* (*Comradeship*, December 1910: 36–37, 44–46). An article on the CHA centre at Park Hall, Hayfield, in April 1911 refers to villagers being encouraged to discuss 'strange writers called Ruskin and Kropotkin', while November found Ruskin being quoted in an article on 'The Daylight Saving Bill', which was closely followed by an contribution on Morris and the Pre-Raphaelites (*Comradeship*, April 1911: 74–75; November 1911: 19–22). In February 1912 an account of a sunny walk from the Hebden centre to Malham and Gordale Scar began with earnest debate: 'Ruskin gripped us. A discussion on the St George's Guild was cementing friendship...' (*Comradeship*, February 1912: 59) In February 1913 a 'holiday sketch' brought together Ruskin and Coniston, a link that was also made elsewhere in the magazine (*Comradeship*, February 1913: 56–57). Ruskin then featured strongly in the March 1914 issue, quoted in an article on Mark Rutherford, and invoked in descriptions of the CHA's Swiss centres as an expository authority on Alpine geology and a predictor of the impact of tourism on Swiss mountain villages, with reference here to Finhaut (*Comradeship*, March 1914: 55, 58).

These are only the most direct and literal references to Ruskin in the pre-First World War issues of *Comradeship*, and a high proportion of the articles are Ruskinian in tone, whether they deal with the beauties of landscape and nature, with the value of walking as a route to deeper understanding than faster and less strenuous modes of transport could provide, with folklore, popular memory and history, with opposition to the extension of mountain railways and roads, with geology, close observation, experiment or the capacity to marvel in tranquillity. Locations celebrated in the text often have Ruskin associations, from the Lake District to Mont St Michel and the Valais. There are other gods on the CHA's Olympus, of course: articles about and regular allusions to Wordsworth, Charles Kingsley (a particular favourite of Leonard himself), William Morris, Richard Jefferies and Patrick Geddes can be juxtaposed to give an overall flavour. But the heavy front-loading of didactic references to Ruskin's corpus of ideas, and the steady flow of allusions thereafter, mark him out as the dominant figure. The sheer range of CHA contributors and collaborators was impressive, ranging from Hobson and Abercrombie to Redfern, Cecil Sharp and F.J. Marquis, the Tory social worker who later became Lord Woolton (*Comradeship*, March 1914: 62; December 1920: 12–13; Brown, 1965: 8). There was a distinct Quaker and pacifist undercurrent (for example, Geddes was presented to readers by Ernest Ewart Unwin, a Leeds University graduate and science teacher in Quaker schools who was a wartime conscientious objector and eventually became a leading educationalist in Tasmania), and Leonard himself joined the Society of Friends before the First World War (http://adbonline.anu.edu/biogs/A120340b.htm; Speake, 1993: 34).

By the eve of the First World War the CHA's history was becoming complicated by its increasing popularity, and in 1913 Leonard seceded, with a display of amicable rhetoric, to form the HF. This division seems to have been a response to the recruitment of new members who did not understand the CHA's ideals, chafed against the disciplines of early rising and compulsory communal rambling arrangements, and offended some of the established membership by boisterous horseplay, practical jokes, the rowdy singing of popular songs 'on the march' to the disruption of contemplative tranquillity, and an unseemly flirtatiousness between the sexes. Worries about these issues were already being aired in *Comradeship* during 1910–1911 (*Comradeship*, December 1910, February 1911). The CHA had been, from its origins, a predominantly middle-class organisation that sought to enhance social mixing by providing, unobtrusively, subsidised or free holidays for designated 'deserving' people who could not afford its modest but potentially onerous charges. J.L. Paton, in 1921, presented the CHA as a 'Toynbee Hall of the open air, where you could rub shoulders with others and share life with them', cross-referring to a self-consciously Ruskinian project to bring education and fulfilment to London's East End through university people of the sort that had worked, as undergraduates, on Ruskin's Hinksey Road repair and improvement scheme in Oxford. The ideal was to bring the classes together in harmony, while transcending political and religious conflict by subordinating it to the higher ideals of shared healthy outdoor pleasure: 'You get your ultra-marine blue Tory, your ultra-red Bolshevik, your ultra Catholic and your Church-going "Kensitian"... I used to find the young fellows on the CHA discussing the most explosive subjects in the open air without coming to blows or even to sarcastic speech' (*Comradeship*, February 1921: 9). 'Kensitians' and Catholics would indeed form a potentially explosive mixture: the former were adherents of John Kensit, the aggressively anti-Catholic founder of the Protestant Truth Society, killed by a chisel thrown at a characteristically violent outdoor meeting in Birkenhead in 1902.

CHA holidays were particularly popular with single women seeking safe, respectable forms of modified 'bohemianism' (in the form of relaxed dress codes, liberation from the tyranny of fashion, and mixing with men on equal, comradely terms), and (it was often suggested) in pursuit of the right sort of husband. It had tended to 'preach to the converted', and its energetic holidays, relying on the shared values of the participants, had made no discernible inroads into the popularity of the commercial seaside, although 100 members from Blackpool itself, which had a strong contingent of resident ramblers, gathered for a 'town reunion' in 1914 (*Comradeship*, March 1914: 50). Its membership was strongly skewed towards industrial Lancashire and the West Riding of Yorkshire, growing out of earlier organisations like the rambling club of Manchester YMCA, although a London CHA Club had been founded in 1901, with 'a study of Ruskin's works' featuring among the early discussion papers. The London group held a 'William Morris celebration', followed by 'a Ruskin centenary lasting a week', in 1918, a year before the membership reached a peak at 700 (Brown, 1965: 1–2, 20–23).

However, even a modest admixture of the sort of secular hedonism that would have been perfectly acceptable in the Clarion Fellowship was enough to generate conflict and the sending of polite letters of exclusion addressed to 'unsuitable' people. Already in 1909 veterans of the CHA's earliest days were looking back in nostalgia at the original Ambleside and Keswick arrangements of 1893: 'Those were simple, Spartan holidays, where we munched hard wheaten biscuits, tramped eighteen miles without a murmur, and didn't criticise the primitive ways of our landladies' (*Comradeship*, April 1909: 49). Leonard's establishment of the HF was an attempt to reassert these values in the face of increasing pressure to compromise them, as the CHA expanded and attracted a less principled and more comfort-seeking public. How far the CHA's mainstream membership, as opposed to those who contributed to *Comradeship* and reinforced the 'official' ideology of the movement, was fully attuned to the founding values must remain an open question; but this evidence suggests that the appeal of what might be called 'Ruskinian' holidaymaking remained self-limiting (Taylor, 1997: 212–217).

Ruskin became less visible in the pages of *Comradeship* after the First World War. The Ruskin Museum at Coniston was mentioned in 1920 (*Comradeship*, December 1920: 6–7), and Ruskin was quoted in 1922 (*Comradeship*, November 1922: 11–12) and 1923, alongside (among others) Darwin and Kingsley, in a piece on 'The Call of the Flowers' which refers to the 'Spirit of Beauty' and the need to protect the countryside from spoliation (*Comradeship*, May 1923: 9–10). Direct references dry up thereafter, although there is much mention of places that might be familiar from Ruskin's writings, from the Peak District and Malham to the Jura; and recognisable themes and preoccupations recur frequently, for example in an article on the need to experience Switzerland on foot rather than from a car or charabanc (*Comradeship*, May 1924: 12–13). The powerful influence Ruskin exercised on the CHA's official literature at the beginning had fed into a broader common stream, and become assimilated into a set of shared values from various interacting sources; but the role of his writings in the construction and legitimising of what might be called 'CHA values' was indispensable.

From the CHA followed further developments in this distinctive field of cultural tourism, but its values were not the only ones on offer. Alternative provision targeted at working people, but with a different agenda, came from the Workers' Travel Association (WTA). This organisation, which was founded in 1921 and began its holiday operations in 1922, brought together leading figures in the Labour movement (drawn from trade unions and the Labour Party in alliance with the Co-operative movement) to offer organised, affordable overseas travel to working-class people who would otherwise have been unable to make the journeys (Barton, 2005: 157–162; Williams, 1960). Leading figures included J.J. Mallon of Toynbee Hall, the Oxford University settlement in London's East End, which from the founder Canon Barnett onwards had strong ties to Ruskin. From 1887 onwards its Toynbee Travellers' Club took students of limited means to 'foreign parts', including Belgium and Spain as well as Florence and Venice. When it was wound up as 'no longer necessary' in 1913, the Workmen's Travel Club, offering shorter European trips to 'the genuine working man', provided an element of continuity, while Toynbee

Hall provided office space and clerical services to the fledgling WTA after the war (Pimlott, 1935: 155–161, 217–218).

The WTA soon moved off in a different direction, away from the Ruskinian influences of Toynbee Hall itself. The management committee soon boasted Labour Party luminaries and future ministers such as Ernest Bevin, J.R. Clynes, Margaret Bondfield and Jimmy Thomas. By 1926 the National Council included Fenner Brockway, Ramsay MacDonald and Ellen Wilkinson. Bevin himself acted as tour leader for the Rhine cruise of 1930, which had 250 bookings (Workers' Travel Association 1924: 1; 1926: 6; 1930: 5–6). This was a parallel venture to that of the CHA, but the overtly Ruskinian values and agenda were conspicuous by their absence. The central stated aim of this non-profit-making organisation was to pursue international peace and mutual understanding by facilitating foreign travel, including the provision of language classes. In 1929 its annual report made the proud claim that, 'WTA members are drawn from every trade and profession. In our parties are to be found workers by hand or brain in every walk of life. Our parties reveal a true democracy, and no little of our success is due to that feeling of fellowship which our methods tend to create'. In outline, these were similar aspirations to those of the CHA; but the dominant ethos was different, as was the pattern of destinations and tours. By 1924 the WTA had a small spring centre in San Remo and four summer centres, in Paris, St Malo, Geneva and Arona, a lake resort in northern Italy. The last of these had strong Ruskin associations: he had sketched, and followed in Turner's footsteps, there. WTA tours – a new venture in 1924 – went to Italy, Switzerland and Russia, but especially (8 of the 13 in that year) to Belgium, taking advantage of the organisation's strong links with the Belgian working-class movement. In 1932–1933, 40% of all WTA bookings were to Belgium (Workers' Travel Association, 1924: 1–3; 1929: 7; 1932–1933: 5). Belgian seaside resorts were a favoured destination, especially Ostend, and the use of fashionable locations such as Biarritz, Nice and San Sebastián (in 1931 'the outstanding success of our Continental Centres') hints that one of the WTA's undeclared aims was to make the haunts of international high society accessible to the workers (Workers' Travel Association, 1931–1932: 3, 6). Alpine destinations included Ruskin's Chamonix, but as a winter sports centre; and the WTA's satisfaction at the success of its Swiss tours in 1926 arose because 'they include, in addition to a great deal of sightseeing, definite opportunities for meeting co-operators and seeing Co-operative institutions and factories in Berne, and facilities for seeing something of the Swiss Labour Movement, especially at Berne and Lucerne. In these two towns the parties stay at the Volkshaus, which is, of course, the local Labour centre' (Workers' Travel Association, 1926: 2). By 1929 the WTA was also organising 'Motor Tours' within Britain, to places like Ilfracombe and Bournemouth and through Scotland (Workers' Travel Association, 1929: 6) and in 1931 it began to organise 'Sunshine Cruises' to Spain, Portugal and North Africa (Workers' Travel Association, 1931–1932: 3). A revealing breakdown of WTA holiday bookings by cost in 1931 found that the cheapest holidays, costing under £5, accounted for only 8% of the total. A further 34% came in at between £5 and £9, and 26% cost £15 or over (Workers' Travel Association, 1931–1932: 6). In every respect this was a far cry from the distinctive, enduringly Ruskinian ethos of the CHA: it was about the democratisation of holiday types and destinations that had hitherto been out of reach for working people, but without the emphasis on the 'Spartan' or the simple life, with a strong commitment to comfortable travel and urban sightseeing, and with an overwhelmingly materialist ideology. The WTA did provide some 'cheap hostel accommodation in the countryside for the less well off', for example at Hope in the Peak District, which also had a CHA centre from 1916 onwards (Speake, 1993: 83; Taylor, 1997: 251). Despite the connotations of the CHA's name, it was the WTA that attracted the practical support of the international labour movement, including the Co-operators. But with a peak of 13,835 'persons booked' on overseas holidays in 1930, a figure that halved as the depression bit deeply in the following year, and a total of 12,119 booked 'at home' in 1932, it was no more 'popular' in numerical terms than the CHA (Workers' Travel Association, 1931–1932: 2; 1932–1933: 1).

The WTA did offer immediate strong support for the new inter-war venture in popular holidays whose ethos most resembled the CHA and HF, however. When the YHA was founded in 1930 the WTA was represented on the YHA Council by its General Secretary; and the two organisations were clearly seen as complementary, not mutually competitive (Workers' Travel Association, 1930–1931: 9). Other organisations with a seat on the Council included the YMCA, YWCA, Boy Scouts, Boys' Brigade, the Camp Fire Girls of the British Isles, Toc H, the Educational Settlement Association, the National Association of Boys' Clubs, the Council for the Protection of Rural England, and the Geographical Association: an impeccable representation of the religious and political establishment. Alongside them, along with the WTA, were various bodies that were aligned with the 'outdoor movement', assorted heterodoxies, and the Left: the Labour Party League of Youth, the Cyclists' Touring Club, the Federation of Rambling Clubs, the Fell and Rock Climbing Club, the Order of Woodcraft Chivalry, the Sunlight League, the Young Friends Committee, and the Workers' Educational Association; and there were also representatives from the CHA and HF (Youth Hostels Association, 1931).

The YHA was an impeccably respectable organisation, the entirely acceptable face of the working-class 'hiking' fashion that attracted media attention in the 1930s. Its immediate inspiration came from Germany before Hitler, and it shared the internationalist aspirations of both the CHA and the WTA; but its core aims were those of the CHA in its own origins: to help young people from the 'great industrial towns' who did not have access to cars to stay overnight in affordable accommodation and 'get into the really good country' beyond day-tripper range, thereby recovering access to their 'lost heritage'. It was initiated in 1929 by the Liverpool and District Ramblers' Federation, but developed into a national organisation within a few months and soon gained practical and financial support from the National Council of Social Service, the National Trust, the Cadbury Trust and the Carnegie Trust, among others. The first national secretary, St John Catchpool, a Quaker and former sub-warden of Toynbee Hall, was very effective at recruiting this kind of support (Heath, 2004). The YHA was also capable of inspiring enthusiasts to do voluntary work to prepare new hostels for their visitors. Its founding President, recruited by Catchpool, was the Cambridge historian Professor G.M. Trevelyan, whose brother had made basic accommodation available for walkers from Tyneside at the family home in Northumberland, Wallington Hall. Ruskin had strong connections with an earlier generation of the family, particularly through his close friend Lady Pauline Trevelyan, and had been a frequent visitor to Wallington. G.M. Trevelyan was a strong supporter of the National Trust, while recognising its limitations; and the rise of the YHA coincided with the Trust's diversion of energy into the acquisition and endowment of threatened country houses, although Trevelyan continued his role as chairman of the Trust's Estates Committee. The YHA charged a very small membership fee of 2s 6d (12.5p) and a basic rate of 1s (5p) for a night's lodgings, and thereby made remote areas of the British countryside accessible to the urban working classes, while excluding motorists (but not cyclists, as was originally suggested), requiring mobility between hostels after a three-night stay, expecting members to contribute task work to the maintenance of the hostels in return for cheap accommodation, and remaining hospitable across imagined boundaries of class, age and gender. A self-organised YHA holiday was much cheaper than anything the WTA had to offer. The YHA was a great success, growing impressively during the 1930s and even more rapidly after the Second World War: it had 130 hostels in operation within two years, and by 1939 it already had 80,000 members. It was an early user of film to get its message across, and 'Youth Hails Adventure', its earliest effort, was at pains to emphasize the movement's potential for class reconciliation, its seductive combination of freedom and discipline, and its essential wholesomeness and innocence (Youth Hostels Association, 1931; Youth Hostels Association, 1932; Youth Hostels Association film archive, 'Youth Hails Adventure'; Taylor, 1997: 235, 250–254).

It soon became clear that the YHA was a development on an altogether new scale. It had clear affinities with the CHA, but offered greater flexibility and freedom, with the opportunity to move in and out of larger groups, enjoying the communal experience when preferred but with the power to make arrangements as individuals, in couples or in small groups. It was also cheaper than any of the alternatives. As might be expected by the early 1930s, the direct, visible influence of Ruskin himself was much diluted; but the presence of the ubiquitous T.A. Leonard as a Vice-President, alongside Patrick Abercrombie and the Archbishop of York, guaranteed that some of the CHA ethos would be shared by its more vigorous successor. A handsome illustrated record of the YHA's progress, published as early as 1932, opened with a William Morris poem about 'the end of the village', and emphasized the pursuit of health in body and mind through the enjoyment of 'our own countryside' and its protection against litter and 'ugly erections', while returning to 'simpler standards of living' (Youth Hostels Association, Illustrated Record, 1932a, b, c). In classic Ruskinian vein, another pamphlet urged that to know 'this amazing England, a man must travel it slowly and keep his intimate touch with its age and loveliness. To know it thus, mile after mile, is to love it deeply; and to love it is to safeguard its beauty, for ourselves and for those who come after us' (Youth Hostels Association, pamphlet, November 1932).

With the passage of time, the direct traces of Ruskin's influence on popular holidaymaking become fainter, and increasingly intermingled with contemporary and subsequent developments, some of which were themselves inflected through Ruskin's ideas. We can investigate it most convincingly through the 'outdoor movement' of the late 19th and early 20th century, which fed into a heady brew of idealistic socialism and nonsectarian nonconformity which issued forth most productively in the 'New Liberalism' of Edwardian Britain. But we do not find Ruskin everywhere among the votaries of the 'outdoor movement': wherever the dominant ethos comes from trade union organisation, from the Fabian Society, from the secular and Marxist left, or from the mainstream Labour Party as it coalesced in the early 20th century, he is difficult to find, even in the 1890s. The most positive and congenial relationships between Ruskin's legacy and the development of new kinds of popular tourism can be found in the Co-operative Holidays Association; and it is not too fanciful to suggest that these influences carried through to help to shape the formative years of the Youth Hostels Association. It would be dangerous to go beyond this; but it remains an important, enduring and productive legacy.

References

Aron, C. (1999) *Working at Play*. New York: Oxford University Press.

Bann, S. (1990) *The Inventions of History*. Manchester: Manchester University Press.

Barton, S. (2005) *Working-Class Organisations and Popular Tourism 1840–1970*. Manchester: Manchester University Press.

Berghoff, H. *et al.* (eds) (2002) *The Making of Modern Tourism: The Cultural History of the British Experience, 1600–2000*. London: Palgrave.

Brendon, P. (1991) *Thomas Cook: 150 Years of Popular Tourism*. London: Secker and Warburg.

Brown, S. (comp.) (1965) *A History of the London CHA Club*. London: London CHA Club.

Carew, S.J. (comp.) (1968) *J.L.P.: A Portrait of John Lewis Paton by his Friends*. St John's, Newfoundland: Memorial University.

Carver, S. (2003) *The Life and Works of Lancashire Novelist William Harrison Ainsworth, 1805–1882*. Lampeter: Edwin Mellen.

Chandler, A. (1970) *A Dream of Order*. Lincoln: University of Nebraska Press.

Chew, D.N. (1982) *The Life and Writings of Ada Nield Chew*. London: Virago.

Clarion (1891–1892) Manchester.

Clarke, A. (1916) *Windmill Land*. London: J.M. Dent.

Clarke, A. (1920) *Moorlands and Memories*. Bolton: Tillotsons.

Cockram, G. (2007) *Ruskin and Social Reform*. London: I.B. Tauris.

Comradeship: The Magazine of the Co-Operative Holidays Association, December 1907 to October 1927, Greater Manchester County Record Office, B/CHA/PUB/1/1.

Cross, G. and Walton, J.K. (2005) *The Playful Crowd: Pleasure Places in the Twentieth Century*. New York: Columbia University Press.

Darby, W.J. (2000) *Landscape and Identity: Geographies of Nation and Class in England*. Oxford: Oxford University Press.

Deacon, B. (2001) Imagining the fishing: Artists and fishermen in late nineteenth century Cornwall. *Rural History* 12, 159–178.

Durie, A.J. (2003) *Scotland for the Holidays: A History of Tourism in Scotland, 1780–1939*. East Linton: Tuckwell.

Durie, A.J. (2006) 'Scotland is Scott-land': Scott and the development of tourism. In M. Pittock (ed.) *The Reception of Sir Walter Scott in Europe* (pp. 313–322). London: Continuum.

Eagles, S. (2007) 'The insinuating touch of influence': Aspects of Ruskin's political legacy. In C. Casaliggi and P. March-Russell (eds) *Ruskin in Perspective* (pp. 83–100). Newcastle: Cambridge Scholars Publishing.

Fraser Rae, W. (1891) *The Business of Travel*. London: Thomas Cook.

Goldman, L. (1999) Ruskin, Oxford and the British labour movement, 1880–1914. In D. Birch (ed.) *Ruskin and the Dawn of the Modern*. Oxford: Oxford University Press.

Graham, J.W. (1907) *The Destruction of Daylight*. London: Allen.

Graham, J.W. (1920) *The Harvest of Ruskin*. London: Allen and Unwin.

Gray, F. (2006) *Designing the Seaside*. London: Reaktion.

Greater Manchester County Record Office (GMCRO), B/CHA/ADM/1/1, CHA Minute Books, 1895–1899.

Hanley, K. (1992) Ruskin's views: Gloom and glory in Kirkby Lonsdale. In K. Hanley and A. Milbank (eds) *From Lancaster to the Lakes* (pp. 72–93). Lancaster: Centre for North-West Regional Studies.

Hardy, D. and Ward, C. (1984) *Arcadia for All*. London: Mansell.

Heath, G. (2004) Catchpool, (Egerton) St John Pettifor (1890–1971). In B. Harrison (ed.) *Oxford Dictionary of National Biography*. Oxford: Oxford University Press.

Hobson, J.A. (1898) *John Ruskin: Social Reformer*. London: J. Nisbet.

Hollett, D. (2002) *The Pioneer Ramblers, 1850–1940*. Manchester: North Wales Area of the Ramblers' Association.

Howell, D. (1983) *British Workers and the Independent Labour Party, 1888–1906*. Manchester: Manchester University Press.

Joyce, P. (1991) *Visions of the People*. Cambridge: Cambridge University Press.

Leonard, T.A. (1934) *Adventures in Holiday Making*. London: Holiday Fellowship.

Liddington, J. (1984) *The Life and Times of a Respectable Radical: Selina Cooper, 1864–1946*. London: Virago.

Lowenthal, D. (2009) Patrons, populists, apologists: Crises in museum steward-ship. In L. Gibson and J. Pendlebury (eds) *Valuing Historic Environments* (pp. 19–31). Aldershot: Ashgate.

McGurn, J. (1987) *On Your Bicycle*. London: Murray.

Mandler, P. (1999) 'The wand of fancy': The historical imagination of the Victorian tourist. In M. Kwint, C. Breward, J. Aynsley (eds) *Material Memories* (pp. 125–141). London: Berg.

Manton, K. (1997) Establishing the fellowship: Harry Lowerison and Ruskin school home, a turn-of-the-century socialist and his educational experiment. *History of Education* 26, 53–70.

Marshall, J.D. and Walton, J.K. (1981) *The Lake Counties from 1830 to the Mid-Twentieth Century*. Manchester: Manchester University Press.

Murphy, G. (1987) *Founders of the National Trust*. London: Christopher Helm.

Percy, J. (1991) Scientists in humble life: The artisan naturalists of south Lancashire. *Manchester Region History Review* 5, 3–10.

National Archives, MT6/1721, additional material in Your Archives Beta Version.

Pimlott, J.A.R. (1935) *Toynbee Hall: Fifty Years of Social Progress*. London: J.M. Dent and Sons.

Prynn, D. (1976) The Clarion Clubs, rambling and the holiday associations in Great Britain since the 1890s. *Journal of Contemporary History* 11, 65–77.

Pye, D. (1995) *Fellowship is Life*. Bolton: Clarion.

Rawnsley, H.D. (1902) *Ruskin and the English Lakes*. Glasgow: James MacLehose and Sons.

Readman, P. (2001) Landscape preservation, 'advertising disfigurement' and English national identity *c*. 1890–1914. *Rural History* 12, 61–83.

Redfern, P. (1907) *Tolstoy: A Study*. London: A.C. Fifield.

Rose, J. (2001) *The Intellectual Life of the British Working Classes*. New Haven, CT: Yale University Press.

Rubinstein, D. (1977) Cycling in the 1890s. *Victorian Studies* 21, 47–71.

Ruskin, J. (1907) *Unto This Last* (new edition with an introduction by J.A. Hobson). London: Cassell.

Salveson, P. (1996) *Will yo' come o' Sunday Mornin'? The 1896 Battle for Winter Hill*. Bolton: Transport Research and Information Network.

Salveson, P. (2008) *With Walt Whitman in Bolton*. Huddersfield: Little Northern Books.

Salveson, P. (2009) *Lancashire's Romantic Radical: The Life and Writings of Allen Clarke/ Teddy Ashton*. Huddersfield: Little Northern Books.

Scott, E.H. (1931) *Ruskin's Guild of St George*. London: Methuen.

Seaside Watering Places (1885) London: L. Upcott Gill.

Snape, R. (2002) The national home reading union 1889–1930. *Journal of Victorian Culture* 7, 86–110.

Snape, R. (2004) The Co-operative Holidays Association and the cultural forma-tion of countryside leisure practice. *Leisure Studies* 23, 143–58.

Speake, R. (1993) *A Hundred Years of Holidays*. Manchester: Countrywide Holidays.

Spence, M.E. (1957–1958) The guild of St George. *Bulletin of the John Rylands Library* 40, 147–201.

Spence, M.E. (1959–1960) Ruskin's friendship with Fanny Talbot. *Bulletin of the John Rylands Library* 42, 453–80.

Stephenson, T. (1989) *Forbidden Land*. Manchester: Manchester University Press.

Taylor, H. (1995) Footpath protection societies in mid-nineteenth century textile Lancashire. *Manchester Region History Review* 9, 25–31.

Taylor, H. (1997) *A Claim on the Countryside*. Edinburgh: Keele University Press.

Tebbutt, M. (2006) Rambling and manly identity in Derbyshire's Dark Peak, 1880s–1920s. *Historical Journal* 49, 1125–1153.

Toulmin, V. (2006) *Electric Edwardians*. London: BFI.

Unwin, E.E. Entry in *Australian Dictionary of Biography*. On WWW at http://adbonline.anu.edu/biogs/A120340b.htm. Accessed 11.04.09.

Waller, P.J. (2006) *Writers, Readers and Reputations: Literary Life in Britain 1870–1918*. Oxford: Oxford University Press.

Walton, J.K. (1974) The social development of Blackpool, 1788–1914. PhD thesis, University of Lancaster.

Walton, J.K. (1983) *The English Seaside Resort: A Social History, 1750–1914*. Leicester: Leicester University Press.

Walton, J.K. (1995) The National Trust: Preservation or provision? In M. Wheeler (ed.) *Ruskin and Environment* (pp. 144–164). Manchester: Manchester University Press.

Walton, J.K. (1996) The National Trust centenary: Official and unofficial histories. *Local Historian* 26, 80–88.

Walton, J.K. (1998) Canon Rawnsley and the English lake district. *Armitt Library Journal* 1, 1–17.

Walton, J.K. (2007) *Riding on Rainbows: Blackpool Pleasure Beach and its Place in British Popular Culture*. St Albans: Skelter Publishing.

Ward, D. and Hardy, C. (1984) *Arcadia for All*. London: Mansell.

Waters, C. (1990) *British Socialists and the Politics of Popular Culture*. Manchester: Manchester University Press.

Wellings, M. (2004) Kensit, John (1853–1902). *Oxford Dictionary of National Biography*. Oxford: Oxford University Press.

Williams, E.F. (1960) *Journey into Adventure*. London: Odhams Press.

Workers' Travel Association, Annual Reports for 1924–1925, 1929, 1930–1933, British Library.

Yeo, S. (1977) A new life: The religion of socialism in Britain 1883–1896. *History Workshop Journal* 4, 5–56.

Youth Hostels Association (1931) Address by Professor G.M. Trevelyan, O.M., the President of the Association, on the Wireless, January 21st 1931, British Library WP15123.

Youth Hostels Association (1932a) Advertising Leaflet, British Library.

Youth Hostels Association (1932b) Pamphlet, British Library, accession stamp, November 1932.

Youth Hostels Association (1932c) *Illustrated Record of the Progress of the YHA*. British Library.

Youth Hostels Association film archive (*c.* 1932) Youth Hails Adventure.

Chapter 7
Ruskin and Brantwood

This chapter examines a further dimension of Ruskin's relationship with cultural tourism through the development of Brantwood, his home on Coniston Water in the English Lake District between 1872 and 1900, as a 'house museum', secular shrine and commemorative tourist destination. Alternative (and more accessible, on some assumptions) potential domestic places of commemoration at Herne Hill and Denmark Hill in the south-east London suburbs were demolished before the First World War, the latter to form part of the site of Ruskin Park (Jackson, 2006). The development of Ruskin's domestic territory in these guises adds an extra dimension to our understanding of his impact on cultural tourism more generally, in a local setting which reached out to make contacts and carry influences and sentiments across the globe, and from which wide ripples of significance and, perhaps, irony can be seen to flow. Brantwood's complex history as a place of pilgrimage associated with Ruskin's memory began at the turn of the century and combined all three characteristics, with an increasingly obvious and necessary concern towards the end of the 20th century to draw in a wider tourist public and to cater for more general interests, presenting Brantwood as a kind of 'stately home' with all the additional attractions that go with that market, including meals, souvenirs and creatively reconstructed gardens (Mandler, 1997). It is a particularly interesting illustration of the problems of presentation, marketing and authenticity that can arise when a destination derives its significance from the literary, philosophical and artistic reputation of a controversial figure, whose work demands specialised cultural capital for full appreciation and whose representation in the outside world fluctuates widely over time, especially in terms of visibility and accessibility to a broad popular market. Research is also made difficult by the limited scale and scope of the available archive for Brantwood itself during its period (since the early 1930s) as a tourist destination and educational institution, dedicated to the display of Ruskin's work and the presentation of his ideas in his own domestic setting; and this chapter will not cover the whole range of potential questions outlined above, especially as regards the changing internal arrangements of Brantwood as presented to the public, and the nature and composition of collections and their presentation.

As we saw in Chapter 5, Ruskin made his own distinctive contribution to the development of tourism in the English Lake District. He added his weight to the construction of the region as a literary landscape and, above all, as a haven of peace, simplicity and rural virtue that deserved to be protected from the incursions of the new industrial society through the spread of extractive industries, reservoirs and railways, and reserved for contemplation and healthy exercise. His opposition to railway extension, whether or not in conjunction with mining and quarrying, carried considerable moral force, although it would be hard to demonstrate that it actually tilted the scales against any particular development. But his rhetorical interventions both furthered existing campaigns, and fed into the development of campaigning organisations that made life increasingly difficult for promoters of economic development of a kind that might threaten existing landscapes and social arrangements. (Marshall & Walton, 1981, Chapter 9; Richards, 1995) His targets included the 'wrong' sort of tourists, those who lacked the cultural, moral or indeed spiritual capital to benefit from experiencing the Lake District landscape and ambience, who might spoil the experience for others by engaging in the sacrilege of drunken or disruptive behaviour in this special setting, and whose presence might generate demand for inappropriate kinds and levels of urban development and investment in commercial popular entertainment. His own presence in and writings about the Lake District, however, provided an endorsement of the area's attractions for serious-minded lovers of landscape and tranquillity, and his own expressed preferences directed the journeys and the gaze of others, while his fame and writings generated a culture of commemoration after his death, associated with places with which he was identified. His followers, especially Canon Rawnsley, took all this further by contributing to the burgeoning guidebook market of the late nineteenth and early 20th century (Walton, 1998). His biographer and former secretary W.G. Collingwood also produced what was effectively a polished, literary guide-book to the region; and *The Lake Counties*, first published in 1902 and revised in 1932, then went through three further reprints in the next 10 years, the last one in the very difficult publishing circumstances of the middle of the Second World War, before appearing in its final guise in 1949 (Collingwood, 1949; Parker, 2001). Like Wordsworth before him, though with less obvious dramatic irony, Ruskin helped to sustain and expand the tourist presence about which he expressed such strong reservations; and Brantwood, as it became a destination for tourists in its own right, eventually made its own distinctive, if low-key, contribution to this process.

Brantwood's status as a tourist destination depends overwhelmingly on the Ruskin connection, although it has other claims to fame. It is in no sense an architecturally distinguished house. As James D. Symon remarked, it is 'a plain house, still declaring its cottage origin. For the house beautiful, in what Ruskin called the vulgarly aesthetic sense, he took no care...' (Symon, 1977: 70). Nor has it ever been a highly popular des- tination: at just under 30,000 per year its visitor numbers are little more than half the English Heritage national average for 'Historic Houses', and within the Lake District it is outscored comfortably not only by (for exam- ple) the Lakeland Pencil Museum and the Barrow Docks Museum, but also by Lakeland literary destinations such as Dove Cottage and Beatrix Potter's Hill Top, as well as Blackwell, the Ruskin-influenced Baillie Scott Arts and Crafts house on Windermere, although it runs slightly ahead of Wordsworth House at Cockermouth (http://www.tourismtrade.org.uk). Its attractions lie in its location, on the east side of Coniston Water with magnificent views across the lake to Coniston Old Man and adjoining Lake District fells, which led Ruskin to buy the house without setting foot in it when it came on the market (he knew the area but not the house), and of course in its association with Ruskin himself. But its detachment from the core of Lake District visitor honey-pots, and its limited access and car parking facilities, also help to keep visitor numbers down.

The core of the house was a cottage of six to eight rooms, built in 1797; it acquired various piecemeal additions in the 1830s and 1850s before Ruskin added a distinctive room with a turret, followed by a lodge and a dining room, during the 1870s, as well as designing and building a lodge for his valet. Subsequent additions, a large artist's studio at the back and a second floor for the whole building, were driven more by Ruskin's cousin, Joan Severn, her husband Arthur, and their growing family as Ruskin himself became increasingly reclusive and uncommunicative from the late 1880s onwards; and the Severns themselves added a conspicuous bay window in 1905 (Dearden, 1960; Hanson, 1987b; Pevsner, 1969: 108–109). The newspaper executive, novelist and topographical writer Frank Singleton, writing (significantly) in 1954, blamed Ruskin for what he saw as 'the ugliness of everything' in the house and its architecture; but the artist's studio (which combined 'the worst features of a disused billiard room, a forgotten railway station and an atheistic church') was created for Arthur Severn (Singleton, 1954: 69). This is a strikingly different percep- tion from that of John Howard Whitehouse, who had bought Brantwood in 1931 to be a national Ruskin memorial, as expressed in his 'account of the exhibition rooms' in 1937: 'The alterations which Ruskin made to the house were of a very attractive and successful character. They included a new dining room ... and a great studio for Arthur Severn, who was a painter of distinction ... The whole place is fragrant with Ruskin's memory' (Whitehouse, 1937: 9–10). Taking this a step further, Bruce Hanson, the joint curator of Brantwood for most of the 1980s, remarked in an interview in 1987 that when the alarm systems were installed it turned out that 'almost every wall had been an outside wall at some stage', that the present house is very much Ruskin's creation, and that it might be argued to constitute, by the nature of its development and relationship with the landscape, an example of 'organic architecture', a term which Hanson ascribed to Ruskin himself (Hanson, 1987b). Singleton's comments show that this last observation would not have commanded universal approbation, at least in the post-war generation.

As presented to the public, the contents of the house are very closely identified with Ruskin in evocative and interesting ways, and the extensive gardens also call forth significant Ruskin associations, while their layout and content, as recovered and re-imagined over the last twenty years, constitute an attraction in their own right. But this is a classic example of a destination whose distinctive attributes, within the context of a tourist region, are bound up with the perceived relationship between personality and place, and its celebration and commemoration (Moore, 2000). As Hanson commented, Ruskin is at the core of Brantwood's importance as a place to visit; but, as we shall see, there are other interesting personal associations alongside those with Ruskin himself.

Nor is Coniston a village of particular distinction in itself. Sir Nikolaus Pevsner described it as having 'the Lake District character of, say, Ambleside: a village, a few old-established white hotels... a totally townish shopping street, and a village church' (Pevsner, 1969: 108). Its main external claims to fame, Ruskin apart, involve the industrial archaeology of Coppermines Valley (Holland, 1987), the quality of the surrounding scenery, and the associations with Donald Campbell's attempts on the world water speed record between 1956 and 1967, and with Arthur Ransome's *Swallows and Amazons* (Wardale, 1998). But the main attraction that distinguishes the village itself, apart from the impressive Ruskin memorial cross in the churchyard, is the Ruskin Museum. This was founded in 1901, the year after Ruskin's death and at the behest of W G. Collingwood, at a point when his visibility and influence, on national and international stages, were close to their peak. Its displays emphasize his importance in terms of religion and ethics; the propagation of an integrating, interdisciplinary, holistic view of the world; the derivation of the foundations of real value and happiness from understanding, truth, equity and pride in work well done rather than from profit, the cash nexus and the accumulation of material possessions; and his perceived anticipation of an array of subsequent concerns, from the minimum wage to the National Health Service to environmentalism (http://www.ruskinmuseum.com/ruskin.htm).

What matters most for present purposes, then, is the association between Ruskin and Brantwood. We need to remember the highly significant ways in which Ruskin's reputation changed during and after his occupancy of the house, as he moved from being predominantly an art critic and architectural writer to opening out a new identity and constituency as social commentator and heretical political economist (Hilton, 2002). We have seen that it was during the 1860s that his writings played a part in stimulating tourism on a novel scale to the destinations he had exalted, as his writings were adopted by key elements of the tourist media to direct the tourist gaze and to legitimise journeys and destinations. The ironies and apparent paradoxes inherent in this process are manifold, although we saw in Chapters 5 and 6 that it is both easy and dangerous to exaggerate Ruskin's hostility to railways. Some have thought it a paradox that Brantwood's view across the lake to Coniston Old Man also included quarries, mines and the railway station, which had opened in 1859, when the Furness Railway also introduced a tourist steam yacht, the *Gondola*, on Coniston Water. As the guide-book writer Baddeley put it, the view was marred by 'the mines and quarries, which abound almost the whole way up the Old Man' as well as the 'blocks of sheds' around the station (Baddeley, 1907: 26). There is no evidence that Ruskin minded this, which is a further reminder not to stereotype his views too easily, although in 1888, in an apparently paradoxical passage that suggested a selective direction of his own westward gaze from Brantwood, he expressed his pleasure in 'the view of the lower reach of Coniston Water, not because it is particularly beautiful, but because it is entirely pastoral and pure. Were a single point of chimney of the Barrow ironworks to show itself over the green ridge of the hill, I should never care to look at it more' (Symon, 1977: 70–71). This is a reminder of his perpetual awareness of the proximity of Barrow and its industrial storm-clouds, but he tolerated the local mines and quarries, and used the Coniston branch line to start and finish longer railway journeys (Hilton, 2002: 862). Today's Brantwood management embraces the restored *Gondola* and urges visitors to use it, and this is not a contradiction. Indeed, the steam yacht, together with the lake ferries, has become an important conduit of visitors to Brantwood since the building of a landing jetty for that purpose in the mid-1980s, especially given the restricted road access and parking facilities at the house (Johnson, 1989).

When he purchased Brantwood, Ruskin was highly visible in his guise as architectural and artistic critic and creator of evocative and inspiring descriptions of buildings, skies, 'nature' and landscapes. His more popular (but overlapping) appeal as moralist, prophet and alternative political economist developed during his time at Brantwood. It had begun most powerfully with *Unto this Last*, which brought his work to its widest and most earnest audiences during the late 19th and early 20th century, exerting an influence not only on romantic socialism but also on the founders of the Labour Party through cheap editions, evening classes, chapel reading groups and followers of William Morris, It reached its peak as he himself fell silent towards the end of the 19th century. After his death, his reputation remained high on a broad front until the First World War. As we saw in previous chapters, it fell into eclipse with remarkable speed during the 1920s and 1930s, as all things Victorian became deeply unfashionable. Lytton Strachey's debunking of Victorian reputations with the publication of *Eminent Victorians* in 1918 had knock-on effects on a broader front, although a Ruskin centenary celebration was held a year later at the Royal Academy, when John Howard Whitehouse mused about whether Ruskin's influence was really in decline, or whether he had become less visible as a taken-for-granted 'part of the lexicon of modern progress', a point of view that might already have seemed anachronistic to some (Waller, 2006: 221). One indication of Ruskin's post-war loss of credibility and visibility can be found in the *Daily Herald* photographic archive, where the only material on him is a single cropped portrait used in 1929 in a mid-January issue of this Labour and Socialist newspaper, and marked on the back 'Socialist in theory, but not in practice'. The paper's slender 'Coniston' file mentions neither Ruskin nor Brantwood, and is dominated by contextual photographs of the lake to provide background for reports on the pursuit of the world water speed record (National Media Museum). Another indicator of Ruskin's loss of currency is the only cartoon in the British Cartoon Archive to mention him, a David Low satire of 1930 on the atavistic procedures and values of a Royal Academy selection committee which features the Mayor of Mudpush and the Secretary of the Painters' and Paperhangers' Union, which includes an elderly academician's comment on a portrait presented for consideration, 'Now what would Ruskin have said?' (British Cartoon Archive LSE1478) It was about this time that Cyril Connolly referred to Ruskin as 'the forgotten man of the nineteenth century' (Pemble, 1995: 189).

   Brantwood remained in the hands of Ruskin's cousin Joan Severn and her husband Arthur, who had looked after him during his difficult final decade. They disregarded Ruskin's will, which 'earnestly prays' that they would they would 'accord during thirty consecutive days in every year such permission to strangers to see the house and pictures as I have done in my lifetime' (35.xlvii), and they gradually sold off important items from Ruskin's collections, especially his Turner paintings, to fund a lavish lifestyle for themselves and their children. In 1925, after Joan Severn's death, her husband left Brantwood for London before himself dying in 1931. During these years Ruskin's Guild of St George made a sustained but unavailing attempt to buy the house as a memorial (Association for Liberal Education, *c.* 1966; Dearden, 1986; Hanson, 1987a). It is interesting that no evidence has been found for any expression of interest by the National Trust, despite the importance of Ruskin to its founders and their ethos. By the late 1920s, the Trust's leadership had passed to a new generation, and the policy of acquiring and maintaining threatened country houses was still a thing of the future. In any case, Brantwood was not a 'country house' in the conventional sense, it lacked the necessary endowment of rental income from an associated estate, and neither its architecture nor its associations would have appealed (to put it politely) to James Lees-Milne, who was to become the driving force behind that project, and whose preference for Georgian country houses and Conservative traditionalism was never dissimulated (Lees-Milne, 1975; Murphy, 1987; Walton, 1995).

During 1930–1931 a series of sales of Ruskin's collections and manuscripts took place at Sotheby's in London and at Brantwood itself, and the house's future viability as a Ruskin shrine with authentic contents, at a time when all things Ruskinian were out of favour (at least in Britain), depended on the intervention of John Howard Whitehouse, an educationalist and former Liberal MP, the founder of the Ruskin Society of Birmingham and the educationally distinctive Bembridge School on the Isle of Wight, where he assembled a leading collection of Ruskin manuscripts, drawings and related materials, a former secretary of Toynbee Hall and Warden of the Manchester University Settlement, and a longterm admirer of Ruskin (and temporary admirer of Mussolini, in the mid-1920s). He was editor of the Ruskinian journal *Saint George* between 1898 and its closure in 1911; a trustee of the Guild of St George, having taken part in the earlier negotiations over the Guild's proposed Brantwood purchase; and the author of celebrations of Ruskin's work. After the trustees of Arthur Severn's will put the Brantwood estate up for auction and failed to find a buyer, at a particularly inauspicious moment for selling such a property, Whitehouse bought the house with 250 acres in 1932 as an international memorial to Ruskin, whose reputation extended far beyond the British Isles, and used the site to house part of his extensive Ruskin collections, many of which he had acquired at the Brantwood auctions. At the same time he founded the Ruskin Society, and three years later the Friends of Brantwood. In April 1934 the house was formally opened, by the Liberal M.P. Isaac Foot (a former pupil of Bembridge School), as an educational centre and museum for the preservation and display of Ruskin's treasures and mementoes, and for the propagation of his philosophy, under the legal umbrella of the Brantwood Education Trust Ltd (Eagles, 2007: 95; Dearden, 1959: 144, 1986; Waller, 2006: 217; Whitehouse, 1937: 6–7). During most of the Second World War, the pupils and staff of Bembridge School were evacuated from the Isle of Wight to Brantwood, and an attempt was made in 1944 to hand the estate over to the permanent custodianship of Oxford University, with which Ruskin had strong academic connections. This was aborted after three years, and in 1951 the estate was returned to Whitehouse (Dearden, 1959: 145, 2004). Under his stewardship its main role came to be the provision of short courses for educational organisations: his hopes that it might be used for conferences on national and international issues were not fulfilled (Whitehouse, 1937: 6–7).

We know little of the (apparently limited) educational provision until after Whitehouse's death in 1955, when the management committee of

Brantwood came under the chairmanship of R.G. Lloyd, a senior Liberal politician and barrister with impressive expertise in patent law, who became Lord Lloyd of Kilgerran in 1973 and had a brief stint as chairman of the Liberal Party (*Times*, 1991). Lloyd's interest in Ruskin seems to date from a brief early spell of teaching at Bembridge School; and in 1986 James Dearden, custodian of the extensive Ruskin collections that Whitehouse had also assembled at Bembridge, was full of praise for Lloyd's involvement at Brantwood: 'Lord Lloyd has been tireless in the personal care and attention which he has given to Brantwood. It is thanks to him and his co-trustees that it is still possible to maintain Brantwood as a national memorial to Ruskin and to hold small residential courses there' (Dearden, 1986). Lloyd was a very influential figure in the development of Brantwood between the mid-1950s and his death early in 1991. As well as chairing the Brantwood trustees, he acted as chairman of the Ruskin Association and of the trustees of Bembridge School; but although he was the apparent heir to so many of Whitehouse's concerns, it is hard to find a remotely similar level of ideological commitment to Ruskinian principles in his stewardship of Brantwood. In 1976, admittedly, he was capable of mounting a fierce but unfocused defence of Ruskin in a House of Lords debate on trade unions and labour relations, accusing no less a figure than Lord Goodman of misquoting Ruskin, and provoking an unedifying row about matters that were completely irrelevant to the question under discussion. He concluded his intervention by remarking bitterly that, 'We are in the technology age and Ruskin does not count in this' (Hansard, 1976).

This was an unusual, and perhaps revealing, outburst; but we are offered much fuller insight into how Lloyd saw his relationship with Brantwood through his extended intervention in another House of Lords debate, in July 1975, on the problems facing colleges that offered short-term residential courses during the inflationary conditions and government spending cuts of the mid-1970s. Lloyd used his experience of Brantwood to illustrate current problems and plead for some special measures of central government financial assistance, but he began by presenting his view of the nature of the estate and his family's involvement in it (Hansard, 1975):

> The duty of the Brantwood Trust is to look after the home of John Ruskin at Coniston in the Lake District. It is a very ugly house with about 30 to 40 rooms and 250 acres of land in a beautiful situation... (About 18 years ago) it became a hobby of myself and my wife to convert this almost derelict house and its grounds into something more habitable. We were fortunate in that after spending thousands of pounds on the property, we were able to encourage one national institution to take it over at a peppercorn rent and to run it for a few years. Financial difficulties arose and at that stage the trustees – myself and my colleagues – felt unable to accept a large grant for

capital improvements that had been generously offered to us because at that time, which was over 10 years ago, we did not think that the financial stability of the Trust was adequate to support further capital improvements.

I was then fortunate in becoming associated with principals of technical colleges and universities, and with an admirable staff we were able to build at Brantwood a project which involved giving courses to some 30 students at a time. At the same time the house had to be held open for the public to visit and look around and see the pictures and the other Ruskiniana. This was happily going forwards until about 18 months ago, when the cost of living went up, the salaries of staff rose immensely and we also found that the local authorities and the universities were unable – or unwilling – to increase their payments for charges for these residential students.

At this point the Trustees were obliged to close down these courses 'to a large extent' and rely on a much reduced income from day visitors and tourists, with their endowment of 'only a few hundred pounds' sufficing only to replace the slates that were blown away in winter gales.

This is revealing in several ways, not least because of the oral and possibly unscripted nature of the intervention. Lloyd moves to and fro, apparently unthinkingly, between regarding Brantwood as a family enterprise and recognising the role of the other trustees. It is not even clear whose money was spent on the refurbishments of the 1950s. He betrays no sense in this passage of the distinctive nature of Ruskin's thought, preferring to focus on the beauty of the artistic content of the collections and the grandeur of the site, although he shows no liking for the house itself, in striking contrast with the affectionate appreciation that was to be displayed by Bruce Hanson. He is at pains to emphasize the straitened circumstances of the Trust, especially at the point where he took over the chair, the 'almost derelict' condition of the estate in the mid-1950s, and the struggle to keep it afloat economically, staggering from crisis to crisis. Some of this may well be exaggeration for effect or to magnify his personal contribution to the 'rescue' of Brantwood, but there is no doubt that the finances were enduringly shaky, and these sustained problems may help to explain his financial caution when efforts were subsequently made to expand existing activities and invest in new ones.

Lord Lloyd's intervention made some impact on the House, although more concern was expressed for the parlous financial condition of two other specialist short-term residential course providers, Attingham Park and Newbattle Abbey. He made a further parliamentary reference to Brantwood in 1982, in opposition to a clause in a national heritage bill which appeared to make bodies like the Trust liable to pay Corporation Tax; and here he emphasized the Trust's role in 'maintaining and keeping open to the public the old home of John Ruskin ... (and) upholding the cultural heritage of the Lake District ...', an early and perhaps pioneering use of this term (Hansard, 1982). Here again, though in shorter compass, we may note the tone of what is expressed, and the nature of what is left unsaid. These contributions to debates in the House of Lords offer some useful insights into Lloyd's attitudes and priorities in his relationship with Brantwood and its Trustees, and provide some assistance in understanding what lay behind the developments between the 1950s and the 1990s that are discussed below.

The early impact of the Lloyd regime was soon apparent. By 1959, after some basic improvements to the amenities, the use of Brantwood as a visitor centre offering short residential courses was 'in the early experimental stages', with reading parties, field studies, and courses on landscape painting, philosophy, religion and social problems being envisaged (Dearden, 1959: 145). By 1961 it had become the Council for Nature's first holiday and conference centre, and the resident lecturer, Stanley Jeeves, laid great emphasis on Ruskin's role as critic of industrial society, and on what was described as 'countryside education' (Brantwood & Coniston, 1965; Jeeves, 1961). Further improvements were made in the facilities during the mid-1960s, when most of the year was occupied by short courses under the auspices of the Association for Liberal Education, bringing students in from further and higher education institutions all over England, including art colleges, teacher training colleges and the Hampton School of Needlework. A week's programme for engineering apprentices in 1966 included visits to the Barrow shipyards and the Windscale nuclear establishment, discussions on the costs and benefits of industrialisation and on racial and industrial conflict, walks on the fells and a single evening visit to a 'local hostelry'. Two weeks in mid-August were set aside to accommodate visiting families, and special terms were offered for artists, composers, writers and students, especially in early Spring and Autumn (Association for Liberal Education, 1966; Brochure of Brantwood, c. 1965). Further improvements to the residential amenities took place during the mid-1960s (including a car park), and this was clearly the main focus of Brantwood's activities at this point (Brantwood for Visitors, 1966). From the mid-1930s onwards Brantwood had been open to visitors who wanted to view the house and collections, and by 1959 it was open to the public daily, except on Sundays. But it was never a popular visitor attraction at this stage, and even in 1983 it only drew in 12,000 visitors per year to the house and collections, putting into perspective Lloyd's comments on the need to depend heavily on the income from day visitors (Dearden, 1959: 145, c. 1960; Hanson, 1987b; Johnson, 1989; Whitehouse, 1937: 8, 41–42).

Whitehouse's intervention, together with Lloyd's continuing interest, kept Brantwood, alongside Bembridge, as a focal point for sustaining Ruskinian ideas, values and traditions, although it will become clear that

the extent to which it was visited or recognised as an interesting and important location, beyond a relatively narrow circle of *cognoscenti*, was very limited. It proved easier to present Ruskin to a wider public in his guise as art
critic and architectural and travel writer, through his collections and his
own artistic output, and later through associations with the depiction of
ecology and the natural world, than through his roles as social critic and
alternative political economist. This perception, after all, seems to have
applied to Lord Lloyd himself. It became particularly the case during the
generation after the Second World War, as the essentially Victorian cultural
capital (especially the detailed textual knowledge of the Bible) necessary
to access Ruskin's published work (which runs to 39 large volumes in
the standard library edition), and derive full understanding of its allusions,
became an increasingly scarce commodity. Early post-war scholarly
accounts of Ruskin might still be broadly celebratory, although Joan
Evans's influential biography of 1954 was less than positive. It dominated
the field until the revival of interest in Ruskin's work from the mid-1970s
onwards, including Robert Hewison's *John Ruskin: the Argument of the Eye*
in 1976, which helped to create a propitious climate for the revival of
Brantwood from the early 1980s (Abse, 1980; Evans, 1954; Hewison, 1976;
Hunt, 1982; Leon, 1949; Rosenberg, 1980). The content of Evans's book
helped to generate a prurient interest in the reasons behind the dissolution
of Ruskin's marriage on grounds of non-consummation. Frank Singleton
was well aware of this in 1954, commenting on 'the tremendous, menda-
cious conspiracy with himself and the rest of the world about his sex life'
(Singleton, 1954: 69). This issue, together with the evidence of his enduring
emotional interest in young girls, tended to dominate casual awareness of
his life, sometimes combined with feminist attacks on his perceived attitudes to the role and status of women. It has also been enduringly difficult
to extract a coherent philosophy from Ruskin's immense, evolving, sometimes self-contradictory body of work, which can be represented as ranging right across the spectrum from paternalist Tory to fierce socialist. This
both makes Ruskin potentially many things to many people, and hampers
the production of a simple, uncontroversial promotional message.

It is interesting, and even curious (on some assumptions about Ruskin
as paternalist Tory or founding influence on the Labour Party), that some
of the most prominent advocates of the propagation of Ruskinian ideals
through Brantwood, from Whitehouse to Lord Lloyd of Kilgerran and
including Hanson, curator during the transitional decade of the 1980s,
were Liberal in party affiliation, and laid emphasis on the ethical, character-
forming, educational and (at least in Hanson's case) 'green' aspects of the
Ruskin message (Hanson, 1987b; Hilton, 2002: xviii–xix; *Times*, 1991). But
a kind of elective affinity between Ruskin, the 'New Liberals' (including
Whitehouse) who emerged in the late 19th century and advocated enabling
social legislation, a protective safety net of pensions and health care, and a

modest measure of redistribution of unearned wealth through taxation, and (for example) the foundation and early development of the National Trust, can be identified quite readily, and would benefit from further investigation (Hall, 2003).

It was not until the 1970s and especially the 1980s that the wheel of intellectual fashion began to gather sustained momentum in Ruskin's favour, and during the latter decade Brantwood began to emerge as a tourist destination with a message, over and above its other identities. From a low point of increasing dilapidation, neglect of the collections and uncertainty about identity or message in the early 1970s, when the Trustees were still very short of money, the house began to attract investment, academic interest and a new clarity of focus on what was important and communicable about Ruskin's living legacy. The crucial transition can probably be identified with the decade or so beginning in 1983, with the appointment as managers of Hanson and Diamond, who presided over a trebling of visitor numbers to 34,000 or 35,000 between 1983 and 1989. The local *Westmorland Gazette* estimated a further increase to 60,000 by 1994. At this point, however, the house and garden were still being run on a tight budget, even as a series of grants and awards paid testimony to the enterprise and success of the new regime; and in 1989 Brantwood won the National Art Collections Award. But tensions developed between the management team and Lord Lloyd, as the latter expressed public impatience with the cash-flow problems associated with investment, and resisted plans to bring the Bembridge collections to Brantwood (Hanson, 1987b; Hewison, 1990; Johnson, 1989; *Westmorland Gazette*, 1994). Lord Lloyd died in 1991. Many of Hanson and Diamond's initiatives have been extended under the subsequent management of Howard Hull, involving interest groups, exhibitions, and particularly developing the gardens, and always with an eye to sustaining visitor numbers. Hanson had succeeded in recruiting the interest of a wealthy Ruskin enthusiast and philanthropic industrialist, H.A. Cann, who has since endowed Brantwood's future financially and contributed generously to the Lottery-funded Ruskin Library at Lancaster University, both of which are run by the Ruskin Foundation. The growing involvement of Lancaster University from 1990 onwards, with the development of the Ruskin Library in 1998, to which the Bembridge collections were transferred, together with the definition of a close working relationship between Brantwood and the University, left Brantwood with more of a 'stately home' than an academic role, while sustaining its position as a vehicle for displaying and propagating Ruskin's ideas. Yet the Ruskin Centre at Lancaster that had been established to promote the serious academic study of Ruskin from an interdisciplinary point of view has since been cut back, so that there too what remains are the curatorial activities directed to what have become known at the John Howard Whitehouse Collections and related exhibitions.

Ruskin has rivals for identification as the most 'iconic' resident of Coniston: especially now Donald Campbell, whose death at the beginning of 1967 while attempting a new world speed record on water led to his becoming a 'local hero' and achieving an (on certain assumptions) improbable posthumous place of honour in the Ruskin Museum, which is now planning an extension as a shrine to Campbell's recovered boat *Bluebird* and a commemoration of Campbell's 'courage and endeavour' (http:// www.ruskinmuseum.com/campbell.htm). His was a very different way of responding to the Lakes from Ruskin's – it was about playing with technology, speed and power and making use of the landscape and location to that end, and the conflict between these ways of enjoying the Lake District and the contemplative pleasures of walkers and seekers after 'Nature and Nature's God' has been an enduring theme in the region's history, with Ruskin and Campbell at opposite poles (Walton & O'Neill, 2004). Coniston also has Ruskin-related associations from an earlier period: with W.G. Collingwood, for many years Ruskin's secretary and among other things a Norse and Anglo-Saxon expert and historian of the Lake District, helping to define a distinctive imagined linguistic and cultural identity for the region; with his son R.G. Collingwood, the philosopher of history; and also with Arthur Ransome, author of the enduringly popular (and nostalgia-inducing) *Swallows and Amazons* children's stories, which are set partly on Coniston Water and its attendant peak Coniston Old Man. Ransome, a glamorous and mysterious figure in his own right, apparently learned to sail in W.G. Collingwood's boat the 'Swallow' (Parker 2001; Wardale, 2000; Wawn, 2000). The most obvious direct Brantwood association is with William James Linton, the wood engraver and democratic political campaigner who owned the house from 1852 and edited the *English Republican* from it for a few years in the 1850s, eventually selling it to Ruskin after leaving for the United States in 1867 (Smith, 1973).

How visible were Ruskin and Brantwood as contributors to the development of the Lake District tourist trade during the 20th century? We have already indicated some of the paradoxes of Ruskin's personal role on the wider stage. We now chart the changing visibility of Brantwood and Ruskin in Lake District guide books from Ruskin's original purchase of the house to the point at which, in the mid-1980s, Brantwood really emerged as a tourist destination of a distinctive kind within a wider 'historic house' genre, as well as a commemorative and celebratory shrine with a mission to educate by articulating and disseminating the tenets and principles of its resident sage.

Brantwood was of no special relevance to Lake District visitors before Ruskin became established there. Black's *Guide* of 1868 mentions it only in passing, as one of several houses with 'beautifully wooded grounds' on the eastern side of the lake (Black, 1868: 74). After Ruskin's arrival it took some time for his presence to register or become relevant to guidebook writers or compilers. The 1880 edition of Murray's Hand-book to Lancashire has much to say about 'char', the characteristic fish of the English Lakes, in its Coniston Water variety, and about views and mountain walks, but the only literary allusion it makes under the Coniston heading is to 'Mr Gresley's novel *Coniston Hall*', set at 'the old seat of the Flemings' near the head of the lake. Gresley was a prebendary of Lichfield Cathedral and a religious controversialist within the Church of England, and (briefly) a prolific novelist during the 1840s; but although he is long forgotten, it is interesting that his virtual presence at Coniston was of greater interest in 1880 than Ruskin's actual one, even though Ruskin had been at Brantwood for nearly a decade, for both Ruskin and Brantwood are invisible in this detailed county survey (Gresley, 1846; Murray, 1880: 190–191). They were also absent from Jenkinson's *Guide* in the same year, which was entirely concerned with walks and ascents in the neighbourhood (Jenkinson, 1880: 43–47).

By 1891 Ruskin's presence at Brantwood was at last becoming visible to guidebook compilers. Baddeley singled out the views of the Old Man of Coniston from Brantwood as particularly 'grand', although he added Ruskin's name to those of two earlier inhabitants, W.J. Linton and 'Gerald Massey, the poet', merely as 'last, but not least' (Baddeley, 1891: 98). Massey lived briefly at Brantwood during 1857–1858, and this Chartist and Christian Socialist, well-known in his time and indeed a correspondent of Ruskin's, who later experimented with spiritualism and looked for relationships between Christianity and the religions of ancient Egypt, was not usually incorporated into a Brantwood story from which Linton himself was to be increasingly marginalised (Shaw, 1995).

The key transition in Ruskin's guide-book visibility spans the turn of the 19th century, the period of Ruskin's greatest influence on a wider public through the social message, the cheap editions and the evening classes. Indeed, the 1909 edition of Baddeley had changed the balance of its coverage completely: it made no mention of Linton or Massey, but laid heavy emphasis on Ruskin: 'Coniston will for all time be the place most closely associated with this great author and critic. His residence, Brantwood, where he died, is on the east side of the lake...' The house itself remained inaccessible to the public during the Severns' tenure, but the foundation of the Ruskin Museum in 1901 was given extensive treatment, and the manner of presentation indicated the way in which the new facility diverted attention away from Brantwood itself, with drawings, manuscripts and minerals contributed by the Severns from the house ('interesting and valuable articles'), and supplemented by exhibits from Collingwood, taking pride of place. A note of levity was introduced by the postscript which completed the summary of exhibits: 'Lastly, the professor's umbrella' (Baddeley, 1909: 103). The Museum was within easy reach of the railway station, while a visit to Brantwood would involve either a boat trip or an awkward and circuitous journey around the head of the lake. The Black's *Guide* of 1907, which was 'edited' by Baddeley but displayed significant textual differences, did mention Linton and Massey, as well as the time spent by Tennyson on honeymoon at nearby Tent Lodge; but the main emphasis at Brantwood was on Ruskin himself, 'the great teacher and writer', who was credited with 'nearly forty years' in residence, a considerable exaggeration (Baddeley, 1907: 26–27).

Even at the turn of the century, Ruskin's increased visibility in publications for tourists was far from universal, despite the extensive coverage afforded to his death and funeral in 1900, which reached the pages of the *New York Times* (*New York Times*, 25 January 1900). An outstanding exception, which perhaps proves the rule, was the work of Ruskin's disciple Canon Rawnsley, who wrote eloquently in 1902 about the beauties of Brantwood's grounds and views, and the depth of Ruskin's attachment to the place and its associations (Rawnsley, 1902: 30–45 and chapter 3). But the book in question was more about Ruskin than about tourist destinations or associations; and it is interesting that Collingwood's *Guide* has little to say about Ruskin in relation to Brantwood while discussing Coniston and district, merely acknowledging in passing the years he spent there, while quoting him appreciatively and at length in other contexts. But he had already covered this ground elsewhere, not least in his successive biographies of Ruskin, which began with an 'outline' in 1889 and culminated in the standard work, first published in 1900, which went through four more editions between 1905 and 1922, and his *Ruskin Relics* of 1903 (Collingwood, 1949: 62). More representative was the prolific topographical writer A.G. Bradley, writing in the year after Ruskin's death, who took no notice at all of Ruskin or Brantwood, although he was eager to retrieve the memory of (Alexander) Craig Gibson, 'a country doctor' with a 'passion for dialect studies and some genius for writing poems both of a humorous and pathetic nature' who was based at Coniston in the 1840s, and whose writings debunked the romantic view of local peasant virtues that was ascribed to Wordsworth and Coleridge (Bradley, 1924: 196–202). Gibson has become almost invisible beyond the British Library catalogue, where we learn that his book on the 'folk-speech' of Cumberland 'and adjacent districts' was twice reissued after its initial publication in 1869, although he does feature prominently in the current on-line 'community profile' for Coniston provided by ePodunk UK. Here he is described as 'writer and poet' and is placed ahead of the two other chosen local worthies, Ruskin himself ('poet and philosopher' on this occasion) and R.G. Collingwood, 'historian' (at the expense of his father, Ruskin's former secretary W.G. Collingwood) (Gibson, 1869; http://uk.epodunk.com/profiles/england/coniston/3001563.html).

The acquisition of Brantwood by John Howard Whitehouse in 1932 was done with a view to its being 'opened… to the public as an international memorial'; and this was soon reflected in guidebook commentaries, although it took time for the exact position to be clearly communicated (Dearden, 2004). By 1936 the Ward Lock *Red Guide* could highlight the growing significance of Brantwood as an attraction in its own right, alongside the Ruskin Museum, where, 'One wonders, however, what Ruskin would have said to the "penny-in-the-slot" turnstile by which one gains admission to the museum!' This is a good illustration of the combination of stereotype and trivialisation which was beginning to surround the fading image of Ruskin as a remote technophobe and a presumably censorious Victorian sage. As to Brantwood, 'The house contains many treasures associated with Ruskin, and is open daily, 10–12.30 and 2–6.30, 1s (5p). A part of Brantwood is used as a guest-house.' Ruskin, here, was 'the great writer' (Ward, Lock, 1936: 90–91).

In the late 1930s the new *Handy Guide to the English Lake District* indicated the low-key but ubiquitous nature of Coniston's relationship with Ruskin. His name was everywhere. Boating was available from the Ruskin Pier, and the Ruskin Institute offered bowls and billiards as well as the Ruskin Museum itself, while the grave was still highlighted as a place of pilgrimage. Ruskin was described as 'artist and poet, critic and political economist', and at this point Brantwood, with its museum, was described as 'a hostel belonging to the Ruskin Society', which 'may not be visited without permission', in contrast with the generous opening hours that were promised by the Ward Lock guide. Ruskin, though mentioned here, was accorded half a sentence in the general section on 'Literary Pilgrimages', although this was eccentric even for the time in giving more space to the Keswick-based novelist Hugh Walpole, then at the height of his visibility, than to anyone else. As we saw above, for more than a generation from the late 1930s Brantwood became much more a residential educational foundation than a didactic tourist attraction (Palmer, *c.* 1937: 9, 42–45). For H.H. Symonds, who held a strong and perhaps inflated view of the importance of Ruskin to Coniston's economy (on a par with copper, sheep and climbing), Brantwood itself in the mid-1930s was nevertheless relegated to the status of 'a museum piece' (Symonds, 1933: 217, 233). It was, however, given star billing by Arthur Mee in the Lancashire volume of his highly popular 'King's England' series in 1939, which took Ruskin's importance as read and drew readers' attention to Brantwood's status as national memorial, which 'we may use . . . as a guest house, live in the rooms in which Ruskin lived, walk about his gardens, look out on the hills that gave him inspiration and delight'. Here we have an important illustration of the enduring power of Ruskin's reputation in patriotic educational circles, to set against the evidence of decline elsewhere (Mee, 1939: 74–77). It was at this point, too, that the geographer Vaughan Cornish, classifying and celebrating the various kinds of English landscape to offer guidelines for the shaping of the post-war National Parks, referred to 'Ruskin by the shore of Coniston' keeping alight the flame of worship of wild landscape that Wordsworth had ignited, 'and to these, more perhaps than to any other prophets of the century now past, we owe the faith ... that the beauties of Nature are a source of inspiration unclouded by intellectual error and available for all men' (Cornish, 1937: 88; and see also Matless, 1998).

Brantwood was, however, almost invisible through the post-war generation. Frank Singleton's survey of *The English Lakes* in 1954 did pay sustained attention to Brantwood, but in a spirit of 'how are the mighty fallen', referring to 'the rats that scurry across the remains ... in this his fallen day', musing on the ironies of his legacies, and concluding that, although it was still 'the chief object of pilgrimage on this side of the lake' (which was actually damning with the faintest of praise), 'You escape with relief from Brantwood' (Singleton, 1954: 67–72). Singleton's comments about Ruskin's invisibility to the rising generation were to be reflected in the Geographia guide of the mid-1960s and *The Observer* 'Time Off' guide of 1967, both of which mentioned the Ruskin grave and museum without saying who Ruskin was, and referred to Brantwood's general location without mentioning access or content (Taylor, n.d.: 71; *The Observer*, 1967: 41). The Ward Lock *Red Guide* entry for Coniston in 1975 highlights the Ruskin Museum and his grave in the churchyard, although mention of Brantwood is relegated to the 'Walks round Coniston' section, where it is described as 'for over a quarter of a century the home of John Ruskin. The great writer died here'. The house's role as a museum, presenting 'many articles associated with Ruskin' and open to the public daily for a 'small charge', is mentioned alongside its current role as 'a centre for Adult Education' (Hammond, 1975: 65–66). But a great deal more was made of the nearby beauty spot of Tarn Hows, although Coniston Old Man and the neighbouring mountains were themselves ignored. These were very low-key years for Brantwood, whose management seemed unsure of what its purpose might be, with Ruskin himself in the depths of eclipse after the rapid fall in his intellectual stock during and after the inter-war years. In about 1980, the house's tiny gift shop resorted to selling gonks bearing the legend 'I've been to JR's house', seeming to identify Ruskin with J.R. Ewing, the villain of the television series *Dallas*, then at the height of its popularity (personal recollection). It would be hard to imagine a more inappropriate association.

Brantwood emerged again from these shadows from late 1982 onwards, under the new management regime of Hanson and Diamond, who were eager to use the house, collections and gardens as means for propagating ethical and ecological aspects of Ruskin's social thought and emphasizing its contemporary relevance, producing a new video to this end (Hanson, 1987b). The house's increasing visibility by the mid-1980s was both highlighted and furthered by the journalist and biographer Hunter Davies's *The Good Guide to the Lakes*, where it appeared in the 'Literary Lakes' section.

Davies endorsed the way in which 'the new curator, Bruce Hanson, is transforming it into an excellent museum and country house', which might soon 'rival the other Lake District big guns (Dove Cottage, Hill Top and Rydal Mount)'. The book shop and tea rooms were singled out for praise, and the new Wainwright Room, celebrating the author of a walkers' illustrated *vade mecum* to the Lakes, pointed up another of the ways in which Brantwood was moving beyond the passive display of Ruskiniana to make itself attractive to more mainstream tourist markets (Wainwright was certainly more 'mainstream' than Ruskin) while propagating 'Ruskinian' messages in the process (Davies, 1984: 152–153). For these purposes Bruce Hanson made every effort to draw parallels between Ruskin and Alfred Wainwright, especially in terms of nature conservation and the prevention of cruelty to animals, although the attention to precise detail in their otherwise contrasting styles of illustration might also have been emphasized. But there was no getting around the fact that Wainwright's own first visit to Brantwood had been in connection with the establishment of 'his' exhibition (Hanson, 1987b). Hanson and Diamond were, indeed, acutely aware that in trying to 'bring Brantwood back to life' they had to recognise the limited appeal of Ruskin and his works in their own right, and the Wainwright exhibition was part of a strategy to make Brantwood attractive to other markets and in more conventional ways, so that visitors could 'discover' Ruskin as part of a wider menu of attractions (Hanson, 1987b). During and after the 1980s Coniston's Ruskin Museum also emerged from a long period in the doldrums, which had culminated in its being identified as one of the collections most at risk in north-west England. It subsequently attracted £850,000 in development funding before reopening in transformed guise in 1999 (http://www.ruskinmuseum.com/ruskin.htm).

All these new directions reflected changing attitudes to Ruskin as writer, prophet and potential tourist attraction, along with growing and more positive academic and media interest, and the recruitment of new custodians who understood the potential of their inherited collections and were eager to unlock it. Exactly how these developments occurred, and what their wider comparative significance might be, remains an opportunity for further research. Meanwhile, this chapter has drawn attention to the importance of this particular type of 'historic house' as a potential subject for historical research into the changing relationships between destination identities as home, shrine, embodiment of a life's work, and (on several potential levels) tourist attraction. The story invites comparison with 'house museums' elsewhere, especially those commemorating or celebrating, perhaps with greater external visibility, lives that might be thought to be of similar complexity and cultural significance, such as Bateman's (Rudyard Kipling), Down House (Charles Darwin), or even Chartwell (Sir Winston Churchill), all of which passed into the custodianship of either the National Trust or English Heritage, a process which in itself communicated a sense of national importance, while Brantwood remained in the hands of its Trustees, just as Wordsworth's Dove Cottage did, in the absence of a readily accessible university or similar focus for patronage and publicity (Buczacki, 2007; Cannadine, 2002 and compare Cross and Walton, 2005, Chapter 6). Teasing out the changing nature of the tensions and contradictions entailed in these processes, over time, and in relation to the personal conflicts and contradictions that were also involved, constitutes an important and revealing kind of research project, a micro-history or history from within of this kind of tourist destination, that offers great promise for further development.

An examination of Brantwood's history as a tourist destination sheds further light on the complex relationships between Ruskin and the development of tourism. Just as other influences have been more visible, so have similar destinations been more popular and easier to market. This should not surprise us, given the idiosyncrasy and relative inaccessibility of Ruskin's last home, and the increasing difficulties encountered in assessing his legacy and presenting his work to new generations. Since it opened its doors in the 1930s, Brantwood has provided for several overlapping niche markets, some of which are attracted by aspects of its history and location that do not require an acquaintanceship with Ruskin and his work. What is perhaps more surprising is the degree of influence Ruskin did acquire over the content, flow and gaze of British tourism in Western Europe during his period of greatest visibility between the mid-1840s and the First World War; but we saw in Chapters 5 and 6 that this was focused firmly on certain well-defined themes and social groups, and that it would be rash to extrapolate it further, even in Venice and other cities of northern Italy. We return to these and related questions in the concluding chapter.

References

Abse, J. (1980) *John Ruskin: The Passionate Moralist*. London: Quartet.

Association for Liberal Education (1966) Brantwood Courses. Cyclostyled typescript in Brantwood Archive.

Association for Liberal Education (n.d., c. 1966) *A Short History of Brantwood*. Twickenham College of Technology, copy in Brantwood Archive.

Baddeley, M.J.B. (1891) *The English Lake District*. London: Thorough Guides.

Baddeley, M.J.B. (ed.) (1907) *Black's Shilling Guide to the English Lakes*. London: Adam and Charles Black.

Baddeley, M.J.B. (1909) *The English Lake District*. London: Nelson.

Black, A. (1868) *Black's Picturesque Guide to the English Lakes*. Edinburgh: Adam and Charles Black.

Bradley, A.G. (1924, first published 1901) *Highways and Byways in the Lake District*. London: Macmillan.

'Brantwood, Coniston' (September, 1965) Association for Liberal Education and Council for Nature, Leaflet in Brantwood Archive.

'Brantwood for Visitors' (1966), printed leaflet in Brantwood Archive.

British Cartoon Archive, University of Kent (1930) David Low, *Evening Standard*, 7 April, LSE1478.

Brochure of Brantwood (n.d., *c.* 1965), in Brantwood Archive.

Buczacki, S. (2007) *Churchill and Chartwell*. London: Frances Lincoln.

Cannadine, D. (2002) *In Churchill's Shadow: Confronting the Past in Modern Britain*. London: Allen Lane.

Collingwood, W.G. (1949) *The Lake Counties*. London: J.M. Dent and Sons.

Cornish, V. (1937) *The Preservation of our Scenery*. Cambridge: Cambridge University Press.

Cross, G. and Walton, J.K. (2005) *The Playful Crowd: Pleasure Places in the Twentieth Century*. New York: Columbia University Press.

Davies, H. (1984) *The Good Guide to the Lakes*. Caldbeck: Forster Davies.

Dearden, J.S. (1959) *Brantwood, in Cumbria* (pp. 141–145). Brantwood Archive.

Dearden, J.S. (*c.* 1960) Brantwood: A brief history for visitors. Leaflet, Brantwood Archive.

Dearden, J.S. (1986) Brantwood in the twentieth century. Leaflet, Brantwood Archive.

Dearden, J.S. (2004) Whitehouse, John Howard (1873–1955). *Oxford Dictionary of National Biography*. Oxford: Oxford University Press.

Eagles, S. (2007) 'The insinuating touch of influence: Aspects of Ruskin's political legacy.' In C. Casaliggi and P. March-Russell (eds) *Ruskin in Perspective* (pp. 101–114). Newcastle: Cambridge Scholars Publishing.

Evans, J. (1954) *John Ruskin: A Biography*. London: Jonathan Cape.

Gibson, A.C. (1869, reprinted 1873, 1910) *The Folk-Speech of Cumberland and some Districts Adjacent*. London: J.R. Smith.

Gresley, W. (1846) *Coniston Hall*. London: The Englishman's Library.

Hall, M. (2003) The politics of collecting: The early aspirations of the National Trust, 1883–1913. *Transactions of the Royal Historical Society* (Sixth series) 13, 345–357.

Hammond, R.J.W. (ed.) (1975) *Lake District: A Ward Lock Red Guide*. London: Ward Lock.

Hansard (1975) House of Lords Debates, Residential Colleges, Lord Lloyd of Kilgerran, 2 July, cols. 320–321.

Hansard (1976) House of Lords Debates, Trade Unions and Labour Relations, Lord Lloyd of Kilgerran, 24 Feb., col. 663.

Hansard (1982) House of Lords Debates, National Heritage Bill, Lord Lloyd of Kilgerran, 16 Dec., col. 798.

Hanson, B. (1987a) *Brantwood*. Coniston: Brantwood Trust.

Hanson, B. (1987b) Tape of interview conducted by W.R. Mitchell, W.R. Mitchell papers, J.B. Priestley Library, University of Bradford.

Hewison, R. (1976) *John Ruskin: The Argument of the Eye*. London: Thames and Hudson.

Hewison, R. (1990) Ruskin heritage under the hammer. *Sunday Times* 18 February.

Hilton, T. (2002) *John Ruskin*. New Haven, CT: Yale University Press.

Holland, E.G. (1987) *Coniston Copper*. Milnthorpe: Cicerone.

http://uk.epodunk.com/profiles/england/coniston/3001563.html.   Accessed 16.06.07.

http://www.ruskinmuseum.com/campbell.htm. 16.07.07.

http://www.ruskinmuseum.com/ruskin.htm. 15.07.07.

http://www.tourismtrade.org.uk. Accessed 16.06.07.

Hunt, J.D. (1982) *The Wider Sea*. London: Dent.

Jackson, H. (2006) A brief history of Ruskin Park. On WWW at http://www.londongardenstrust.org/index.htm?features/ruskin2006.htm. Accessed 19.04.09.

Jeeves, S. (1961) A wish fulfilled through nature. *Lancashire Life* (pp. 63–64). Brantwood Archive.

Jenkinson, H.I. (1880) *Tourists' Guide to the English Lake District*. London: Edward Stanford.

Johnson, P. (1989) Putting the money on Ruskin. *Sunday Times*, 7 May.

Lees-Milne, J. (1975) *Ancestral Voices*. London: Chatto and Windus.

Leon, D. (1949) *Ruskin, the Great Victorian*. London: Routledge.

Mandler, P. (1997) *The Fall and Rise of the Stately Home*. New Haven, CT: Yale University Press.

Marshall, J.D. and Walton, J.K. (1981) *The Lake Counties from 1830 to the Mid-Twentieth Century*. Manchester University Press.

Matless, D. (1998) *Landscape and Englishness*. London: Reaktion.

Mee, A. (1936) *Lancashire: The Cradle of our Prosperity*. London: Hodder and Stoughton.

Moore, K. (2000) *Museums and Popular Culture*. London: Continuum.

Murphy, G. (1987) *Founders of the National Trust*. London: Christopher Helm.

Murray's Hand-book for Lancashire (1880) London: John Murray.

National Media Museum, Bradford, *Daily Herald* archive, files on 'Coniston' and 'John Ruskin'.

New York Times, 25 January 1900, Funeral of John Ruskin.

Palmer, W.T. (n.d., c. 1937) *The Handy Guide to the English Lakes*. London: Handy Guides.

Parker, C. (2001) W.G. Collingwood's Lake District. *Northern History* 38, 295–314.

Pemble, J. (1995) *Venice Rediscovered*. Oxford: Clarendon Press.

Pevsner, N. (1969) *North Lancashire*. Buildings of England: Penguin.

Rawnsley, H.D. (1902) *Ruskin and the English Lakes*. Glasgow: James MacLehose and Sons.

Richards, J.M. (1995) The role of the railways. In M. Wheeler (ed.) *Ruskin and Environment* (pp. 123–143). Manchester: Manchester University Press.

Rosenberg, J.D. (1980) *The Darkening Glass: A Portrait of Ruskin's Genius*. New York: Columbia University Press.

Shaw, D. (1995) *Gerald Massey: Chartist, Poet, Radical and Freethinker*. London: The Buckland Press.

Singleton, F. (1954) *The English Lakes*. London: Batsford.

Smith, F.B. (1973) *Radical Artisan: William James Linton, 1812–1897*. Manchester: Manchester University Press.

Symon, J.D. (1977, first published 1911) *John Ruskin: His Homes and Haunts*. Folcroft, PA: Folcroft Library Editions.

Symonds, H.H. (1933) *Walking in the Lake District*. London: W. and R. Chambers.

Taylor, R. (n.d., revised between 1958 and 1966) *The Lake District: Britain's Largest National Park*. London: Geographia.

The Observer (1967) *Time Off in the Lake District and the Yorkshire Dales*. London: Hodder and Stoughton.

Times (1991) Obituary of Lord Lloyd of Kilgerran, 1 February.

Waller, P.J. (2006) *Writers, Readers and Reputations: Literary Life in Britain 1870–1918*. Oxford: Oxford University Press.

Walton, J.K. (1995) The National Trust: Preservation or provision? In M. Wheeler (ed.) *Ruskin and Environment* (pp. 144–164). Manchester: Manchester University Press.

Walton, J.K. (1998) Canon Rawnsley and the English lake district. *Armitt Library Journal* 1, 1–17.

Walton, J.K. and O'Neill, C. (2004) Tourism and the lake district: Social and cultural histories. In D.W.G. Hind and J.P. Mitchell (eds) *Sustainable Tourism in the English Lake District* (pp. 19–47). Sunderland: Business Education Publishers.

Ward, Lock and Co., Limited (1936) *A Pictorial and Descriptive Guide to the English Lake District*. London: Ward, Lock.

Wardale, R. (2000) *Arthur Ransome and the World of the Swallows and Amazons*. Skipton: Great Northern.

Wawn, A. (2000) *The Vikings and the Victorians: Inventing the Old North in Victorian England*. Cambridge: D.S. Brewer.

Westmorland Gazette, 29 April 1994.

Whitehouse, J.H. (1937) *Ruskin and Brantwood: An Account of the Exhibition Rooms*. Cambridge: Cambridge University Press and the Ruskin Society.

Chapter 8
Conclusion

John Ruskin has never been a presence in Tourism Studies. His continuing invisibility is signalled by his absence from the list of 'Giants of Tourism' in a book intended to promote awareness of tourism's history by highlighting the contribution of 'historic' figures. Apart from a chapter on 'early significant figures' such as Marco Polo and Ibn Battuta, the only biographies to reach back beyond the 20th century are those of Beau Nash, Baedeker (but not Murray), Thomas Cook and John Muir (Butler & Russell, 2010). The Grand Tour has a central place in the abbreviated, conventional versions of tourism history that are briefly fed to students, but Ruskin's important role in the Victorian development and refinement of what to see, and how to see it, is by-passed. Coverage moves straight on to Thomas Cook and his alleged invention of popular tourism and the 'package tour'. The influence of Ruskin's writings and ideas on tourist routes, destinations and above all perceptions is discussed in works of literary history and criticism, by (for example) Fussell, Buzard and Pemble, but this seems not to have passed across into Tourism Studies.

It is arguable that the absence of any previous serious consideration of Ruskin in Tourism Studies is indicative of a wider neglect of the Humanities, brought about by the focus of the discipline on business rather than culture, except where the latter can be instrumentalised for commercial purposes. Sociological approaches such as that of Urry have largely proved complicit in this restricted focus: 'Commerce and culture are indissolubly intertwined in the postmodern' (Urry, 2005: 77). Our study suggests that the incorporation of awareness of the extensive body of work on guidebooks and travel writing, viewed from a broadly historical and literary perspective, would significantly deepen and enrich the field; that Ruskin's influence would form an important dimension of this process; and that understanding of literary, historical and aesthetic research would gain equally, in its turn, from such an interdisciplinary leavening. Most writing on Ruskin within the Humanities, after all, tends to avoid his connections with tourism, just as it draws back from his inconvenient heresies about the proper relationships between economics and morality. We hope that this book may build bridges between these various approaches. The authors of this volume surprised themselves by the extent of their agreement about the key issues and arguments. One of us is a Roman Catholic distributist with a deep distrust of Mammon and the unregulated market place, while the other is a libertarian socialist with a strong commitment to the empowerment of democracy through critical liberal education. Ruskin, as it turned out, provided us with extensive common ground, which we entered from opposite poles but tilled in common, fortified by shared values derived from the Humanities.

While Ruskin's engagement in so many different areas is open to a variety of cross-disciplinary investigations, we are keen to emphasise the seriousness of his radicalism as a social and cultural critic. He stands apart from the rise of middle-class tourism as directed by Murray and Cook, for example, but his idiosyncrasy is founded on an important alternative tradition of Romantic anti-capitalism, and the uses of Christian discourse to investigate an agenda for social and political thought which has subsequently been lost or obscured. Victorian Britain was often publicly identified with Evangelical Protestant seriousness, and many of Ruskin's writings fitted in well with this official posture, saturated as they were in biblical allusion and metaphor. These were Ruskin's levers to battle against the commodification of leisure and to announce the possibility of relating to, and even participating in, the joy of creative freedom. Recognising this, we have tried to re-evaluate the tradition of 'anti-tourism', finding it more formidable and potentially right-minded than did Buzard, who invented the term and examined its ambivalences. Unlike the industrial and academic machine, Ruskin does not shy away from confronting the historical otherness of national pasts. His legacy has been a diaspora of strands of influence – both on British cultural travel in Europe and on domestic and popular tourism.

Ruskin inhabits a crucial moment of social and technological history when access to the traditional arts and to artistically desirable landscapes was becoming democratised, through the readier dissemination of the printed word and the availability of cheap visual images as well as through the falling costs and challenges of travel in terms of time, money, organisation and cultural capital. Though it is difficult to tease out Ruskin's specific influence from the general *zeitgeist*, he certainly made an original contribution to ways of seeing, which has had an important afterlife. He defined an energetic kind of sightseeing, which differed from the energetic busy-ness of the Cook's tour or the prescribed rituals of 'verifying' one's Baedeker or Murray in its peremptory prescription for the interpretative and diagnostic. He required a kind of perception which expanded from an actual scene or object to its cultural associations to its moral significance, seen in the light of overarching themes of historical process, Biblical myth and scientific 'laws'. All this depended on sustaining and developing a full spectrum of physical and mental experience, and it is with the intention of reconstructing the idea of such a potential, extending to the reading of his written texts and visual mediations, that we have ourselves spent much time and space in detailing it in the present work.

Ruskin was a demanding guide, and he knew it. Ruskin's gaze required the full, fiercely detailed commitment of the disciple, at a level which could rarely be attained or sustained. But, as we have argued, his influence was widely felt in terms of where to go, what to see, and how to appraise, evaluate and be inspired by the object of the gaze. Most people experienced it in diluted and simplified form, sometimes through his own ambiguous incorporation into commercial tourism through interventions in the guidebook market and the appropriation of selective quotations, and sometimes through a dual recognition that Ruskin was both a deity to be placated and a fallible judge who might be challenged. Most were overawed by his mid- and late Victorian reputation, and by the dizzying power of his rhetoric, in combination with the sheer density of his appreciation of light and colour and his deployment of interpretative detail. This applied both to the cultural tourist in Europe, trying to come to terms with demanding itineraries through the cathedrals, churches, museums and galleries of northern France or Italy, and to the idealistic pursuer of nature and the simple life in the Alps or through the uplands of (especially) northern England, where Ruskin's main influences on popular tourism (the tourism of the lower middle and aspiring working classes) were brought to bear.

We have tried to bring a canonical figure of obvious historical and philosophical significance, surrounded by an aura of controversy and myth, into a new field of vision. Ruskin should be a figure of great importance not only in tourism history, but also in Tourism Studies as a wider discipline. His incorporation into this expanded framework of understanding and discussion should form part of a wider rapprochement between Tourism Studies and the Humanities. We hope that this book will have furthered such an enterprise and encouraged such developments.

References

Butler, R. and Russell, R. (eds) (2010) *Giants of Tourism*. Wallingford: CABI.
Urry, J. (2002) *The Tourist Gaze* (2nd edn). London: Sage Publications.

Index

Abbeville (Prout), 45
Adam and Eve and Fig Tree, the Ducal Palace,
  106
aesthetic approach, 8, 9
Aiguilles, Chamonix (Crawley), 48
Alhambra in Granada (Roberts), 47
Allen, George, 52, 62
– *Amiens from the river* (Ruskin), 117
Alps Western Switzerland
– interpretation of places, 92–101
– knowledge, 93
– Romantic encounter, 94
anti-tourism, 2
architectural analyses, 146
– drawings and illustrations, 57
– social implications, 40
artist. *See also* specific titles
– Ruskin as, 134
artistic dicta, 146
associationism, 10

Baedeker, Karl
– guidebooks and handbooks, 52, 80–82
– tour leader and market, 5, 14, 28–29, 148,
  202
Bas-relief of the Apostles and the Lamb, St.
  Mark's, 109
Bible of Amiens, 125
– Intelligent Traveller's section, 52
Blandy, Louise Virenda
– *Copy of Fra Angelico,* 102
Brantwood on Coniston Water, 21, 41
– association with Ruskin, 99, 169, 179–197
– contents of house, 182
– core of house, 181
– history, 197
– John Howard Whitehouse intervention,
  188–189, 193–194
– Lord Lloyd's intervention, 187–188
– Ruskin Museum, 171
– Ruskin purchased, 41, 183
– Ruskin's presence, 192
– Ruskinian ideals, 189
– tourist destination, 180–181, 197
– view across lake, 136
Brantwood Trust, 186
Britain
– domestic tours through, 36
Britain and Western Europe

– tourism development, 1
Byzantine influences, 11, 115
– architecture, 91, 103–104, 105

Ca' d'Oro, Venice (Ruskin), 75
Carpaccio, Vittore
– *Dream of St. Ursula,* 114
– *Presentation in the Temple,* 116
Casa Contarini Fasan (Ruskin), 46
CHA. *See* Co-operative Holidays
  Association (CHA)
Chamonix, 32, 38, 143
– composed first book, 40
– development, 139
– purchased field, 99
– revisiting, 92–95, 98, 172
– tourist trade, 36, 140, 141, 167
– travel pattern, 138
Choir Stalls, Amiens Cathedral, 130
Clarion Cycling Clubs, 156
collections sales, 185
colour symbolism, 76
columns of San Marco and San Teodoro, 108
combination principle, 74, 165, 174, 194
communal gaze, 6
Coniston Water. *See* Brantwood on
  Coniston Water
continental tours, 35
– final, 43
– first, 38
Cook, Thomas
– consumerist package, 14–15, 154
– facilitating education and recreation, 5
– his travel business, first tour, and
  motivation, 31–34
– Temperance movement and widening
  social access, 19–20
– tourist literature and influence on
  tourism, 134–148
– tours and mass tourism, 1, 133
Co-operative Holidays Association (CHA),
  160–169
copper-plate mezzotinting, 64–65
Copy of Fra Angelico (Blandy), 102
Copy of the central part of Tintoretto's
  'Crucifixion' (Ruskin), 103
Cottage near Altdorf (Ruskin), 61
Crawley, F.
– *Aiguilles, Chamonix,* 48

Crests of the Slaty Crystallines
   (Turner/Ruskin), 73
critic influence, 134
cross-disciplinary investigations, 202
Cuff, R.P. (engraver)
– *Growth of Leaves* (Ruskin), 17
– *Sculptures for Bas-reliefs of the North Door of
   the Cathedral of Rouen* (Ruskin), 121
cultural touring, 31, 135
– approach, 2
– art and high moral purpose, 154
– constructions, 2
– enlightenment, 28
– geography, 84
– historical leaps, 84
– and moral improvement, 154
– restoration, 123
– role, 3
– Ruskin Moment, 43–52
– through landscape and architecture, 154

daguerreotypes, 63
– *Aiguilles, Chamonix* (Crawley), 48
– *Detail of S. Denis and Angels, Rheims
   Cathedral* 63
– *Maria della Spina, Lucca* (Ruskin), 63
– *S. Denis and angels*, 121
– *St. Mark's and Clock Tower*, 62
destiny and dilemma, 8
*Detail from Tintoretto's 'Adoration of the
   Magi': Magi and Cherubs* (Ruskin), 101
*Detail of S. Denis and Angels, Rheims
   Cathedral* (Ruskin), 63
domestic tours through Romantic margins
   of Britain, 36
drawing
– power of notation and description, 56
– style, 44
dreaming mind, 16
Dream of St Ursula (Carpaccio), 114
dream-vision, 71
Dr. Syntax Tumbling into the Water
   (Rowlandson), 70
Ducal Palace, 105

Edinburgh, from St. Anthony's Chapel
   (Turner), 78
Edwardian outdoor movement
– Ruskin influences, 156
English Lake District. *See also* Brantwood on
   Coniston Water
– tourism development, 136, 150, 161–167,
   180
engraving, 64
– *Amiens from the river* (Ruskin), 117
– *Crests of the Slaty Crystallines*
   (Turner/Ruskin), 73
– *Edinburgh, from St. Anthony's Chapel*
   (Turner), 78

– *Growth of Leaves* (Ruskin), 17
– *Kirby-Lonsdale Church Yard* (Turner), 87
– *Lake of Como* (Turner), 46
– *Sculptures for Bas-reliefs of the North Door of
   the Cathedral of Rouen* (Ruskin), 121
– *Simple Topography* (Turner/Ruskin), 72
– *Turnerian Topography* (Turner/Ruskin), 72
Europe
– architecture, 40
– Grand Tour, 1
evangelical Christianity, 15
evangelical and realist predisposition, 68
evangelical stress on hard work, 12
experimentation, 70

family travels, 37
– horse-driven vehicles, 49

General View of Amiens Cathedral
   (Kaltenbacher), 126
Giessbach Falls 1816, 96
Giotto
– *Marriage of St. Francis and Poverty*, 113
Golden Virgin, Amiens Cathedral, 129
Goodall, Edward (engraver)
– *Lake of Como* (Turner), 46
Grand Tour, 3, 12, 25–26, 138, 201
– Europe, 1
– Ruskin's approach, 13
Growth of Leaves (Ruskin), 17
growth pattern
– self-realisation and fruition, 17
Guide to the Cathedral, 127
guidebooks, 52
guides, 203
– leading feature, 79
– Ruskin as, 78–88

Hand-book to Northern Italy, 52
Heath, C. (engraver)
– *Kirby-Lonsdale Church Yard* (Turner), 87
historical influence, 12
historical picture, 77
History of Venice, 42
Hugot, Charles
– *Vue Général d'Amiens, Prise de la Citadelle*
   (Hugot), 125

ideological position, 20
illustrations
– architectural analyses, 57
– insights over time and travelling, 58
– *Stones of Venice*, 66
imagination
– combinations, 69
– literalism and visual, 72–73
– and reality, 86
influences, 142–146
– on ethical socialist movement, 157

– on mainstream middle-class continental
    tourism, 148
– Victorian and Edwardian outdoor
    movement, 156
– on working-class apostles, 159
integrating interpretative gaze, 87
interpretation of places, 91–131
– Alps: Western Switzerland and Savoy:
    Nature's Lost Eden, 92–100
– Northern France restoration in
    architecture, 117–131
– Venice: the Fall of Art, 100–117
invented techniques, 57
Italian tour of 1846, 5

joy of travel, 1–21
– argument, 12–21
Judgement of Solomon, the Ducal Palace, 108
Jungfrau from Interlaken (Ruskin), 47

Kirby-Lonsdale Church Yard (Turner), 87

Lake District. *See* English Lake District
Lake of Como (Turner), 46
landscape
– art analysis, 62
– defined, 56
– *Modern Painters*, 62
*Last Judgement Tympanum of St Maclou,
    Rouen*, 120
Leafage in the Vine Angle (Ruskin), 104
Le Glacier des Bois, Chamonix (Ruskin), 95
Lever, Charles
– tourist habits, 20
Lily Capital, St. Mark's (Ruskin), 105
literal topography, 71
literalism and visual imagination
– interplay between, 72–73
living legacy, 190
Loch Achray and Ben Venue (Ruskin), 58

Mackmurdo, A.H.
– *Sepulchral Slab of Galileus de Galileis, Santa
    Croce, Florence*, 85
Maria della Spina, Lucca (Ruskin), 63
Marriage of St. Francis and Poverty (Giotto),
    113
medieval Christian society, 118
Mer de Glace, Chamonix, 32
Miller, W. (engraver)
– *Edinburgh, from St. Anthony's Chapel*
    (Turner), 78
Modern Painters, 38, 40, 56, 57, 138
– landscape art analysis, 62
morality
– aesthetic, 11
– improvement, 154
– significance, 102
– various styles and periods, 104

mosaic approach, 73
motivation of readers, 18
Mountain Glory, 98
Murray, John
– guidebooks and handbooks, 5, 27–34, 41,
    52, 79–85, 88, 145–146, 192
– Switzerland handbook, 139–144

National Home Reading Union (NHRU),
    160–169
natural composition principle, 60
Near Blair, Athol, Scotland (Turner), 64
NHRU. *See* National Home Reading Union
    (NHRU)
*Northern Porch, West Front, Amiens Cathedral,
    Before Restoration* (Ruskin), 122

Ornaments from Rouen (Ruskin), 66

Parsons, Nicholas T.
– guidebooks and handbooks, 20, 24
– historical contexts, 24–34
– Venetian school, 100
Pass of Faido (Ruskin), 72
perceptions, 67
piazetta near St. Mark's Square, 108
picturesque theory and practice, 69
picturesque travelling
– vantage point for vision, 50
Pilgrims of the Rhine, 44
Plan for the western Porches, Amiens Cathedral
    (Ruskin), 131
polymath, 4
Pontifices. Clerus. Populus. Dux mente serenus
    (Fairfax Murray), 78
popular tourism and Ruskin, 154–175
Presentation in the Temple (Carpaccio), 116
profitable travelling, 49
prophet
– Ruskin's life as, 196
Protestant undercurrents, 25
Prout, Samuel
– *Abbeville*, 45

Queen of Sheba and Solomon (Veronese), 113

radicalism and Victorian high seriousness, 13
railways
– comments on impact, 136–137
– Ruskin's contributions to campaigns
    against, 150
readers' motivation, 18
realist predisposition, 68
recording and representation
– travelling, 44
religious art
– symbolic content, 114
religious demarcations within Switzerland, 97
religious topography, 83

representational field
– metonymically continuous, 76
Roberts, David
– *Alhambra in Granada*, 47
– *West Front, Amiens Cathedral, France*, 123
Romantic margins domestic tours, 36
romantic and religious content
– truthfulness, 59–60
Romantic anti-capitalism, 3
Romantic encounter with Alpine scenery, 94
Romantic gaze, 7
Romantic writer and artist, 48–49
Rouen Cathedral
– stained glass, 119
Rowlandson, Thomas
– *Dr. Syntax Tumbling into the Water*, 70
Ruskin, John, 46. *See also* specific areas e.g. Influences; specific titles of art and books
– *Amiens from the river*, 117
– as artist, 134
– authority on historic buildings and art treasures of northern Italy, 148
– *Ca' d'Oro, Venice*, 75
– *Casa Contarini Fasan*, 46
– *Copy of the central part of Tintoretto's 'Crucifixion'*, 103
– *Cottage near Altdorf*, 61
– *Crests of the Slaty Crystallines* (Turner), 73
– *Detail from Tintoretto's 'Adoration of the Magi': Magi and Cherubs*, 101
– *Detail of S. Denis and Angels, Rheims Cathedral*, 63
– double brougham, 50
– engagement, 202
– final continental journey, 43
– first continental tour, 38
– *Growth of Leaves*, 17
– guidebooks, 52
– *Jungfrau from Interlaken*, 47
– *Leafage in the Vine Angle*, 104
– *Le Glacier des Bois, Chamonix*, 95
– *Lily Capital, St. Mark's*, 105
– *Loch Achray and Ben Venue*, 58
– marriage to Effie Gray, 39
– *Mornings in Florence*, 51
– *Northern Porch, West Front, Amiens Cathedral, Before Restoration*, 122
– *Ornaments from Rouen*, 66
– *Pass of Faido*, 72
– *Plan for the western Porches, Amiens Cathedral*, 131
– *Pontifices. Clerus. Populus. Dux Mente Serenus*, 78
– *Sculptures for Bas-reliefs of the North Door of the Cathedral of Rouen*, 121
– *Shoot of Spanish Chestnut at Carrara*, 65
– *Simple Topography* (Turner/Ruskin), 72

– *State of Snow on Mont Blanc*, 94
– *Study of Portal and Carved Pinnacles, Cathedral of St Lô Normandy*, 65
– *St. Wulfran, Abbeville*, 119
– *Temperance and Intemperance in Curvature*, 67
– *Trees and Rocks*, 61
– *Troutbeck*, 60
– *Villa, Sommariva, Cadenabbia*, 62
– *Vine. Free, and in Service*, 104
– *Vine Angle, the Ducal Palace*, 107
Ruskin gaze
– sightseeing with Ruskin, 68–78
Ruskin Institute, 194
Ruskin Moment, 24–52
– cultural travelling, 43–52
– historical contexts, 24–34
– tours, 34–43
Ruskin Museum, 194
Ruskin Museum at Coniston, 171
Ruskin Pier, 194
Ruskin Society, 194
Ruskin's approach
– Grand Tour, 13
Ruskin's cultural travelling, 43–52
Ruskinian ideals
– through Brantwood, 189

S. Denis and angels, 121
Savoy Nature's Lost Eden
– interpretation of places, 92–100
Sculptures for Bas-reliefs of the North Door of the Cathedral of Rouen (Ruskin), 121
self-improvement, 18
self-realisation and fruition growth pattern, 17
Seven Lamps of Architecture, 57
Severn, Arthur, 181, 184, 185, 192
Severn, Joan, 181, 184, 185, 192
Shoot of Spanish Chestnut at Carrara (Ruskin), 65
sightseeing
– defined, 202
– with Ruskin, 55–88
– Ruskin as guide, 78–88
– Ruskin gaze, 68–78
– visual representation, 55–67
Simple Topography (Turner), 72
Slade Professor of Fine Art at Oxford, 41
social access
– traditional cultural experience, 19
social implications
– architectural analyses, 40
soft-ground etching, 66
St. George, 110
St. George and the Dragon, 111
St. Mark's and Clock Tower
– daguerreotype, 62
St. Mark's Rest, 42

Starke, Mariana, 27
State of Snow on Mont Blanc (Ruskin), 94
Stones of Venice, 57
– illustrations, 66
St. Salvador piazza, 111
St. Wulfran, Abbeville (Ruskin), 119
Study of Portal and Carved Pinnacles,
    Cathedral of St Lô Normandy (Ruskin), 65
sun's drawing, 63
Switzerland, 92
symbolic content
– religious art, 114

Temperance and Intemperance in Curvature
    (Ruskin), 67
Thomas Cook's First Tour of Switzerland
– map, 32
Three Western Porches, 126
Titian's *Assumption*
– mind changes and contradictions, 115
touring, 34
– Brantwood, 180–181
– Brantwood's history, 197
– Ruskin Moment, 34–43
– structured, 82
– through Romantic margins of Britain, 36
tourism
– authenticity quest, 4
– defined, 2
– and Ruskin, 154–175
tourism development
– Britain and Western Europe, 1
– English Lake District, 136, 150, 161–167,
    180
Tourism Studies, 1–2
– Ruskin's absence, 201
tourist
– destination, 197
– destinations and Ruskin, 133–150
– gaze, 6
– *vs.* traveller, 2, 135
Tourist in Spain, 44
traditional cultural experience
– widening social access, 19
traveller *vs.* tourist, 2, 135
travelling
– practices specialised instruction, 45
– recording and representation, 44
– Ruskin's preference, 137
Trees and Rocks (Ruskin), 61
Troutbeck (Ruskin), 60
Turner, J.M.W., 46
– *Crests of the Slaty Crystallines*, 73
– *Edinburgh, from St. Anthony's Chapel*, 78
– *Kirby-Lonsdale Church Yard*, 87
– *Near Blair Athol, Scotland*, 64

– *Simple Topography*, 72
– *Turnerian Topography*, 72

Uhlrich, H. S.
– *Bas-relief of the Apostles and the Lamb, St.*
    Mark's, 109
– *St. George*, 110
Urry, John, 5, 6, 7, 8, 27, 28, 55, 135, 201

Venetian artefacts
– measuring and recording, 106
Venetian Gothic architecture, 103
Venetian political history
– Ruskin's scheme, 112
Venice: the Fall of Art
– interpretation of places, 100–117
Veronese, Paulo
– *Queen of Sheba and Solomon*, 113
Victorian period
– culture, 8
– development, 201
– and Edwardian development, 155
– and Edwardian outdoor movement, 156
– high seriousness, 13
– Ruskin influences, 156
– social critic, 48–49
Villa, Sommariva, Cadenabbia (Ruskin), 62
Vine. Free, and in Service (Ruskin), 104
Vine Angle, the Ducal Palace (Ruskin), 107
visibility in publications for tourists, 193
visual imagination, 72–73
Vivarini epoch, 115
Vue General d'Amiens, Prise de la Citadelle
    (Hugot), 125

walking
– Ruskin's preference, 138
western eurocentric area, 5
West Front, Amiens Cathedral, France
    (Roberts), 123
Whitehouse, John Howard
– Brantwood acquisitions, 193–194
Whitehouse's intervention
– Brantwood, 188–189, 193–194
Workers' Travel Association (WTA),
    171–173
worldview, 10
writer
– Ruskin's life as, 196
WTA. *See* Workers' Travel Association
    (WTA)

Youth Hostels Association (YHA), 162,
    173–175

zeitgeist, 5, 202